THE FIXERS

T.A.S.

for

Julia and Naomi

A.M.M.Y.

for

Charles, Alexander and Charlotte

The Fixers

Crisis Management in British Politics

TREVOR SMITH and ALISON YOUNG

Dartmouth

Aldershot • Brookfield USA • Singapore • Sydney

Published by
Dartmouth Publishing Company Limited
Gower House
Croft Road
Aldershot
Hants GU11 3HR
England

Dartmouth Publishing Company
Old Post Road
Brookfield
Vermont 05036
USA

British Library Cataloguing in Publication Data
Smith, Trevor
 Fixers:Crisis Management in British
 Politics
 I. Title II. Young, Alison
 320.941

Library of Congress Cataloging-in-Publication Data
PCN number 95-83677

ISBN 1 85521 726 0

Printed and bound in Great Britain by
Hartnolls Limited, Bodmin, Cornwall

Contents

Preface

This book is the first detailed account of the role played by fixers in crisis management in British politics since 1945. It examines the circumstances in which fixers are called in, how they become fixers and the attributes they possess, and how they go about dealing with the crises they are asked to handle. While some have written autobiographies and others have had biographies written about them, they and their activities have not been considered together until now, nor has fixing *per se* been an explicit theme in any of these books.

We also trace the recent trend whereby individual fixers are being increasingly augmented by corporate fixers, in the form of management consultants, employed by government to assist in coping with crises that are now established as an endemic feature of political life. This parlous condition results in no small measure from the growing constitutional deficiency of governmental arrangements that is widely perceived not just by the *cognoscenti* but also by the general public. Sleaze is but one of the symptoms, for constitutional decrepitude also manifests itself in the growing judicial intervention into the actions of government, the advent of professional lobbyists, and the emergence of what is tantamount to a *nomenklatura* composed of those who serially move between the roles of civil servants, party *apparatchiks*, ministerial henchmen, MPs, think tankers, lobbyists or management consultants. Fixers and fixing are viewed in the context of this somewhat kaleidoscopic contemporary milieu.

In writing what in large part amounts to a group biography many debts are incurred to the subjects themselves, others familiar with them, and to previous authors. Accordingly, we record our grateful appreciation to those who kindly agreed to be interviewed by us: the late Lord Franks, the late Lord Goodman, the late Sir Roy Griffiths, Lord and Lady

Plowden, Lord Rayner and Lord Young of Dartington. These constitute the subject matter of six of the ten chapters.

Others who gave freely of their time and experience were: Leighton Andrews, Sir Louis Blom-Cooper QC, Charles Clarke, Nigel Clarke, Dr Tony Flower, Andrew Gifford, Ian Greer, Lord Merlyn-Rees, Sir Patrick Nairne, Jill Pitkeathley, Eirlys Roberts and Peter Willmott. We acknowledge their assistance.

Dr Andrew Massey and Julia Smith read earlier drafts of the entire *ms.*, while Leighton Andrews, Anthony Barnett, Stuart Weir and Charles Young read particular chapters. In absolving them for responsibility for any errors of fact or interpretation, we thank them for their advice.

It will be apparent to the reader that we have relied heavily on literary and journalistic sources to inform and supplement our own endeavours and we hope to have made full reference to them. In particular, we are grateful for permission to quote extensively from four sources: to Chapmans Publishers to cite extracts from Arnold Goodman, *Tell Them I'm On My Way*; to Weidenfeld and Nicolson for dispensation to quote from Kathleen Tynan, *The Life of Kenneth Tynan* and for similarly allowing us to quote from Sir Nicholas Henderson, *The Birth of Nato;* and the extract on page 31 is taken from *Dancing with Dogma: Britain Under Thatcherism* by Ian Gilmour, published by Simon & Schuster London in hardback and paperback, copyright (c) Ian Gilmour, 1992.

Thanks are also due to the directors of the Joseph Rowntree Reform Trust Ltd for a grant to support our research and, not least, we pay warm tribute to Mrs Margaret Connolly and Mrs Julie Cummins whose efficiency and professionalism in producing endless drafts and preparing the final *ms* for printing are beyond praise.

In the lengthy gestation of the book we thank both our families for their support and forbearance and happily dedicate it to them.

T.A.S
A.M.M.Y.
August 1995

1 Fixers and Fixing

On the death of Oliver Franks in October 1992 the obituarists' fulsome praises were accompanied by remarks to the effect that we would not see his like again. In a sense they were right. His type of public servant had become an almost extinct species. But just as he was not the first of his kind so he was not the last for in the same year Sir Bernard Tomlinson had been chosen by Virginia Bottomley, the Health Secretary, to report on the rationalisation of London's hospitals in the hope of extricating her from the controversy that threatened to engulf her. Similarly in April 1993 Education Secretary John Patten appointed Sir Ron Dearing to rescue him from the furore provoked by his proposals for pupil assessments and league tables of schools' performance. Governments and ministers faced with crises still summon outsiders to help resolve them, though different kinds of people are pressed into service today from those of thirty or forty years ago. Fixers and fixing, it seems, are alive and kicking.

This is hardly surprising for both are as old as government itself. They exist and survive because government institutions, this side of paradise at least, are less than perfect. Man-made constitutions cannot cater for all eventualities and when crises arise, when the system fails, then the firemen - the Rasputins or Red Adairs of politics - are called in.

The business of government and its institutions is essentially about routine politics. Parliament is there to mediate between the governors and the governed; the Law Courts arbitrate between the claims of conflicting parties, be they civil disputes between individuals or corporations or criminal ones between the state and those who infringe its rules; while the executive branch of government, the Cabinet and the civil service, seeks to adjudicate between the competing items on the public agenda. In the conduct of foreign affairs, ministers and diplomats are employed to negotiate with their counterparts in other nation states with the aim of concluding settlements which may be enshrined in treaties or other agreements. Thus politicians, diplomats, judges and civil servants are in their various spheres involved in the activity of regular fixing. In this book we are not concerned directly with what might be called the routine activity of fixing: many books have and will continue to be written about such processes and those involved in them. Instead, we are focusing on those people called in to deal with a crisis; recruited to handle issues that routine processes have failed to deal with. Usually these crises involve two types of problem: impasse or 'hot potato' problems.

Politics and politicians have to deal with the problems other groups have found insoluble. Indeed problems only reach the political agenda after architects, bankers, farmers, industrialists, physicians, scientists and all other occupational groupings have failed to deal with them. Political problems, then, are by definition the most difficult of all and by their very nature are often intractable; all that politicians or governments can hope for is some contrivance or adjustment that will make things tolerable for a further period. Constitutions, of course, are meant to provide the framework within which the thorny problems of politics are processed and decided about. The formal Constitution of the United States of America was one of the most considered and, as it has turned out, lasting experiments in constitution-making, but, despite the ingenuity of the Founding Fathers, it resulted in a system that is not easily worked on a day-to-day basis. Frequently it creates paralysis, or political 'gridlock' in President Clinton's phrase, in the form of impasse between the White House and Congress. All manner of informal devices have had to be invented to overcome such blockages and enable the system to function. The British have tended to believe that their unwritten constitution was more flexible, adaptive and altogether operationally superior to that of the Americans, but now there is a growing acknowledgement across the political spectrum that British arrangements have become sclerotic and are in need of major reconstruction. Part of the evidence for this constitutional decay in the post-1945 period is to be seen in the greater incidence of fixing, the use made of fixers and the changing character of the fixers themselves. To keep the system working there has been an importation of American-style personnel, in the form of henchmen, ideologically sympathetic policy advisers, lobbyists and management consultants, all of whom in their different ways are fixers.

In today's complex society, as Anthony Sampson points out in his latest and most pessimistic edition - *The Essential Anatomy of Britain: Democracy in Crisis* - 'decisions always seem to be taken somewhere else'

(Sampson, 1992, p.14) The concept of ministerial responsibility, for instance, increasingly recognised as something of a fiction in the post-war years, is now accepted as almost totally inoperative. Sexual scandal and/or other indiscretions may force a minister from office, but even faced with unambiguously bad policy blunders there is a marked reluctance to admit responsibility and resign. One reason for the undermining of this convention and other such constitutional pillars is that modern government is overloaded. The British state got big without anybody thinking about it, as Peter Hennessy has put it (Hennessy, 1990b, p.14). Despite recent attempts to push back the boundaries of the state, it now occupies every corner of national life and there has been no corresponding remodelling of constitutional checks and balances by way of compensation. Within the executive branch of government it is true that various methods of coping with overload have been tried: rather like buttresses added to the exterior of a shaky building. Ministerial advisers, think tanks, and policy units have flourished in attempts to shore up the practice of modern government both in the formulation of policy and its execution.

These additional props for an overloaded government machine are not new. They take a number of forms. One variant is a Prime Minister's Office. Lloyd George had his 'garden suburb'; Churchill had a staff of people under Lindemann; Attlee had the Central Economic Planning Staff (CEPS) till it was removed to the Treasury with Stafford Cripps. The Central Policy Review Staff (CPRS) was set up in 1970 when the Heath government came in; it was working for ministers collectively, aiming to give a new angle on interdepartmental issues. Its remit was to 'think the unthinkable', but its tendency to do just that led to a number of political storms. Mrs Thatcher thought very little of the CPRS and scrapped it in 1983; 'you should have talked more to M & S', she reportedly said (Blackstone and Plowden, 1988, p.46). There was also the cabinet policy unit which Harold Wilson set up under Bernard Donoughue in 1974. This was slimmed down in the Thatcher years but she relied on other special advisers, including Sir Anthony Parsons on foreign affairs, and Sir Alan Walters on economics. It is not only the central capability of government which is overloaded; this is also true in the departments. Since about the mid-1960s most ministers have had young political advisers in their offices. Think Tanks also proliferated in the 1970s and 1980s - imitations both of the earlier Fabian Society and its right wing analogue the Institute of Economic Affairs. The Thatcherite Institute for Policy Studies and the even more free-market Adam Smith Institute, together with the more recent foundation of the left-of-centre Institute for Public Policy Research all play their part in the *demi-monde* of political life. Norman Lamont when Chancellor of the Exchequer appointed a team of economists of differing views, known as the 'seven wise men', to act as an independent, broadly based sounding board.

Advisers and think tanks are co-opted in these ways to help underpin an increasingly creaking system by feeding in ideas for policy making in a continuing attempt to forestall political problems from reaching critical levels. Those problems that cannot easily be anticipated and spring up suddenly as crises are often dealt with by judges or senior barristers, when they are taken out of their everyday judicial or legal work, and appointed to undertake official investigations. In recent years public inquiries have frequently been resorted to by government. Lord Denning, for example, in 1963 was asked to investigate the Profumo scandal that threatened to bring down the Macmillan government. Lord Scarman inquired into the 1981 Brixton riots. Lord Taylor reported on the 1989 Hillsborough stadium football disaster. Lord Woolf analysed the 1991 Strangeways prison riot. In 1993 Lord Donaldson was appointed to look into the *Braer* oilspill off the Shetland coast and Lord Justice Scott's enquiry was set up to inquire into the Matrix Churchill arms to Iraq affair. As Sir Louis Blom-Cooper QC, himself a veteran of many inquiries particularly in health and welfare matters, has observed:

> The instinct to reach for the solution of a public inquiry stems from a desire to distract the critics or deflect criticism, or to expose some fraud, fault or act of maladministration. It also arises out of the need expeditiously to restore public confidence in government or in public administration, or to scotch ill-founded rumours of scandal, by an independent investigation of the events under scrutiny. The urge is also to establish the facts other than by established methods, such as coroners' inquests, litigation (including judicial review) or criminal proceedings. (Blom-Cooper, 1993, p.204)

Public inquiries, presided over by judges or barristers - with or without the assistance of technical assessors - are clearly one of the main techniques of crisis management. They are a form of fixing by last resort, not least because of the enormous costs involved: the Clyde Inquiry of 1992 into alleged child sex abuse in the Orkneys cost £6 million and was inconclusive. Public inquiries, however, will be appointed when the pressure of public concern forces the hand of government to be seen to be seriously addressing a major problem. Perhaps the main reason why governments are reluctant to use public inquiries is that, once empanelled, they become 'loose cannons' so far as Whitehall is concerned and that very independence is thus a double-edged sword: on the one hand it gives reassurance to the public, but on the other it allows for potentially radical criticisms and proposals to be made that will place further strains on government.

Routine fixers, like judges, thus sometimes find themselves playing the role of crisis fixers. They differ from other types of crisis fixers in two important respects: first, as has just been remarked, they are able to exercise considerable independence and secondly, although they are given a good deal of latitude about their *modus operandi* (particularly since 'the virtual abandonment' of procedures set up by the Tribunals of Inquiry (Evidence) Act of 1921, (Blom-Cooper, op. cit., p.206) they will bring and are expected to bring an essentially legal approach to the task in hand.

It is the other type of crisis fixers and their methods that we shall focus on. They range from individuals to specialist firms: from those such as Lords Franks and Plowden on the one hand, to the management consultants and lobbyists on the other. Together they comprise a group who are called in to effect compromises, make adjustments, and facilitate accommodations between different sets of political actors, including sometimes the public. Their freedom of manoeuvre is usually more constrained than that of public inquiries and is often dependent on their own skills and judgement as to how far the boundaries of a particular mission can be stretched. Unlike their judicial counterparts they rely on informal techniques and at times have to get their hands dirty.

Crisis fixers such as these are referred to *en passant* in numerous commentaries on British politics and they have featured in both biographies and autobiographies, but hitherto they have not been considered as a group in their own right nor have their actions been studied alongside one another. This omission is perhaps the last *lacuna* in the study of British political life. It is a surprising gap since so much attention has been paid in the last decade or so to crisis management and damage limitation on the one hand and to the related issues of government overload and constitutional reform on the other. For the last half century government it seems has been moving progressively from a system where there were sporadic crises to one where crisis is now endemic.

Between the wars probably the most famous fireman was Walter Monckton. Known as 'old oil tank' among lawyers in the Temple,

Monckton was a conciliator *par excellence*. In 1933 he had negotiated on behalf of the Nizam of Hyderabad for the princely states over the scheme for a federal India and, although the scheme was not adopted, he emerged with his reputation greatly enhanced. As legal adviser to King Edward VIII during the Abdication Crisis he acted as confidant and go-between. He gained the trust not only of the King and Mrs Simpson but the respect of Baldwin, the Prime Minister, and Beaverbrook, who were totally at odds on the issue. It was probably Monckton who kept the press quiet and played a major part in contriving a settlement acceptable both to the individuals involved and the institutions, notably the government and the established church. His skills ensured that the monarchy did not become a publicly contentious issue and retained unimpaired its formal position at the apex of the country's constitutional arrangements.

Part and parcel of his negotiating skills were his gift of lucid expression, commonsense and an ability to manipulate networks effectively. Edward VIII's private secretaries were his contemporaries at Harrow, while he was himself at Oxford with the King. His ambitions to become Attorney General and Lord Chancellor, neither of which were achieved, led him to abandon the usual fixers' politically neutral stance. He was elected to Parliament, with some difficulty. In 1951, as Churchill's Minister of Labour - a post which he was horrified to be offered, 'his virginal political status turned out to be a priceless asset' (Birkenhead, 1969, p.270) and he was seen as a great success becoming a personification of what would later be known as 'Butskellism'. His brief was to preserve industrial peace: 'On what terms did you settle the dispute?' 'Theirs of course old boy'.

Pre-eminent among crisis fixers in the post-war period, was Oliver Franks, a philosophy professor recruited as a temporary civil servant in 1939 and who within five years rose meteorically to become Permanent Secretary to the Ministry of Supply. For the next forty-seven years he was to be in and out of Whitehall fixing solutions for governments over a wide range of problems. Edwin Plowden, an industrialist and another war-time civil servant, undertook similar tasks as did, on a smaller scale, his wife Bridget. From the 1960s onward Arnold Goodman became a familiar and very public fixer attending to the needs of governments of both political hues. Recently Lord Goodman and Lord Plowden have published their autobiographies and Alex Danchev has written a biography of the late Lord Franks. To a greater or lesser extent, these provide fleshed-out portraits of their subjects but they do not analyse in detail the *modus operandi* employed by the fixers nor, of course, can they make comparisons and contrasts between the subjects themselves as we are seeking to do.

A major distinction between Monckton and his post-war successors, however, is that as an Harrovian and a High Church Anglican he was undoubtedly both of and in the Establishment. Franks, Plowden and Goodman by contrast were not. None of them attended a Clarendon public school, while in terms of religious affiliation they were respectively Congregationalist, Roman Catholic and Jew. Thus although they were ultimately to enter into the Establishment, at the outset they were not of it.

Much has been written about what exactly comprises membership of the Establishment. Schooling, status and snobbery all play a part, but like any elite it must adapt to survive and newcomers may be admitted without the requisite background, especially if they possess specific and scarce skills. Networks - and the political Establishment is only one of these - are an important part of the story. Jeremy Paxman tells an amusing tale of Lord Plowden being visited by someone (John Hoskyns, who was to be head of the PM's policy unit 1979-82), who had decided to go into politics and wanted advice. After a brief talk, Plowden suddenly asked 'Who are you?' This was a coded way of saying, 'I've looked you up in *Who's Who* and you're not there!' He is now. (Paxman, 1991, p.83)

Another view of the Establishment, quite widely subscribed to, sees it in institutional terms as 'the English constitution and outlying agencies built round it to assist in its protection' (Hugh Thomas, quoted in Ranelagh, 1992, p.38). Commentators as far apart politically as former Marxist Martin Jacques and ex-mandarin Sir Frank Cooper define the Establishment as a grouping whose *raison d'etre* is to resist change. Small wonder then that the Thatcher years saw an alteration in the methods for choosing and using fixers. Crisis fixers, then, tend to come from the ranks of outsiders: indeed were they insiders they would be part of the problem. Although times are changing routine fixers were traditionally drawn in large numbers from the long standing gene pools of Eton, Christ Church and the Guards or their equivalents in terms of schools, universities and professions.

The personalities alluded to so far have all been official crisis fixers, called in by government. We shall also be examining the activities of one very unofficial fixer in the form of that highly maverick and perpetually youthful personality Michael Young. With his keen eye for failures in the system he spotted the need to create a consumer movement in Britain, something which he achieved almost single-handed. He has also made a considerable impact on the course of educational, social and health policy. Whereas official fixers are essentially reactive, by being pragmatic, incrementalist and consensual, Michael Young was, by contrast, an initiator who promoted a series of quite radical departures. In some sense he could be described adequately enough as being a very fertile pressure group begetter rather than as a self-propelled unofficial fixer, but it is the range and magnitude of the problems he addressed that earn him the designation of fixer and inclusion in the pantheon: the impact of the whole of his undertakings is far greater than the sum of its parts.

Michael Young is highly unusual but not unique; in the pre-war years John Maynard Keynes performed both the formal fixer role later taken on by Franks, or Goodman or Plowden and the informal role later to be played by Michael Young. Keynes sought through his public pronouncements and pamphleteering to plug the gaps which he perceived government had ignored; equally he was from time to time called in by government to advise them formally.

Although for the most part Michael Young is an unofficial fixer, he has much in common with his official counterparts. His origins were modest and he attended Dartington, the progressive school founded by one of the richest women in the world. Like many of the others he, too, became a life peer and like them is not especially enamoured of the House of Lords; contributions to its debates are either sparse or almost negligible. It is Whitehall and Downing Street and not Westminster that attract them. Ministerial life in any case is shorter than a fixer's career. All of them either avoided or were unable to have a direct and sustained relationship with political parties and Parliament. If they are public men, then they are private public men as opposed to MPs who are public public men or women.

Franks, Plowden, Goodman and Young came to prominence in the post-war consensual world. By the mid-seventies oil price shocks and continuing economic decline were beginning to make governing more difficult; political crisis seemed permanent. Many reforms were tried and most failed. The Thatcher years brought a change of atmosphere, pace and emphasis to this aspect of political life as to all others. The fixers up to then had often been used to chair committees of enquiry or royal commissions. Such bodies, consisting of that sub-section of the Establishment known as the great and good, would be appointed to examine a major issue and, with the help of a few civil servants, gather information, facts and opinions, deliberate on them and report. Though widely perceived as a way of 'dodging' an issue, postponing a tricky problem or simply as a method of throwing a sop to public opinion which would shortly find another cause for concern, such inquiries were set up at the remarkable rate of twenty-five per year in the 1950s and 1960s and considerable recourse to them was made in the 1970s. But these committees and commissions were instruments of consensus. In co-opting outside help on policy making and on social problems for instance, they invited interested parties to give their views and recognised implicitly that bureaucracy is not naturally innovative. But, with few exceptions such as the Robbins Report on expanding higher education, they were only capable of promoting piecemeal reform. Margaret Thatcher had no time for such enquiries. Her dislike of the old guard of the Establishment, distrust of the civil service and determination to introduce radical change meant that these kinds of old style fixers were redundant. She was not interested in discussing *what* to do, for she knew her own mind, but rather *how* to do it. In its way conviction politics was meant as an alternative remedy to this kind of fixing, but it was not enough: fixers could not be dispensed with, both in the 'what' of policy formation and especially in the 'how' of policy implementation.

A new breed of fixer began to be put to work behind the scenes, this time in group form and usually as management consultants. These were to provide the extra resources that could be drafted in to assist the overstretched civil service while, in addition, they could bring an outsider's perspective and experience to bear on the issues which were proving intractable. But even this movement away from the individual towards the corporate fixer threw up two people who kept alive the notion that an individual could make a significant contribution, while simultaneously representing the new breed of manager: these were Derek Rayner and Roy Griffiths. Like the other individuals they were not of the Establishment, coming as they did from relatively modest or even humble social origins. What was different, however, was that they had spent almost all of their careers in management and especially retailing in which, interestingly, both had reached to top positions as outsiders; Rayner was the first non-Sieff to lead Marks & Spencer, while Griffiths was the first non-Sainsbury to lead that grocery chain. Together they reflect the transition of fixers from the individuals to consultants.

After the war it had seemed natural to send for Franks and Plowden when difficulties arose because they knew the working of the government machine and spoke the same language: 'The thing about the language of Whitehall is that it makes it unnecessary very often to carry arguments right through to the end, because so many assumptions are shared' (William Plowden quoted in Kellner and Crowther-Hunt, 1980).

Derek Rayner and Roy Griffiths, appropriately enough as times were changing, were 'headhunted'. Rayner was suggested to Heath by Sieff as a suitable person to advise on improving procurement in 1969-70 though his real fame did not grow till he worked for Heath's successor from 1979 to 1983. Griffiths told a story about noticing when he was addressing a BIM dinner that there were an unusually large number of civil servants present; he was approached by Sir Kenneth Stowe, DHSS permanent secretary, about chairing an enquiry into the NHS.

We can see a progression from Franks and Plowden as representatives of a high-minded post-war consensus through to Rayner and Griffiths, the supermarketeers and heralds of the era of the management consultants. This marked the end of the post-war period. For the most part, the great and the good were put out to grass in the Thatcher years.

Accordingly, Rayner and Griffiths were not asked to chair committees of enquiry with all the deliberation that that implies. They took no evidence, they did not write lengthy reports - in fact they were only tangentially concerned with policy. Efficiency was the name of the game and these two were professionals at it, though their approaches were fundamentally different, even opposed. They moved quickly and expected fast results, especially Rayner. Coded reports were a thing of the past; the direct management approach had arrived.

The rise of the management consultants and their associated accountancy firms as the new 'firemen' of government was paralleled by the rise of the lobbyist profession. As government came to resemble the Hapsburg Empire in its last stages so new conduits had to be channelled between the politicians and an influential segment of the public, namely big business and especially multi-national companies. The lobbyists were there to thread their way through appropriate parts of government and make representations on behalf of their clients, operating at parliamentary, civil service and ministerial levels. They, like the management consultants, are outsiders and like the consultants are also the beneficiaries of the unravelled and dishevelled system of government.

The barriers to effective government that result directly from our outmoded and largely redundant set of constitutional arrangements are now widely recognised across the political spectrum. Calls for radical reform no longer come solely from the centre and left but emanate also from the wet and dry wings of the right. A broad spectrum coalition is emerging for a major review of the system. From left of centre various proposals of the Labour Campaign for Electoral Reform, the Institute for Public Policy Research, Charter 88, the Liberal Democrats and the Democratic Audit are echoed in the right of centre reform programmes of the European Policy Forum and in the writings of Ferdinand Mount, Norman Stone and Paul Johnson. There is a growing sense that fixing and incremental adjustments, however ingenious or extensive, will not suffice for much longer.

It may well be at some future date, following extensive constitutional reform of a root and branch kind, that the system will return to one where crises are sporadic and relatively contained and therefore amenable to the ministrations of an individual fixer. In the meantime, however, the archaic constitutional condition of Britain will provide the management consultants and their like with a continuing bonanza and with a monopoly threatened only by the rise of a new set of corporate firemen offering a different range of nostrums. Even so, while awaiting a radical constitutional reconstruction, it is clear that certain crises will arise of a kind that will be within the compass and competence of an individual. The recent use made of Sir Bernard Tomlinson and Sir Ron Dearing to deal with contentious issues in health and education respectively are proof of this. By the same token, the growing reliance on routine fixers in the form of senior judges, such as Nolan, Scott and Woolf, to investigate dramatic, 'hot potato' issues is indicative of further mutations in the contemporary activity of fixing.

2 Oliver Franks: A Man for All Treasons

Baron Franks, OM, GCMG, KCB, KCVO, CBE, PC, will be seen as the undisputed doyen of post-war British fixers. His public career spanned the period from September 1939 to the first Thatcher government. On his death in 1992 lavish praise was heaped on him in the obituaries, not just because of his achievements, but also because he was a prime example of a breed of public servant that was rapidly becoming extinct. If the eulogies were for the individual they also saluted the passing of an age that had afforded expansive opportunities for the talented generalist to display his versatility to the full. As *The Times* observed:

> The golden days of that elegant old network have gone, with its sinecures making possible service to the state interspersed with periods of intellectually rigorous leisure. (17 October 1992)

Over the years Oliver Franks played a wide variety of roles as academic, civil servant, diplomat, Reith lecturer, banker and, above all, fixer. He was offered many more, which he declined, including Governor of the Bank of England, Secretary General of NATO, Director General of the BBC and editor of *The Times*. Press comments were unanimous in their judgement as to the quality of his mind and his professional skills: 'master of all briefs', 'the great inquisitor', 'an alpha treble plus mind', 'last of the spartans'. In a leader *The Times* remarked that:

> He was not just a member of the First XI of the Great and the Good. He was its captain, wicket-keeper and last man in ... we shall not look upon his like again. This is partly because it takes time and age to make the qualities of Greatness and Goodness visible. It is also because of the necessary shift in British public affairs from a citizen to a professional army. The increased activity of public life has destroyed the traditional breeding grounds of the

Great and the Good. Britain did not need them all quite as much
as many of them thought it did. But it will always need men of the
stature of Lord Franks. (17 October 1992)

This reflection on how times changed is fair enough but in representing
Franks solely as a relic of the past it does him less than justice. One of
the reasons why he towered over others is precisely because he was
acutely aware that he was bestriding the changeover from one regime, the
hallmark of which was general *administration*, to a new one, whose main
characteristic would be that of specialist *management*. Echoing, perhaps,
some aspects of James Burnham's thesis proclaimed in *The Managerial
Revolution*, published in 1941, he realised that the bureaucrat was about
to give way to the technocrat. He had a prescient appreciation as to the
likely turn of events and, what is even more to the point, he acted upon
it. He was, therefore, both the intellectual and practical personification of
the historical transfer which was happening. It was this blend of ancient
and modern in his make-up that made him unique: he was at once among
the last of the mandarins and in the vanguard of the management
consultants. As he put it himself: 'The civil servant would have to ac-
uire some of the qualities of the businessman' (quoted in Hennessy, 1990a,
p.124).

His formal training in philosophy and, in particular, his identification
with Kantian ideas, induced in him an almost excessively high valuation
on rational analysis and orderliness and goes a long way to explain why
he despised the world of politics and most politicians. For him, it is a
messy milieu and one made messier by the deficiencies in both character
and intellect of the politicians themselves. The post-war world would
require a new, better trained type of civil servant to offset the antics of
politicians and anticipate the avoidable difficulties thrown up by politics.
The implication is never very far away that unless the system of
government is reorganised to bring in more personnel of the calibre and
outlook of Oliver Franks on a regular and routine basis, coherent,
consistent, and enduring policy outcomes will not be achieved and fixers,
like himself, will have to be resigned to being called back to the service
of the state at frequent intervals.

This somewhat arrogant and disdainful viewpoint was not incompatible
with his origins and early background which contained strong ascetic and
puritanical elements. Born in 1905, he was the son of a Congregational
theologian who was the Principal of the Western Theological College at

Bristol. He and his brother and sisters were encouraged to read, argue and question. The College's library contained thousands of volumes which Oliver read voraciously from the age of eleven. An intellectually rich existence perhaps, but as one of four children whose father earned only £300 a year, it was materially very modest. After Bristol Grammar School, he went to Queen's College Oxford. There he rowed enthusiastically, but also, displaying already the high seriousness which was to be a distinctive Franks characteristic all his life, worked hard and gained first class honours in both Honour Mods and Greats. He was immediately offered a teaching Fellowship which he took up in 1927, after a year spent in Germany. He married Barbara Tanner, a Quaker heiress in 1931. Apart from a stimulating spell as visiting professor at the University of Chicago in 1935 (where he was offered the faculty Deanship) he remained at Queen's until 1937 when he applied for and got at the young age of thirty-two the Chair of Moral Philosophy at Glasgow. A former occupant had been Adam Smith and, as Franks would always proudly proclaim, the only post for which he ever formally applied; all his other jobs were offered to him. Even then, it was not exactly a 'cold' application, for the other philosophy chair at Glasgow was held by his former tutor at Queen's. At Glasgow, as at Queen's and Chicago before, he was a willing and excellent academic administrator as well as a diligent and stimulating teacher.

He retained throughout his life the frugal habits and pious outlook of his upbringing, in stark contrast to many of his Oxford contemporaries. 'Severely cerebral' was one description of him. It was said of Franks in Washington, where his predecessor Lord Inverchapel was known to have enjoyed *risqué* jokes, that Franks was 'the kind of serious intellectual whose austere charm made one wonder whether he would know a dirty story if he heard one' (Brandon, 1988, p.75). His teetotalism was well known, like his forbidding exterior; it was once said of him that when the ice had been broken the water was exceedingly cold. But he did occasionally drink a dry martini in the line of duty and also possessed a notable charm when he chose to use it. He was a shy, private man who was also a confident public speaker, addressing the American Society of Newspaper Editors on Western civilisation without notes and holding them spellbound (Brandon, op. cit., p.75). He was a near-Quaker whose friends wondered, as war approached, whether he would take the pacifist line (Danchev, 1993, p.39) but who then, as a high ranking civil servant, made a major contribution to the production of munitions. He managed, at least to his own satisfaction, to square the circle, praising the Lord *and* passing the ammunition. Later, as ambassador in Washington, he successfully urged Britain's participation in the Korean War. In the last year of his life he became a 'convinced' Quaker, joining the Witney Monthly Meeting as a full member (*The Friend*, 19 March 1993).

Had it not been for the Second World War Franks would probably have remained an academic, perhaps becoming a vice-chancellor and possibly chairman of the University Grants Committee, before a pre-retirement post as head of an Oxford college. As it was by 1945 he had risen to be Permanent Secretary at the Ministry of Supply. Such rapid promotion exceeded even that of Enoch Powell, another young pre-war philosophy professor, who enlisted in the army in 1939 and ended up with the rank of brigadier. In equivalent terms, Franks was a full general and thus three rungs higher.

The Ministry of Supply was to give Franks an in-depth and prolonged experience of middle and senior management. It was concerned naturally with all aspects of weaponry, but was very much more than that, dealing with atomic energy, iron and steel and other metals, and engineering. It also sponsored research which made it the greatest single employer of scientists in Britain and perhaps in the world (Mackenzie, 1950, p.68).

It was thus a complex conglomerate requiring a variety of skills among its personnel. The permanent civil servants were a small minority, being outnumbered twelve to one by the temporaries, who mostly came from business and academic life. 'This partnership of civil servant, don and businessman turned out to be one of the most interesting and fruitful experiments of the war'. (Hancock and Gowing, 1949, p.89). On his arrival Franks, always an avid reader, devoured departmental minutes as an introduction to the ways of Whitehall, together with the twelve volume history of the Ministry of Munitions, Supply's First World War predecessor. For the rest of his life the scholarly approach of wide reading was the prelude to taking up any new practical task. The Ministry had to establish many Royal Ordnance Factories. At the peak in 1942, they employed 300,000 people, many of them young Irish women, 'the largest munitions undertaking in military history' (Calder, 1969, p.324). Provision for their welfare had to be made but production was the main imperative which in turn required an adequate flow of relevant data; it was statistics which were 'the lifeblood of the Ministry of Supply' (Postan, 1952, p.351). Speed was essential. The card game *Racing Demon*, Douglas Jay suggested, would have been good training (Jay, 1980, p.88).

Franks took to all of this with great ease and enjoyment, working even harder than the permanent civil servants and acquiring a reputation as the most competent of the temporaries.

A huge ministry such as Supply naturally faced formidable communications problems. Franks got intensive experience of networking. Though the obvious and formal means of communicating was via committees and minutes, 'far more effective was the close personal contact which existed between a comparatively small number of ministers and civil servants, permanent and temporary ... by lunching, dining and even breakfasting together they ... developed a corporate thought which was more effective than any series of minuted decisions' (Chester, 1951, p.19). In the sphere of economic policy there were probably twenty to fifty people who, if their views coincided, could do almost anything, though ministers, if they wished to assert themselves, got the last word. 'At the top it is personal ability and power rather than any arrangement of committees that really matters' (op. cit., p.26). This network continued to exist after the war, and was the main conduit by which Franks was to be recalled to the colours time and again.

Reflecting on his Whitehall experience in a lecture, he saw the whole process as 'a deliberate and continuous effort to reconstruct the activities of the national economy in the balance thought best to win the war. It was a major essay in management ... the essential point was the strength brought in by people from industry and commerce'. An administrative civil servant needed much more than analytic power and the ability to make proposals. 'He had to take a line, expound it, persuade and convince ... he had to have a keen sense of what was practical and of timing. He had to have the strength of will to take responsibility to translate policies into facts' (Franks, 1947b, p.12).

At this time his views were, to put it mildly, *dirigiste*. Civil Service successes on the home front strengthened belief in the planned economy and technocracy. In many cases his Ministry had put government controllers in place of existing managers, or acquired the equity in a firm by compulsory purchase. The government, said Franks, was '... committed to selecting and defining the ends of the national economy ... it is engaged on a radical redefinition of the function of Government in the economic field and is asserting its job to be the shaping of situations before they arise. In short, it has ... become general manager of the national economy' (Franks, 1947a, p.35). He envisaged a future in which industry and commerce would 'have roles that are extensions of the function of the civil service'.

But this was 1947, the year in which economic complacency was shattered, the *annus horrendus*. Currency and balance of payments crises, added to the worst winter in living memory, were exacerbated by strikes and a fuel crisis. Franks' war-time success gave him the chance to be 'in at the creation' of the post-war economic order, his first really large fixing task.

In June of 1947, General George Marshall, the US Secretary of State, had delivered a speech at Harvard which called for 'a cure rather than a mere palliative' for 'the hunger, poverty, desperation and chaos' in Europe. Marshall proposed that programmes for reconstruction should be devised, developed and agreed by the European nations, with the USA giving 'friendly aid in the drafting of a European programme and ... later support for such a programme'. Ernest Bevin, the British Foreign Secretary, immediately seized the implication of Marshall's speech. Within hours both Britain and the other European states had started to take action. Bevin chose Franks to lead the British team in Paris where the hastily formed Committee of European Economic Cooperation (CEEC) was to meet. Franks became the chairman of the sixteen nation conference. Undertaken as a long vacation task, it was to be the hardest work he had ever done. Against a background of continuing economic crisis, severer rationing and the imminent suspension of sterling convertibility, the conference had to draw up a response to the potential offer of US aid. It had to indicate deficits in vital commodities, how far European needs could be met by increased production and what outside requirements were necessary to ensure this (*The Times*, 18 July 1947). Questionnaires were sent out to all sixteen governments. After six hectic weeks, the first draft was dismissed by the Americans as little more than a shopping list. They wanted measures for achieving financial stability, commitments to reduce trade barriers, a statement of general principles, in other words the first moves towards European integration. A redrafted report, done in a few days and taken to Washington was acceptable enough for the conference not to be reconvened. But the idea of a Customs Union in Western Europe was now on the agenda; indeed when Franks, presenting the final report, said that they had been 'encouraged to find that Europe was not an empty word. They had tried to bring out a common purpose, common principles, common interests' (*The Times*, 23 September 1947), these were the words the Americans wanted to hear and Franks prudently provided them, though he and Bevin knew that it would be politically unacceptable at home.

However much he had hankered after a life at Queen's, his role in getting the Marshall Plan off the ground seems to have rekindled in Franks the desire for greater action. The network - in the form of Edwin Plowden - had little difficulty in persuading Bevin to appoint him to the Embassy in Washington. Franks arrived fresh from his triumph over the Marshall plan negotiations, which he had had to sell all over America, a youthful forty-three. Only Peter Jay was younger at forty and only Ormsby-Gore, later Lord Harlech, had more clout as a friend of President Kennedy. He had, he admitted to Richard Crossman years later, had more power than a senior minister. His appointment made clear not only Bevin's regard for his work in Paris but also a determination to deal bilaterally with the US. It was a basic principle of Bevin's foreign policy that the UK was not just another European country. He also needed Franks in Washington to secure an anti-Soviet pact.

The NATO negotiations, which began in July 1948, were a revolutionary step for the Americans. They gave Franks an ideal opportunity to practise those skills of chairmanship and diplomacy that had been perfected in Paris, especially in view of the looming Presidential election, which effectively tied the hands of the State Department, and gave Franks an opportunity to show what he was made of.

Sir Nicholas Henderson, later himself Ambassador in Washington, watched admiringly while Franks, conducted the other ambassadors, all older than himself, like an orchestra:

> Sir Oliver Franks possessed capacities of intellect and exposition which none of his colleagues could equal or ignore. To him fell the main burden of the negotiations: to make the running until such time as the Americans could take the lead, and to prevent a gulf developing between the European and American sides of the table. ... He, more than any of the other representatives, imparted a sense of collectivity to the negotiations. He sought to lift the discussions from a series of statements of national viewpoints to a plane where all were endeavouring to reconcile minor disparities for the achievement of an aim of great importance to them all ... The methods used to win conviction were those more of the sower than the advocate: he would sow doubts here and there and then when they had taken root he would scatter seeds of his own persuasion in such a plausible way that the other representatives soon felt that

there was no alternative but to gather round and nourish them. (Henderson, 1982, p.42)

A crucial feature of Franks' ambassadorship was his friendship with Dean Acheson who succeeded Marshall as Secretary of State in January 1949. This was to have a major influence on the special relationship over the next four years or so, due largely to the fact that Acheson was a convinced Anglophile - indeed 'indulgent of British weaknesses and affiliations' (Nicholas, 1970, p.887). Acheson, who demanded a very high intellectual standard of people, accepted Franks as an equal. They met regularly in private to discuss affairs of common interest so that they could maintain a degree of confidentiality which would otherwise have been impossible. Though Acheson refused to acknowledge any 'special relationship' there is no doubt that during the Truman presidency Britain's was one which was qualitatively different from US relations with other European states, and that Franks contributed a great deal to this. He was a constant in Washington during a time which saw Herbert Morrison replacing Bevin as Foreign Secretary and later Churchill succeeding Attlee as Prime Minister. He was influential on a number of issues, resisting, for example, pressure from Congress for the UK to participate in the 1950 Schumann Plan.

On the Korean war Franks felt it vital for the British to prove themselves the most reliable ally by sending land forces, even writing privately to Attlee in his own hand to urge this on the Prime Minister. He also played an important part in getting an undertaking from Truman, though admittedly only an informal one, that nuclear weapons would not be used without consultation with the UK and pushed for prior consultation on the use to be made of US bases on British soil - 'no annihilation without representation' (Danchev, 1993, p.132). The formula agreed for this still stood forty years later.

The 1949 devaluation of the pound marked another high point of Franks' influence; Franks, in touch with American opinion, joined the pro-devaluation group, including Hall and Plowden and was present at a cabinet meeting in July 1949 to discuss the issue.

Whatever judgement might be made with hindsight on some of these policy decisions, Franks' ambassadorship was a double success. For the UK he had 'probably earned more respect than any previous foreign representative' (*The Times,* 27 February 1952), and had performed excellently for the Attlee government for four years in trying circumstances. For himself, it was probably the most successful phase of his life and it certainly gave him considerable satisfaction. In conversation with Henry Brandon he compared it with having made a marriage work (Brandon, 1988, p.95). When the time came for him to leave towards the end of 1952, farewells even included a nationally networked radio broadcast (*The Times*, 28 November 1952).

But his 1954 Reith lectures showed that his view of the world was fast being overtaken. The residues of the special relationship and great power status were still clearly visible in his thinking: 'close and effective cooperation between Britain and the United States is the basic condition of an orderly world', he declared. Britain's geography and history, his argument ran, prevented her from abandoning what he called 'the traditions of greatness'. In effect he was setting out Churchill's 'three circles' view of Britain's place in the world. But he pinpointed the date of the Schumann Plan as a key one for post-war Europe though, in his view, Britain could take part in such initiatives only as a 'country' member with fewer obligations. He could at this point have beckoned Britain to its European destiny. Not to do so was a failure of intellectual imagination.

Returning from America, he resisted Acheson's attempts to persuade him to become the first Secretary General of NATO. He also declined several other top posts, including one at the Treasury and the editorship of *The Times*; 'an act of creation every day' would not have suited his temperament, he thought. Instead he was invited to become a director of Lloyds Bank early in 1953, with a view to becoming chairman the following year. His career had already peaked.

At this time he showed signs of hesitancy and ambivalence about what to do next. He had a considerable reputation both as a civil servant and diplomat, and might well have been reluctant to leave the limelight. As chairman of Lloyds Banks and later as the Provost of Worcester College, Oxford, neither of which would fully stretch him, he would be well placed to accept this or that commission from the government and other institutions, which would exercise his skills and ensure that he was never far from the centre stage. From the mid-fifties to the mid-seventies he was a high-ranking member of the Great and Good, exemplified by being one of the first members of the National Economic Development Council, an early life peer and chairing one committee after another.

The first of these was the Committee on Tribunals and Enquiries. Like several of his subsequent enquiries, it was concerned with a major constitutional issue. On this occasion, the subject matter was the 'second yoke' borne by the much governed nation (Greenleaf, 1987, p.626) that is delegated legislation and administrative law. Franks at the time knew little of the law but, as with every other assignment, it was for him another rapid learning experience.

The Franks Committee was the first to investigate the area of administrative law since the Donoughmore committee twenty-five years earlier. Its terms of reference pointed to those decisions which parliament had decided should be subject to appeal, not the purely executive decisions such as that made about Crichel Down, which concerned a piece of land in Dorset acquired by the Crown for military purposes and which the previous owner had failed to get back. But the germ of Franks' enquiry was to be found in that scandal; the *cause célèbre* proved a watershed for the convention of ministerial responsibility. Civil servants had been publicly questioned when the matter was being investigated and the Minister, Sir Thomas Dugdale, had resigned when evidence of maladministration became known. Sir Edward Bridges, a civil service mentor of Franks, thought the time was right for an examination of the field. More and more tribunals and committees, especially on planning and welfare matters, were affecting the lives of more and more citizens. At the level of the ordinary person, the first Franks report produced a number of improvements which were widely welcomed. These were based on the principle that tribunals and enquiries should have three characteristics: openness, fairness and impartiality. To ensure that this was more than a pious hope, it was recommended that a Council on Tribunals should be set up to oversee the machinery of justice. The requirement for openness meant that inspectors' reports, on planning enquiries for instance, should be published and this completely altered the whole ethos of administrative procedures (Delafons, 1982, p.258). The report also supported the idea that there should be an appeal from executive decisions, which later helped to lead to the creation of the office of ombudsman, or Parliamentary Commissioner for Administration, in 1967. One result of these changes was an increase in the number of public enquiries on controversial planning issues.

Apart from the Council on Tribunals, which was seen by some as a new constitutional function, the report did little on a constitutional level. It rejected the view expressed by some top civil servants that tribunals were part of the machinery of government but also denied that they were ordinary courts, thus failing to make a definite choice between judicial and administrative criteria as standards of judgement. Perhaps too much influenced by the writings of Dicey, who 'taught that administrative law is the devil incarnate' (Bridges, quoted in Greenleaf, op. cit., p.625), the Committee was determined not to recommend an administrative division of the High Court because it would create two jurisdictions. Ministerial responsibility must be preserved. To those who took a different view, it was a restatement of the problem rather than a solution, 'relying on comforting, meaningless and apparently indestructible fictions' (Griffith, 1959, p.126).

Behind the scenes Franks was also much in demand at this time by both the Conservative and Labour parties, for advice on financial and banking matters. He was an influential member of the Radcliffe Committee on the monetary system, whose report appeared in 1959. This enquiry had been prompted partly by the 1957 Bank Rate leak which had weakened the position of the Governor, Lord Cobbold. Here Franks was a fixer chosen to back up a routine fixer in the form of Lord Justice Radcliffe; as a banker, he may on this occasion have been chosen for his expertise. The report was highly critical of the Bank and its economic and statistical services. It advocated the recognition of the primacy of the Chancellor over the Governor of the Bank and set the seal of official approval on scepticism about the effectiveness of monetary policy. For those who did not agree with the unanimous neo-Keynesian conclusions of the report, the issues were blurred rather than clarified and its recommendations seemed 'timid and tentative and in some cases obscure and even contradictory' (Seldon, 1960, p.87). Had unanimity perhaps been purchased at too high a price? One commentator discerned too little realism about the pressures of politics and thought the committee revealed their previous experience of public service 'in the emergency of war when the all-consuming purpose of defence implied acceptance of political control no matter how arbitrary' (op. cit., p.107). Interestingly, the Secretary to the Committee was a young civil servant called Robert Armstrong.

Not only was Franks a prominent member of the Committee, but he was also in the running for the Governor's job. Both political parties considered him a possible successor to Cobbold. Gaitskell noted in his diary 'how useful it is to have someone as good as him in a key position in the City' (Gaitskell, 1983, p.460). Conservative ministers made firm approaches to Franks, the intermediary being Lord Plowden. Finally, though clearly very tempted, he declined the Bank to take on the job of Provost of Worcester College, and returned once more to Oxford.

His relationship with Oxford presented another paradox. It was apparently his dearest wish to work there, but he was always keen to accept commissions that would take him away. His attempt to gain the Chancellorship of the University was one of the few real failures of his life. The Oxford Chancellorship election of 1960, occasioned by the death of Lord Halifax, also a former Washington ambassador, was a wholly exceptional event in Franks' life. The only time he stood for public election - by all Oxford MAs - he lost in spite of having considerable support within the university. A large number of heads of houses were for him. Franks, in India for the World Bank, telegraphed that he would accept nomination. Enter Hugh Trevor-Roper, 'arch intriguer' and Regius Professor of History, a post in the gift of the Prime Minister; he took the view that a faction of dons had attempted to fix the election in advance. He proposed to invite Macmillan to stand.

Many letters were written to *The Times*. Some saw the PM as preeminent. Others emphasised Franks' administrative ability and experience and felt the burden of the office would be too great for a serving premier. Macmillan won by 1976 votes to 1697, Trevor-Roper having apparently used every means to get his man in (Sampson, 1967, p.177). Macmillan the hedonist took great pleasure in his victory and told Harold Nicolson that he attributed his success to the fact that *The Times* had published a leader supporting Franks! Hence no doubt the following exchange in the House of Commons. Tony Benn (as he later became) said to the Prime Minister:

> May I also congratulate him on having proved by his own tremendous victory in a ballot held in Latin, open for all to see, that the Establishment has nothing to learn from the Electrical Trades Union?

Macmillan replied:

> Except that on this occasion, I think, the Establishment was beaten. (quoted ibid., p.177)

Franks the fixer was also to undertake commissions from non-governmental bodies. One of his most successful pieces of work was a spin-off from the Robbins report on higher education. Robbins had recommended two business schools linked with well-established educational institutions. Franks was to consult the interested parties and make recommendations on how this might best be achieved. He was called in as an arbitrator (by two old members of the Ministry of Supply network, Lord Rootes and Sir Norman Kipping, both eminent businessmen). Working, unusually for him, alone, he spent a month taking oral evidence - working up to ten hours a day, four days a week - from management and educational bodies, business organisations and individuals. In the course of these consultations he managed to bring together widely divergent views and to come to conclusions which to a large extent satisfied all the parties concerned and which also fitted in neatly with the Robbins recommendations. A joint university/business structure was essential, he argued, so that neither academic nor business people felt their aims were being lost to sight; the new schools should be in major conurbations and offer courses to both graduates and those with business experience. All of this in just eleven pages of typescript was general enough to be acceptable to all. It was clearly an idea whose time had come. The report resulted in the creation of the London and Manchester Business Schools. In May 1964 the final fix came with the appointment of his old friend Lord Plowden to be the first chairman of the London Business School.

Oxford University had also featured in the Robbins Report, being taken to task as 'slow, obscure and different', and was therefore under some pressure to indulge in a bout of self-criticism. Franks was invited to chair an internal enquiry which gave him the chance, some thought, to get his revenge for his failure in the Chancellorship election. The enquiry was conducted with maximum publicity, a strong lead being given by the chairman, which gave him full opportunity to display his skills. He wrote his own terms of reference and had a major part in choosing his fellow commissioners, who included Robert Hall, a former civil service colleague and Oxford don. The remit was very wide, covering organisational and structural matters, the Vice-Chancellor and his functions, admissions, teaching and exams.

Hearings started in early 1965 and these were reported almost daily on the court page of *The Times* and elsewhere in the press too, sometimes sensationally. Many thought Franks had gone too far when the Commission published a statistical report on the pay and perks of dons. The magisterial style of the chairman is still recalled by one witness nearly thirty years later, and in his usual way Franks worked himself and everyone else hard. They went through three-quarters of a million words of written evidence and listened to oral evidence from eighty-two organisations and individuals. They also had assistance from university statisticians and from accountants at Price Waterhouse (Danchev, 1993, p.161); figures as well as facts were grist to Franks' mill.

The final report proposed a complete reorganisation of the university offices and the appointment of a vice-chancellor for a four-year term. It also wanted the abolition of entrance awards, fewer tutorials and more seminars together with a range of other reforms. Reaction was mixed, including some strong criticism: some feared that the commission would have liked to impose a bureaucratic uniformity. Lord Balogh thought that the recommendations would concentrate power in a few hands and reduce democracy, 'We have been bequeathed a chaotic system of government and I cherish it. The university is neither a factory nor a business nor even a Government department' (*The Times*, 23 November 1966). Lord Annan asked the vital question 'Is Franks too much of a civil servant and too little of a politician?' (Annan, 1966, p.395).

In spite of the criticisms, the administration of the university - All Souls apart - was transformed; the austere Franks pointed to privileges and extravagances which should be cut down and set in motion an income redistribution system. On the academic side, success was less marked, though admissions policy was widened, but the proposals for mixed colleges were ignored. The recommendations for alterations in the tutorial system had little impact and the recommendation for the abolition of entrance awards took almost twenty years to implement as did the four-year term for the vice-chancellor.

After these two privately commissioned reports, his next fixer's commission was an official one: a review of the working of Section 2 of the Official Secrets Act. This was the first of several assignments Franks undertook which were very close to sensitive areas of government. This one and the Ministerial Memoirs Committee, like the Tribunals and Enquiries Report so long before, touched closely on that rocky area of British constitutional theory - ministerial responsibility.

Shortly before the announcement of the enquiry four defendants had been acquitted on secrets charges in a case involving the *Sunday Telegraph* and the Nigerian civil war. But the government denied that there was any connection. The 1970 Conservative manifesto had promised to review the Act and the Fulton Report (1968) had also urged greater openness in government, declaring that the convention that only the minister should explain issues in public was damaging. It was no longer tenable that it should be assumed that the minister had full detailed knowledge and control of all the activities in his department. The question of 'open government' and that of Section 2 of the discredited Official Secrets Act were therefore both on the agenda, though only the latter was specifically mentioned in the terms of reference. The results were bound to be unsatisfactory.

The Committee did indeed examine some of the wider aspects, calling Sir Burke Trend, among others, who proclaimed that the dominant feature of Cabinet government was collective responsibility and that it was important not to reveal differences of view between Cabinet members (Leigh, 1980, p.23). But this and other matters, including the question of a general right of access to official information, they declared to be outside their terms of reference and drew back from them, on the grounds that they raised 'important constitutional issues'.

In spite of the subject matter, Franks determined to have most evidence in public, as he habitually did. The committee gathered a great quantity of information, from overseas as well as domestic witnesses. The report when it appeared in 1972 attacked the 'catch all' nature of Section 2 which obscured the distinction between espionage and leaks and proposed an official information act, which would apply only to certain categories of information - defence, foreign relations, cabinet papers and security.

'What we have done', said Lord Franks interviewed on radio, 'is to abandon an attack on all fronts and make it a highly effective attack in depth, only protecting by criminal law a very few subjects of primary importance to the state and to the people'. But though the necessity for change was widely accepted, this proposal was unpopular on all sides. The press found it too timid. The government thought it went too far. Worse, in the case of a breach of security, the decision as to whether a document had been correctly classified would be taken by a minister - which looked like a breach of natural justice. The provisions on official information seemed to some eyes to be drawn so widely as to cover almost any investigation by journalists. Most trenchant was the remark from Richard Crossman, who condemned the report as 'a timid little document' and predicted that the proposals would provide the civil service with 'an infinitely more powerful weapon than the erratic old blunderbuss which has been going off at rare intervals for the past 50 years' (*The Times*, 4 July 1973).

Another contentious issue was that of a public interest defence. Here Franks took a cautious line on a question that was to be hotly debated in the 1980s when the Conservative government was embarrassed by a series of cases, notably that of Clive Ponting. Such a defence, ran the argument, would be likely to be used where difficult political issues were involved, and would be hard to meet without revealing more sensitive information. It might also be used indiscriminately, raising constitutional issues again. The government was in no hurry to allow a debate on the report; indeed almost a year passed before this took place, at short notice and on a Friday. A lack of public interest, changes in government, opposition from the civil service and the wider implications of all such proposals combined to prevent any progress over the next few years. Unlike its Labour predecessor, the Thatcher government used Section 2 far more than previous ones. When a new Secrets Act was finally passed in 1989 the lines were drawn much more narrowly, refusing a defence not only of public interest but of prior publication, criminalising civil servants who leaked information and severely restricting investigative journalism.

Cabinet secrecy was dealt a severe blow by the publication of the Crossman diaries in the summer of 1975 (see chapter 4). The furore which ensued prompted the formation of a committee under Lord Radcliffe, the membership of which included Conservative and Labour MPs and peers and Franks himself, the man for all treasons. It was in effect a rescue operation. As Radcliffe said, it was not a fact finding committee, but a discussion committee. It recommended that subsequent authors of memoirs should not reveal anything which would jeopardize the requirements of national security or foreign policy, or reveal anything which might destroy confidential relationships until fifteen years had passed. They thought the Cabinet secretary should continue to scrutinize memoirs; these recommendations were immediately accepted by Harold Wilson. Apart from Castle and Benn, few followed in Crossman's footsteps until the spate of memoirs that appeared after the ousting of Margaret Thatcher.

Only a year later, the Labour government again faced difficulties when Harold Wilson's 'lavender list' of resignation honours was called into question. As a result, the Political Honours Scrutiny Committee, chaired by Lord Shackleton, was given a new lease of life. Franks sat on it for many years as the Liberal representative with Robert Carr for the Conservatives. There was a tightening up on the award of all honours of CBE and above, but no serious alteration of prime ministerial prerogative in the area of patronage, though, it was said, Jeffrey Archer's peerage was delayed by a year or two.

Franks' penultimate task as fixer was to handle a 'hot potato' issue, namely to examine the feasibility of drawing up a register of immigrants' dependants for which purpose he was joined by two MPs Mark Carlisle and Sydney Irving. As was his wont, Franks wrote to *The Times* in August 1974 inviting evidence. The final report came out in February 1977, an unusually long gestation period, reflecting both the political sensitivity of the issue and the practical difficulties of devising a fair and satisfactory scheme. A younger Franks might have succeeded in squaring the circle, but by now such an outcome was beyond him. The group made no specific recommendations, saying that the only feasible scheme would be discriminatory, not comprehensive, slow and expensive, while it was difficult to determine accurately the likely numbers of dependants involved.

The Falkland Islands Review - the ultimate challenge for which all his previous committees can be seen as a preparation - resulted from a commitment made in advance of hostilities, before the outcome was known, and intended 'to establish the authority of a government at war' ('The unpredictable invasion', *Economist*, 22 January 1983). The committee was one of privy councillors, which was somewhat unusual, and even more exceptionally the members of the committee and the terms of reference were negotiated with the opposition parties. Franks even at this late stage in his life was apparently the only chairman acceptable to all sides. (Had Britain become a republic, it was once suggested, Oliver Franks would have been its first president). The choice was inspired by Robert Armstrong, who had been secretary to the Radcliffe Committee, and had long admired Franks' skills. The old man himself said it was because he was a 'political neuter' (Danchev, 1992, p.ix). But no one else approached his immense authority or his experience of sensitive enquiries. The rest of the committee was made up of two former Conservative ministers, Lords Watkinson and Barber; a former Labour minister Lord Lever; all of these three had some experience of cabinet committees and security aspects of government; Merlyn Rees, was the only MP, but he had been a Labour Northern Ireland Secretary and Home Secretary and on the Official Secrets enquiry with Franks. Each of these, as it was pointed out, could protect the interests of a former Prime Minister. The fifth member was Sir Patrick Nairne, college head and retired mandarin, who some thought was there to protect the interests of the civil servants, but this is to underestimate him. His own modest interpretation is that he had been asked to join the committee to help look after the ageing Franks and make sure he got home safely, since they both lived in Oxford!

The terms of reference were to prove vital and as always Franks and his committee never lost sight of them. 'To review the way in which the responsibilities of Government in relation to the Falkland Islands and their dependencies were discharged in the period leading up to the Argentine invasion of the Falkland Islands on 2 April 1982, taking into account all such factors in previous years as are relevant; and to report'.

Franks knew that his task whatever else it was, was to turn the affair into 'political history' (Danchev, op. cit., p.xvi). Though a military success, it was a failure of diplomacy and of cabinet government. He was keen, it was said, to produce a unanimous report which would maintain his record of having no dissenting minority report attached to any of the enquiries he had chaired. It was to prove touch and go in this case. In the circumstances it was essential that everyone could put their name to what was produced, though this in the end resulted in a failure to be as outspoken as some would have liked.

Franks' first aim was thus to ensure that the enquiry into such a politically delicate matter was non-partisan. Recovering in hospital for a few days from a cataract operation, he thought this over and decided on a 'read in'. He put it to the committee that they could either allow civil servants to select material for them or they could read it themselves; they would have to form opinions on it. And they had access to all the official information from the Treasury, DTI, MoD, Home Office, cabinet papers, monthly intelligence reports and even raw material from GCHQ. It was only after several weeks of intensive reading, assiduously undertaken, Franks having insisted that all five members should put their thoughts down on paper, that they began to hear evidence from civil servants and military men, ministers and former ministers - and the Prime Minister.

Franks gave a very strong lead. 'This time he was running a jury' said one member (*The Times*, 17 January 1983). He consulted the other members of the committee, but he knew what he wanted from them. He had insisted on having a good drafter as secretary to the Committee and on this occasion did not do any drafting himself, though he was definitely in editorial control, taking great care over wording. He questioned toughly and all were impressed by his mastery of detail. They worked at a brisk pace. It was understood they would complete their task by Christmas if at all possible; the Prime Minister had hoped for this, for Franks it was thought would be tiring by then.

The report gave a meticulously detailed account of UK/Argentine relations *vis à vis* the Falklands since 1965; like the intelligence apparatus it paid perhaps too little attention to events in Argentina, but it was the 'most rigorous scrutiny ever' of an episode in British foreign policy (Francis Pym in *The Times*, 20 January 1983). And though the enquiry, contrary to Franks' usual practice, had been conducted under conditions of considerable secrecy, it revealed a good deal which had previously been concealed concerning the intelligence organisations and cabinet committees. It was in Danchev's words, an 'unseasonable tribune for open government' (Danchev, 1993, p.171); the secrecy surrounding the JIC and current intelligence groups was removed.   Secret documents were quoted and the existence of the Cabinet's Defence Committee was formally admitted. It also showed up a lack of collective decision making and a failure over years to discuss a matter which eventually became a crisis. This was the area of which Franks was most critical. It should have been discussed in Cabinet or committee.   Although he was procedurally punctilious Franks in fact pronounced absolution: the Prime Minister and her colleagues were, after all, 'reasonable men'. As the *Economist* pointed out, however, the impossibility of allocating blame to people who had behaved reasonably was not 'a happy constitutional innovation' (22 January 1983). The report suggested a tightening up of reporting and assessment procedures and the possibility of having one minister - not the Prime Minister - responsible for security matters. But its most striking features were the refusal to use hindsight and to apportion blame. The method they used to address the central issue was to ask themselves two questions: could the government have foreseen the invasion on 2 April 1982: could it have prevented that invasion?

To the first question it gave the answer no and to the second a definite answer was not possible.   And as a result they concluded that no blame or criticism could be attached to the government. This conclusion fortuitously appeared alone at the top of the final page of the report. The commonest reaction to the report was that it was a whitewash. 'Franks clears Maggie!' screamed the headlines.   Corelli Barnett in *The Times* summed up the general feeling 'The British Establishment has sat in judgement on the British Establishment and found it not guilty' (Letter, 6 January 1983).

In the words of Hugo Young 'It soothes and reassures by performing the ultimate trick of appearing to be so candid' (*Sunday Times*, 23 January 1983). A fiercer criticism was to come later from the pen of Ian Gilmour, a Cabinet minister at the time of the Falklands campaign:

> The verdict of the Franks Committee of distinguished Privy Councillors which was set up to inquire into the origins of the war was that "we would not be justified in attaching any criticism or blame to the present government for the Argentinean Junta's decision to commit an act of unprovoked aggression in the invasion of the Falkland Islands on April 2nd 1982". There are two explanations for that astounding conclusion. The first is the political atmosphere at the time it was written. The Franks report was published in January 1983. While the committee was deliberating, public enthusiasm for what had been achieved remained high. The committee did not want to tarnish a great victory; had the Falkland operation failed, we can be confident that it would have come to a different conclusion.
>
> The second explanation is more particular. The verdict of the Franks Committee demonstrated the well-known truth that if you ask yourself a silly question you are likely to get a very silly answer. The committee asked the question: "Could the government have foreseen the invasion on 2 April? To which the answer is: of course it could not know what was going to happen on 2 April, unless it possessed unique powers of clairvoyance. The proper question to ask was: did the government through its actions and its inaction run an unnecessarily large risk of war being started? And the answer to that question, as we have seen, is undoubtedly, yes". (Gilmour, 1993, p.307-8)

Both Young and Gilmour are correct in their judgements. Franks with his skills intact and fully exercised, delivered a report that served the purpose intended: the government was off the hook and Franks could seal his career with the private satisfaction of a successful fix.

When he died in October 1992, the plaudits heaped upon him in dozens of obituaries and a leader in *The Times*, matched the honours he received in life. What qualities had made him a topclass fixer?

A first class mind, undeniably, coupled with an outstanding memory. His native intellect had been honed by the voracious reading habits of his teenage years and developed as he plundered the volumes in the well stocked library of his father's theological college. This precocious scholarly propensity was continued and rounded off by the philosophical training he received at Oxford, and further reinforced as a tutor and professor.   Although of a scholarly disposition, he was not, by the standards prevailing at the time, a philosopher's philosopher.   He rejected the emerging school of analytical and linguistic philosophy eagerly embraced by his contemporaries who included A.J. Ayer, Gilbert Ryle and P.F. Strawson.   Nor, though Franks' lectures drew large audiences and his clarity of exposition was renowned, was he a performer in the manner of Isaiah Berlin or A.J.P. Taylor.   He remained an old fashioned moral philosopher who felt that Kant had said virtually all there was to say.

The first tool he applied to fixing, then, was a powerful philosophical cast of mind.   He began with a clean sheet and undertook what nowadays would be termed a zero base analysis.   He would invariably call for evidence or facts.   The evidence would be sought internally from minutes and other material and externally by invitation in letters to *The Times*. Facts were important but were certainly not sacred and even more certainly should not be allowed to speak for themselves.   First, if they were reliable they had an obvious relevance.   The war-time statistical section of the Cabinet Office had rapidly developed good data to assist in the formulation of policy and Franks relied on the statistical skills of Elizabeth Ackroyd and the interpretive expertise of Robert Hall to equip him with the necessary numerate background for successful policy formulation.   But, secondly, Franks quickly appreciated that even questionable quantitative data would help to pre-empt opposition to proposals being advanced.   When calling for questionnaires to be completed by the sixteen European nations involved in the OEEC exercise, he would have known that the information provided was deeply suspect and the margin of error considerable.   But it had to be done in order to accommodate the Americans' susceptibilities.

His requests for evidence from the public and interested parties were again prompted by dual motives.   On the one hand, it would throw up some important data in the form of opinions, experience or harder material, while on the other it would legitimise the project in hand.   It was an exercise in mobilisation as much as in participation.   The distribution of questionnaires to dons for the Oxford enquiry is an example of this technique.   Franks was also careful to clarify or define the limits of any task.   He had a fine sense of the logic of the situation, of, that is to say, the limits of feasibility.   He was a catalyst and an implementer, essentially reactive, attending to others' agendas.   He showed zest and determination of the highest order in war-time Whitehall and post-war Washington. With later official assignments, he appeared to lose some of his spark and had a tendency to trim and possibly over-estimate the difficulties of making radical proposals or coming to radical conclusions. This was certainly true when he was dealing with administrative tribunals where he appeared to fudge or split the difference; and the same judgement has been made of the Falklands Enquiry. On the issue of Oxford reform however, he displayed a large measure of radicalism, enjoying in the process, some alleged, revenge for losing the Chancellorship. His penchant for strictly defining the scope of a task would have been reinforced by watching Lord Radcliffe's chairmanship of the monetary system enquiry which illustrated the importance and effectiveness of getting terms of reference appropriately defined at the outset and then adhering strictly to them. Franks said later: 'We could have gone into all these questions ... but if we had produced answers to all of them, we would have been more than a committee. We would have been divinely inspired. We therefore stuck to our terms of reference' (quoted in Danchev, 1993, p.167).

The exploitation of existing networks and, if necessary, the creation of new ones was another technique he employed to the full. College life, the Queen's connection with Glasgow, the informal dining groups in the civil service, would all have developed his appreciation of team-work. Virtually all his assignments came from the network he had joined, while in Paris and Washington he sought to establish new ones or at least surrogates for them in the form of a network ethos. University and civil service collegiality, coupled with attendance at Quaker meetings, would have served to emphasise the efficacy of bonding people for a common purpose.

Properly reading oneself in before commencing a task was an essential pre-requisite for Franks. He did it at the Ministry of Supply and required the same of his colleagues when approaching the Falklands Enquiry.

He would also allow others to speak at length in the course of deliberations. Partly this was to make them feel their contributions were worthwhile, partly to ensure progress was not disrupted by inconvenient afterthoughts and partly to draw them out as fully as possible to see where they were supportive and where opposed to the outcomes Franks had already decided on. Only one person would be allowed to keep cards up his sleeve. He once remarked: 'The amount of time that people are willing to waste in hearing each other talk is a very important constituent of our political life' (Administrative Tribunals and Enquiries, 1957, p.463). But according to one close collaborator, he also had an 'instinct for the exhaustion point' (Nairne interview), after which he would stop discussion and conclude with a felicitous summation in a way which would maximise his own position and down play any contrary views. Finally, he would play up his own considerable moral authority and recognised stature as a past-master in the noble art of fixing.   His austerity, aloofness, assiduity and singleness of purpose were such as to intimidate lesser mortals, who melted when he chose to step down from Olympus and subject them to his personal charm.

Because 'philosopher-kings' of the new planning sort he had rec-ommended in 1947 were not forthcoming in the civil service, despite many attempts to produce them (such as the Fulton Report, creating the Civil Service College, secondments from Whitehall to business etc.), Franks perhaps would not have been surprised at the enormous recourse to management consultants by governments.   To him this would be a second best option, but nevertheless better than nothing.   If he had to choose, management consultants would be the 'goodies', whereas lobbyists, as politicians *manqué*, would be the 'baddies', not least, of course, because wining and dining, free trips, retainers and back-handers would be deeply offensive to his inherent non-conformist outlook and values.   Equally, however, given the failure to implant the new planner-philosopher-king into Whitehall, he would not have been surprised at the appearance of the lobbyist.

Franks, then, was not simply the grand master of the post-war corps of fixers, he also embodied in his experience, attitudes, modes of operation, and to a marked and unequal degree - foresight - some of the dominant elements of the theory and practice of contemporary government.

3 Edwin and Bridget Plowden: A Couple of Fixers

Edwin and Bridget Plowden constitute a unique duo: his career lasted longer and covered more issues; hers was shorter and largely confined to education and broadcasting but she was invariably described as 'formidable'. His forbears were Shropshire Catholic gentry who remained true to Rome throughout the Reformation and after, while her father had been an admiral and governor-general of Ceylon. A common factor between them was their schooling, which was somewhat unconventional. Edwin was denied a traditional public school education by his American mother, being sent to school in Switzerland instead and then for a spell to Hamburg University, before being repatriated to Cambridge to pursue a well-trodden English path; Bridget had a very patchy education partly provided by a series of governesses which left her underqualified for university. In the long run, however, these experiences were no handicap to either of them in the public service they were to render.

Edwin Plowden's career is a fairly close approximation of Oliver Franks'. The latter may have had a more incisive mind and always sought an academic milieu, the former was clearly highly intelligent and, in a less aloof or austere way than Franks, very adept at getting people to work together not simply because of good inter-personal skills but also by virtue of his ability to translate the views of experts in such a way as to have them put on the agenda and acted upon.

His career, moving in and out of government and to and from industry and commerce, has a distinctly Washingtonian resonance. It began, as with Franks, with a lucky war.

After receiving his economics degree from Cambridge in 1929 he shared the experience of many graduates at the time of the slump. Finding it difficult to obtain appropriate employment, he took work as a handyman, farm labourer and salesman before joining a city firm dealing in potash where he spent the rest of the decade. In 1939 after the outbreak of war, he became a temporary civil servant in the Ministry of Economic Warfare, where Gladwyn Jebb and Hugh Gaitskell also worked.

This was the first and most crucial move from the world of business to the world of government: the pendulum had begun to swing and would do so, with irregular timing, for the next forty years. This pattern can be seen in broad terms that cover all the phases of his career. From 1940 to 1945 he worked mainly in the Ministry of Aircraft Production, first for the irascible Lord Beaverbrook and then for Sir Stafford Cripps, ending up at the age of thirty-seven as Chief Executive. In 1946 he resumed his business career only to be recalled to government service a year later as Chief Planner to Attlee's government, then beleaguered by a major fuel shortage and economic crisis, a post he held until 1953. From 1954 he remained in the public sector as chairman of a nationalised industry, the United Kingdom Atomic Energy Authority. He then migrated back into the private sector first as chairman of British Aluminium and then of Tube Investments (1960-76) as well as keeping a foot in the door of government by conducting a number of official inquiries that included the crucial 1961 report on public expenditure. Finally from the mid-1970s until the mid-1980s he was involved in a variety of agencies involving the police, venture capital and top people's pay.

Plowden had left Whitehall in 1946 and returned to his pre-war employer C. Tennant Sons and Co; but only a year later, with the Labour government facing enormous economic problems, he was asked to return as Chief Planning Officer. He was at first reluctant to accept the post, but was finally persuaded to do so. He drove a hard bargain, securing a salary of £6,500, almost twice that of Bridges, the Permanent Secretary to the Treasury, as well as a car and driver. All the same he had doubts about the job. They were partly due to the exaggerated stories about his power and importance, though Attlee when announcing the appointment, had made it clear that all planning decisions would be taken by the Cabinet not Plowden, who would report to Morrison as Lord President of the Council. At the time Morrison was ill and the role of the Central Economic Planning Staff (CEPS) was unclear, while the Economic Planning Board had yet to be appointed. Power struggles within the Cabinet made dealing with the economic crisis still more difficult and consequently the newly appointed Chief Planner did not have a great deal to do initially. To make matters worse, Morrison did not grasp economic concepts very readily. Not surprisingly, Plowden confided in Cripps in September that he was in despair because the machinery for managing the economy was unworkable and he was thinking of resigning (Donoughue & Jones, 1973, p.414-5 and Plowden, 1989, p.18). However, major changes were about to transform the prospect. Stafford Cripps gained full charge of economic affairs in succession to Morrison, with the title of Minister of Economic Affairs, and then quickly became Chancellor when Dalton's premature press leak forced his resignation. The management of economic affairs thus returned to the Treasury, economic and financial policy were reunited, Plowden and his planning staff moved to the Treasury and almost simultaneously, the Economic Section of the Cabinet Office acquired a new director in Robert Hall. Hall, a Cambridge-educated economist had been in the Supply Ministry with Franks in the war. Douglas Jay, another Supply old boy, was by this time Economic Secretary to the Treasury. Since the wartime networks had carried over to peacetime, Plowden and Hall collaborated easily with each other which made for greater harmony between Downing Street and the Treasury. They were to become remarkably influential both as a double act and in combination with a few other civil servants, such as R.W.B. 'Otto' Clarke. This influence was due to several factors. First, Cripps, though a powerful figure in the government for most of 1947-50, like Morrison, his predecessor, did not really understand economic policy. According to Douglas Jay, though he could have spelled them out, he did not really grasp the arguments for and against devaluation. He was however an immensely hard worker and very effective at pushing through the ideas and policies suggested to him. 'Cripps added the drive and moral fervour' (Brittan, 1971, p.180). The second reason was the shortage of trained economists; with one exception, Plowden's staff were not professional economists. He remembers 'there seemed to be few among the senior Treasury officials who appreciated the difference between looking after candle ends and making economic policy' (Plowden, 1989, p.22). Plowden, like Franks, showed a prescience about the new thrusts and direction of post-war government policy where the economic component of policy would usually be paramount; this would need a more managerial approach.

Plowden looked mainly to Robert Hall for guidance and their close relationship was to continue for many years. Hall was an academic and a diffident man. A good many civil servants found him almost in-articulate, but at his best he had an 'almost feminine intuition for the way the economy was moving' (Brittan, 1971, p.95-6). Plowden was the more incisive and a far better communicator. Hall loaded the gun, and he fired the bullets was how Plowden chose to express it (Plowden, 1989, p.25). Together they were a vital source of support and advice for Cripps: in November 1947 Hall noted in his diary that since Stafford Cripps had taken over, a revolution in government policy had taken place, Cripps 'has been the undisputed master in the field and on the whole Plowden has been his prophet' (Hall, 1989, p.19). The two sometimes got their way almost too easily, Hall thought '... we don't really know enough to justify this faith in us, or more truly lack of faith they have in themselves'. Plowden was in daily contact with the Chancellor and also briefed the Prime Minister directly from time to time.

While later he judged this period as being of only limited success, two particular episodes - devaluation and re-armament - demonstrated the strength of the Hall-Plowden partnership. In 1949 together with Otto Clarke, they were instrumental in persuading other officials and ministers that devaluation was the right course of action. Clarke had favoured this course since the end of the war; Robert Hall was persuaded early in 1949 and he converted Plowden. The campaign to try to persuade other officials and ministers was not easy. Cripps was the last man to be persuaded, he saw devaluation both as a moral failure and a personal humiliation. Eventually most of the Cabinet were won round and Plowden played quite a big part in this (see *The Times,* 3 January 1980). In 1949 pressure from America for a realignment of European rates was growing and as time went on this pressure focused specifically on sterling. Hall and Plowden and two others at a meeting in Franks's study, decided on the new rate of $2.80 which seemed rather drastic, for some opinion had favoured $3.20. They urged strong deflation on the cabinet, though they were only partly successful in this:

> Many cabinet members were loath to accept deflation to the extent required because, like Attlee, they failed to grasp adequately the connection between financial policy and the external account. Others suspected a conspiracy amongst officials designed to force the Labour government to abandon its socialist policies. (Plowden, 1989, p.66)

Predictably there were tensions and threatened resignations in Cabinet over which departments should accept public expenditure cuts. This experience no doubt had an effect on Plowden's later views. It was true that he did try to make Labour ministers abandon their socialist policies and he strongly opposed steel nationalisation, writing to Cripps that it was 'an act of economic irresponsibility' (Morgan, 1984, p.120). He also favoured the strongest possible post-devaluation austerity package, persuading Cripps that agricultural subsidies were a bad thing, resisting any commitment to a global figure for house construction in 1948; later, he backed Gaitskell all the way in imposing the NHS charges in 1951 that prompted the resignations of three ministers, Bevan, Wilson and John Freeman.

Cripps, however, ill and exhausted, fought hard to try and impose the cuts his advisers told him were essential. He was, apart from his austere inclinations, in any case indifferent to the constraints of party in spite of or because of his strong moral sense.

Cripps gone, Plowden got on as well or better with Gaitskell, who admired Plowden's 'sanity and intelligence' (Gaitskell, 1983, p.133). Gaitskell's relations with his civil servants were not in general particularly good, but 'I am perhaps more close to Edwin Plowden than anybody else', he wrote on 22 January 1951 (op. cit.), 'but he in particular has a keen sense of his own independence, perhaps because he is not a permanent civil servant'. Plowden for his part, while paying tribute to Gaitskell's many good qualities, also remembers his arrogance and tendency to get bogged down in detail, behaving more like the wartime civil servant he had been than the minister he had become.

Rearmament was also an issue on which the Plowden team had a major influence. They had become convinced of the need for rearmament as early as April 1950, and the CEPS was instrumental in drawing up the programme which doubled to fourteen per cent the defence share of GNP. The British as it turned out were wildly optimistic about how much aid would be forthcoming from the US. In Plowden's view, British rearmament was as much as anything a political statement to reassure the Americans and the world in general and prevent a third world war. It showed which way foreign policy priorities still pointed. Plowden made a number of trips to Washington with Gaitskell or Attlee in 1950 and 1951 and became one of the 'three wise men' - his colleagues being Averell Harriman representing the USA and Jean Monnet from France - charged with reaching some sort of accommodation between the countries of the newly-formed NATO on the question of reconciling adequate defence with economic capability. Hall was also involved in this exercise, in which Plowden, once again shadowing Franks, placed the NATO treaty on a sounder footing. The negotiations were hard, requiring 'the stamina of a marathon runner and the patience of a saint' (Plowden, 1989, p.128).

Possessing neither of these qualities in any abundance he could not face accepting the job of NATO Secretary General that Franks had also turned down. He certainly was not overendowed with patience as Hall's diaries attest. Sensitive and mercurial, Plowden as portrayed by Hall is frequently 'at the end of his tether' and losing his temper. In the early CEPS days at least he was not very robust physically either, often living on pills and suffering from anxiety, thinking on one occasion that he had an ulcer.

Plowden and to a lesser extent Hall were also involved in early moves towards European economic cooperation. In 1949-50, he came to know Jean Monnet well, being closely involved with him on talks on the Schumann Plan. The CEPS also held talks with their French counterparts. Politically at that time any surrender of national sovereignty was seen as impossible. The talks concentrated on practical and technical questions (Plowden, 1989, p.75), 'rarely touching on wider issues of politics'. In spite of American support for the Schumann Plan, it was seen by the Labour government as too great a commitment - 'the Durham miners wouldn't like it' in Morrison's words. Plowden's verdict is that this should not be seen as a missed opportunity because such a judgement is to use too much hindsight (op. cit.). A clue to Plowden's real feelings is given in his assessment of Monnet's vision: the mechanics were vague, no thought had been given to investment and pricing policies: 'The political principles of the whole arrangement were sacrosanct ... the technical details were all secondary'. Therein lies the difference in emphasis between French and British technocrats between a Plowden and a Monnet: for Plowden technical details were never secondary. He was a manager, a rationalist and as such in many ways naturally opposed to the political. But as a fixer his major attribute was that of a natural go-between, an interpreter - especially of Robert Hall's economic ideas. He also displayed tenacity in sticking to his views in the Whitehall arena. The go-between role fell to him rather often; it was he, following a suggestion of Hall's, who put to Franks the idea of going to Washington as Ambassador. Again when Cripps resigned too ill to continue, it was Plowden who asked Morrison to consider taking over the chancellorship though he can hardly have done this with any enthusiasm.

When the Conservatives came into power and R.A. ('Rab') Butler became Chancellor in 1951, he asked Plowden to stay on. Bridges, Hall and Otto Clarke also continued at the Treasury. Plowden in fact had feared the sack if the Conservatives were elected; indeed he had announced his departure two months earlier, and then immediately regretted it, thinking that he should have become a permanent civil servant (Hall, 1989, p.164). His relationship with Rab was a rather hot and cold affair; Rab's confidence in Plowden was affected by the fact that he could not make up his mind whether to stay or go. Having been a temporary civil servant on a one-year contract for so long was a mixed blessing; he argued that his position gave him greater independence than that enjoyed by an established Whitehall mandarin so that he could afford to 'stick his neck out' (Plowden, 1989, p.170). At the same time he had no pension and consequently hankered for a business job to enable him to secure his financial future. Although Butler described Plowden in his memoirs as 'my faithful watchdog in chief' (Butler, 1973, p.157), and when finally Plowden departed in 1953 praised him to the skies in the House of Commons and said his going weakened his own position and that of the British economy, the facts do not really bear this out. He encouraged Plowden to accept the NATO job, an idea which came from Monnet, but this only served to make him feel that Rab had no confidence in him.

His suspicions were also aroused by the ROBOT scheme hatched by Otto Clarke and strongly supported by Rab Butler; this would have floated the pound and blocked the sterling balances. Neither Plowden nor Hall had been apprised of this plan and when they heard about it they were appalled. Hall thought that Clarke had 'a strong Napoleonic streak combined with a contempt for facts' (Hall, 1991, p.165). The Robot plan when it became known was opposed by others, notably Cherwell and Salter, and both Plowden and Hall were very influential in squashing it. Once it had been put aside, which took most of 1952, the economic measures adopted were similar to what Hall and Plowden had recommended - defence and housing cuts, cuts in imports, a rise in Bank rate - in short a traditional deflationary package, which succeeded in strengthening the reserves and sterling.

Plowden finally left Whitehall in 1953 but he remained in the public sector, becoming first chairman of the UK Atomic Energy Authority. This proved less congenial to him than the more familiar corridors of power in the Treasury. He had no scientific training which provoked the Institution of Professional Civil Servants to pass a resolution in May 1954 taking strong exception to the appointment of a non-scientist. He missed his old job and felt overworked and underpaid, though a salary of £8,500 was quite generous, but he still kept in touch with those who were close to government, and remained influential in different ways. In his own new field he played a major and important role in the agreement which restored the exchange of nuclear information between Britain and the USA - severed by Soviet spy scandals in Britain - and later defended Macmillan's decision to hush up the Penney report on the Windscale accident on the grounds that the agreement might not otherwise have been possible (Horne, 1989, p.54). Plowden was very committed to nuclear power, predicting in 1956 that by 1968 all power might be generated by this means - a wildly exaggerated estimate as it turned out.

He assiduously kept his ear to the ground in civil service and government circles: lunching fortnightly with Robert Hall, poaching staff from the Treasury for the Authority and even in late 1955 being in the position of telling Hall the news of Rab's impending resignation from the Chancellorship. By March 1958, he had been out of Whitehall for five years, but was consulted by the newly appointed Chancellor, Heathcoat Amory. Naturally, he in turn, consulted Hall. His on-off relationship with public service continued; his five year contract with the AEA was due to expire and, as ever, he was keen to get a good job in industry but when asked to stay on for an extra year, he did. In 1959 an election was likely: Gaitskell had sounded Plowden out about the possibility of becoming Governor of the Bank of England. This briefly preoccupied him, but he was then offered the chairmanship of British Aluminium and instead found himself cast once more in the role of go-between, again endeavouring to persuade Franks to accept the job of Governor of the Bank, in the event of a Labour victory.

He was ennobled in 1959 and was given a dinner at 10 Downing Street in January 1960, ostensibly to mark his final departure from the world of public affairs. Within months, however, he was to return to undertake the task which was to gain him his greatest fame.

The 1950s were an ideologically comatose decade, reflected in the Keynesian consensus of 'Butskellism', that according to Rab Butler would 'double the standard of living within twenty-five years' and which would secure in 1959 the return of the Conservative government, for an unprecedented third term, on the hedonistic assurance by Harold Macmillan that the electorate had 'never had it so good'. A year earlier, the resignations of the Chancellor of the Exchequer, Peter Thorneycroft and his two Treasury colleagues, Nigel Birch and Enoch Powell, over increases in expenditure had been a warning, but Macmillan had been able to dismiss them as 'a little local difficulty'. But to those at the centre of affairs there was an acute appreciation that successful electoral economic manipulation and sloganising could not for long disguise an underlying weakness in the economy. This was soon to be identified as the 'stop-go' cycle. Reliance on macro-economic techniques alone it was realised could not deal with the problem: it was a classic example of systemic failure. One of the remedies, it was thought, lay in devising measures for the stricter control of public expenditure; the other being the adoption of Monnet-style indicative planning.

Edwin Plowden was ideally placed to preside over an almost clandestine group of former and current civil servants. He knew Whitehall and the Treasury well; he had experienced the economic crises of the Attlee government; and he was acceptable in terms of the skills and pre-dispositions he would bring to the task.

The subsequent report on the control of public expenditure was a remarkable document and much has been written in both criticism and praise of its modest thirty-five pages. It was unusual in a number of ways and is quite different from the reports issued by most other committees and commissions of enquiry. First, it was clearly an 'inside job', conceived as an internal Treasury enquiry, reporting to the Chancellor, the results of which initially were not expected to be published. The membership was entirely made up of 'insiders' or former insiders in the Whitehall game who were fluent in its language and procedures. The named members of the committee had all served in the civil service before going out into the wider world; but there were also unnamed civil servants on the committee, 'assessors', who included Robert Hall, Evelyn Sharp, Burke Trend and Otto Clarke. These top civil servants were to be responsible for putting into effect the changes which ensued. No evidence was taken in the usual way; instead a series of 'seminars' was held over a period of more than a year. There was a reason for this, as Clarke later wrote, for they were not engaged in an enterprise which required them to find out the facts and to draw conclusions. They were engaged in an altogether larger task, 'the crucial questions are not those of detail ... the real problems are wider: what the machine of government is trying to do, what its attitudes are, what it regards as important and its approach to its work on all matters involving public expenditure ... here is the kernel of the matter' (Plowden Report, 1961, para. 3). In the argot of a later era, in other words, Plowden and his colleagues were seeking a radical change in the culture of economic management, not least in emphasising the need for a more strategic approach. Within the span of a decade, British technocracy was moving closer to its French counterpart.

Otto Clarke exercised the main influence on the working party and was the chief, though unacknowledged, author of its report. It is said he wrote most of it in a single weekend. Later, modestly underplaying his own influence he commented: 'Plowden did, unusually, succeed in pointing out a new course in an important field in public affairs, which has been followed by successive governments and has become part of the structure of public administration'. The Beveridge Report, Clarke recalled, had been produced in a rather similar way and had likewise been chiefly concerned with practical matters. It was formulated by a man who, like Plowden, was 'of great standing and authority and with deep knowledge and experience of the subject matter' (Clarke, 1978, p.38). Beveridge's report was also a major influence on British public administration for many years to come. But there was one vital difference between Beveridge and Plowden. Where the former was a 'one-man band' the latter had to be a team builder who made sure discussion and decisions were participated in by the whole committee. Plowden's report, less than twenty thousand words long, was described by a *Times* leader as 'a tantalising document' (*The Times*, 21 July 1961). Already a statement codifying government policy, it was essentially a summary version of several internally-circulated reports. Written in the understated mandarin style, its prose had been polished to such a degree of smoothness that reading between the lines was essential to decipher its true meaning. Indeed a number of amusing translations were attempted, notably by Professor W.J.M. Mackenzie in the *Guardian* (Mackenzie, 1963).

But in spite of its brevity and opacity, it was a document of immense importance. Its official title *Treasury Control of Expenditure*, belied its dual purpose, for not only was it to lay the foundations for controlling expenditure but it was also to facilitate - Monnet-style - the planning of government spending. The report contained four main sets of proposals that were already being put into effect: a system of forward planning of public expenditure; allied to a strengthening of the collective responsibility for that expenditure; plus the introduction of better management in the civil service; along with the development of better information systems and techniques.

First, there was the 'forward look'. This was the heart of the newly instituted public expenditure survey, first carried out in 1961. Partly inspired by French practice, but also with an eye on the purse strings, the idea was that there should be regular strategic appraisals of public expenditure as a whole looking ahead four or five years. Decisions about the overall level and about individual spending plans were to be taken in the light of available resources. This survey included all central and local government expenditure plus that of the nationalised industries. The survey was first published in 1963 when Reginald Maudling was Chancellor, though the Plowden Committee had originally intended it to be kept confidential. Plowden also stressed the importance of stability in public expenditure, for the previous years had seen wasteful cuts as a result of stop-go economic policies, and spending decisions had been arrived at in a piecemeal way.

The new system was successfully introduced into the repertoire of Whitehall, though it still seemed to have an expansionary bias built into it: it also lacked provision for evaluation so that the rationale of policies went largely unquestioned: the future would resemble the past, only more so.

There were other disadvantages in the Public Expenditure Survey Committee (PESC) system, notably a tendency to think that the numbers produced by the survey constituted control - 'the triumph of technique over substance' as Heclo and Wildavsky put it (1981, p.xxiv). The idea of a forward look became so ingrained that looking back to consider the outturn of a year's survey was given a low priority. And the fact that the survey was conducted in constant prices meant that the effects of inflation were insufficiently attended to - financial control barely existed. PESC also assumed reasonable stability in the economy, national and international, together with a certain level of growth. These assumptions broke down totally following the world oil crisis of 1974, when rising interest rates and escalating wage demands created recession conditions never envisaged by the Plowden group. The 'missing billions' discovered by the Select Committee on Expenditure in 1975 revealed how out of control the PESC system had become.

Alongside the PESC process which departments had to prepare for each year, Plowden hoped to strengthen the hand of the Chancellor, to deal with the 'problem of his having no friends' (Heclo and Wildavsky, p.185), or rather perhaps to spread the responsibility for public expenditure. The group hoped that the system of collective responsibility, which in its view was functioning imperfectly, could be strengthened by the introduction of joint interdepartmental and cabinet committees. A new post was also created, that of Chief Secretary to the Treasury, of sufficient seniority to be in the cabinet to back up the Chancellor in the annual spending round who, in later years, would preside over a 'Court of Star Chamber' to resolve allocation disputes. The Plowden committee appears to have underestimated the political nature of the spending decisions. Otto Clarke, the main architect of the PESC procedure later recognised this:

> Cabinets take their decisions on public expenditure in much the same way as they take their decisions on anything else - push and pull, threats and cajolery, bluff and counter-bluff ... PESC can't change this at all, for this is the nature of political life. (Clarke, 1978, p.xviii).

The third main strand, and one that was to have greatest impact on the thinking of the Plowden committee was the importance of management. Just as the public expenditure survey has had a major influence on most civil service departments since 1961, the stress placed by Plowden on management can be seen as 'the starting point of a process of change in public administration over the following twenty years' (Delafons, 1982, p.264). If public expenditure was to be properly planned and controlled, an improvement in managerial skills of all kinds was necessary: the interdependence of the two was axiomatic to the Plowden group. That the responsibility for this would be located in the Treasury went without saying; it would develop management services and training and introduce new techniques. This would strengthen the Treasury in its dealings with other departments. After the Plowden report was published there were two immediate organisational spin-offs: first, a recasting and simplification of the form in which the estimates were produced, which was welcomed almost unanimously. The second reform was a drastic reorganisation of the Treasury in 1963. It was divided into two: the economic and financial side and the management side, each with a joint permanent secretary in charge. Later, this split enabled the management side, in the charge of the Head of the Home Civil Service, to be detached from the Treasury and become the Civil Service Department, as recommended by the Fulton report in 1968. This reform, as we shall see, was later reversed as a result of Lord Rayner's activities when the Civil Service Department was abolished.

The idea of improving civil service management started to take hold in the 1970s. The Programme Analysis and Review (PAR) system introduced by the Heath government attempted to correct some of the faults of the Public Expenditure Survey system as introduced by the Plowden report. But it imposed excessive demands on civil servants and did not attract sufficient commitment from Ministers. PESC and PAR were but the start of a long series of developments in government techniques to improve the handling of its own spending.

The Plowden committee on Public Expenditure was swiftly followed by another, this time on representational services overseas. The report, published in February 1964, shared several characteristics with Plowden Mark I. It was a private enquiry, though there were possibly fewer insiders on the committee, including as it did a banker and a Unilever director, plus two MPs. Once again the report appeared as a White Paper, though publication had not been expected and once again it was in perfect mandarin prose, plentifully sprinkled with statements of the obvious and others of polished impenetrability. Though the committee had more outsiders than its predecessor, it seems inescapable that the inspiration behind it came from within, where a view had emerged that reforms were overdue and that some adaptation to the requirements of a changing world were essential. The report stressed the importance of economic and commercial work. It focused on three main aspects. First, recruitment, training and conditions of service. A bow in the direction of those concerned about public school domination of the diplomatic service was followed by a meticulous summary of improvements which should be made; in the time-honoured method of pre-emption these had already been mostly implemented. Secondly, the section on policy planning expressed the by-now fashionable view that many issues can be foreseen and some of the most intractable could have been handled better if their implications had been explored more fully in advance: a diplomatic version of the 'forward look'. The committee recommended a staff who would write planning papers, a cabinet office committee and the use of outside experts and consultants. An echo of the CEPS, and not the last Plowden would come up with. The events leading up to the Falklands conflict, as later recounted by Lord Franks, might have been rather different had such a body existed. The proposal was criticised in the Lords by Lord Alport who described it as sinister and likely to interfere with ministerial responsibility. Plowden denied any such intention; but nothing was done.

Third, came the recommendation for the unification of the foreign service, the Commonwealth Relations Service and the trade services into a single Diplomatic Service: this was the logical conclusion of the painstaking report. And the committee duly advocated it, but with quite remarkable pusillanimity decided that the two 'head offices' in London should not be amalgamated, at any rate 'not yet'. Not surprisingly, the report was widely criticised for this non sequitur. It was nonetheless politely received by Plowden's fellow peers, as 'a model of clarity', '... a magnificent report in every respect', but was only debated for an hour and a half in the Commons. It had far less impact than Plowden I: its failure to probe accepted orthodoxies meant that before long another committee was charged with investigating much the same area. The later Duncan Report was much more radical, though its recommendations and indeed its appointment did not please Plowden. Andrew Shonfield, one of the Duncan Committee, later described his experiences and the 'pragmatic fallacy' which can affect members of such enquiries. They plunge into the subject, collect as many facts as possible, think hard and use their common sense. This approach, he suggested, 'derives from a view of public affairs which puts the functions of an investigator on essentially the same footing as those of a common law judge - you are supposed to know all about the theoretical assumptions - all you need is facts' (Shonfield, 1969).

If the report on the diplomatic service was a failure it was because Plowden had been too much of an insider and had yielded too much to the views of the Foreign Office. The real significance of it was in its reinforcement of the new managerial thrust that was sweeping through government, a movement that was to gather momentum for the remainder of the century. Plowden II mimicked many of the proposals set out in Plowden I: the need for better management, for planning capacity to undertake strategic 'forward looks', and the inculcation of a more businesslike approach to policy formulation and implementation.

No sooner had he reported on overseas representation than he was again requisitioned to investigate the state of the British aircraft industry by Roy Jenkins, Minister of Aviation in the new Labour government. The other members of the Committee were the usual spectrum of people, including representatives from banking, industry, trade unions and the navy, as well as two MPs. In his foreword to Plowden's memoir, Jenkins wrote that the primary aim of the enquiry was to 'shine a searchlight of sceptical judgement upon a somewhat cushioned industry' (Plowden, 1989, p.x). He was in effect handing the worthy Plowden a political and economic hot potato. The British aircraft industry was beset with rising costs, long delays and indecision by the government. Several projects were about to be cancelled in favour of American aircraft and the prevailing mood was one of uncertainty. Although the committee took evidence in public - a personal first for Plowden - they mostly took it from civil servants or aircraft industry insiders and never went near a factory. The report when it came out, after some delays and a good deal of speculation in the press, satisfied no one. Lord Jellicoe in the Lords announced magisterially that he would not be able to give Edwin his 'usual alpha plus for this term's report'. In the words of the *Economist* it was a 'great, furry, smothering, suffocating woolly shawl of words' ('Plowden Washes Whiter', 18 December, 1965). A central theme of the report was that the level of government support should be reduced; but the committee was not united on the question of a government shareholding in BAC and Hawker Siddeley, and a minority report by Aubrey Jones MP opposed any government shareholding in the industry. Plowden felt that the report had been misinterpreted - they held the view that Britain should continue to have a substantial aircraft industry, but should no longer try to compete where she was at the largest disadvantage, which pointed in the direction of European co-operation and harmonisation and buying some aircraft from the US.

The aircraft report showed that for the first time he was less than a consummate fixer. Unlike Franks, who ostensibly preferred to go public as far as possible from the outset, Plowden had previously only been involved in more covert missions and clearly was more successful under such conditions. Secondly, unlike the public expenditure and diplomacy enquiries, with aircraft he was required to work with colleagues representing a disparate set of vested interests and, unlike Franks, his skills were unable to achieve a consensus. Following the aircraft report he was never again to be given a major commission although he continued with a variety of smaller tasks.

He devoted much of the next ten years to the chairmanship of Tube Investments, though he remained an active and dutiful public-spirited person in the Lords and elsewhere. He became the first chairman of the London Business School in 1964. In 1968 he followed Franks as chairman of the body monitoring higher civil service pay. He also defended the civil service in the debate on the Fulton report: to him the Fulton portrait of the Administrative Class was untrue and unfair. What the civil service needed was 'clever people with judgement', knowledge was not important. He supported British membership of the EEC whenever he could. Having announced his conversion to the European cause in his maiden speech in the Lords in 1961, he took part in another 'Wise Men' exercise with Carli, Pisani and Hallstein in 1969, which came to the conclusion that there were no insurmountable obstacles to British membership. He finally retired from the chairmanship of Tube Investments in 1974 at the age of sixty-seven.

One last enquiry was entrusted to Lord Plowden, again by a Labour government, this time into the working of the electricity supply industry which was set up in December 1974. The chief recommendation was that the Central Electricity Generating Board and the twelve regional supply boards should be unified. Slow and cumbersome policy-making at the centre was the result of divided responsibilities, but over-centralisation was undesirable. A new Central Electricity Board would aim to provide strong leadership as well as devolving as much as possible to local operating companies. The report was not published till 1976 and appears to have had little practical impact.

He was also vice-chairman of the Edmund-Davies Committee on Police Pay, that reported in July 1978 which led to his becoming chairman of the Police Complaints Board. This was another job which Roy Jenkins organised for him. The quality Plowden would bring was 'his judgement ... but also the authority of his reputation and experience to launch a necessary but controversial scheme' (Plowden, 1989, p.x). Especially useful in the delicate task would be two other qualities which Jenkins saw Plowden as having: a devotion to public duty and a faith that rational discussion could solve nearly all problems. He was probably less welcome in this particular task than any he had yet undertaken. Sir Robert Mark, the Metropolitan Police Commissioner, had voiced the fear that the authority of Chief Constables would be infringed and the Police Federation advised its members not to co-operate. Plowden's approach was conciliatory, stressing that the Board would aim for impartiality. He would not be soft on unreasonable complaints, he said, nor would he 'whitewash' the police (*The Times*, 7 January 1977). There were fewer complaints than expected. In 1980, a report was published on the Board's first three years of operation. It included a recommendation that complaints involving a serious assault should still be investigated from within the police but by a special team; but the compliment from *The Times* that 'this is one quango which has manifestly performed valuable service to the public' (16 July 1980), was no doubt merited. He retired from the PCB in 1981.

Edwin Plowden's career as a fixer closely paralleled that of Oliver Franks. Both were propelled into Whitehall at the outbreak of war where they established reputations for themselves as exceptional administrators. Naturally more personable than Franks, with 'a generous share of human understanding', according to Douglas Jay, some felt that his style was too austere but it was this feature which bonded him so closely to Sir Stafford Cripps and which was further reinforced by their common Christian commitment. Cripps possessed 'a puritan style of highly distinctive kind. After all his Christianity derived from the upper reaches of high Anglicanism rather than from the democratic populism of the chapels' (Morgan, 1987, p.174). They both shared a predilection for planning, modernisation and efficiency. Franks, of course, was also a follower of this school of thought as can be seen from his 1947 lecture on planning in war and peace. But if Franks provided the broad sketch both then and in his later proposals regarding business schools, it was Plowden who filled in much of the detail inventing new control techniques in public expenditure and becoming the first chairman of the London Business School. The two had much in common and even where they differed they often complemented each other. Both, but particularly Plowden, were the heralds of the rise of the management consultants.

Like all fixers Plowden relied upon a close network of influential people both within and outside the government machine. The same group surrounded him through the Whitehall years and those later spent in industry. In this he was more like Arnold Goodman than Oliver Franks whose relationships were emotionally more distant. His partnership with Robert Hall was particularly close and mutually productive and the latter's influence was less strong after Plowden left the Treasury. His own dependence on Hall was vividly illustrated by the remark he made at his friend's memorial service. When asked to speak he said, 'my first instinct was to reach for the telephone and ask Robert what I should say, and would he please write something for me' (Introduction to Hall Diaries, 1991, Vol. II, p.xiii). Plowden's influence would have been far less without the ideas and inspiration of Hall. Without Plowden, Hall's ideas might have found no conduit, no interpreter.

Plowden's networking was not limited to acting as an intellectual and administrative go-between, it was further reinforced by an element of inter-locking appointments. For example, when he became chairman of Tube Investments, he retained Hall as its economic adviser; a fellow board member of the Atomic Energy Authority was Sir Ivan Stedeford, who had been a director of Tennants before the war, a member of the Economic Planning Board, and was later to become chairman of both British Aluminium and Tube Investments - posts in which Plowden succeeded him. His old boy network more than compensated for his lack of an old school tie!

As with his fellow official fixers, Plowden was politically non-partisan serving governments of both colours and enjoying their high esteem. He sits as a cross-bencher in the House of Lords where he has participated in the debates. He does not seem to share the disdain for politicians as a *genre*, which comes through from Franks and is made quite explicitly by Goodman, but this may be because most of his relationships - certainly on the Labour side - were with the more technocratically inclined ministers such as Gaitskell, Cripps and Jay or, in the case of Conservatives with the very moderate, consensual kind as exemplified by Rab Butler. In addition to working with the least ideological minister, he always preferred to go about his fixer tasks in the shadows. Though he spent many successful years in industry after leaving Whitehall, Plowden was in many ways a natural bureaucrat. He shunned publicity and took easily to the secretive ways of Whitehall. Almost an embodiment of the corporatist values of the post war years, he naturally sought consensus. This could on occasion be very successful.

The enquiry into control of public expenditure made use of all the qualities which had been honed over the years since 1940. He was an outsider who was also an insider with almost twenty years knowledge of the internal working of the government machine; a go-between who had so often mediated between civil servants and politicians, the insular British government and the European-minded French, between the US and UK on nuclear matters, between the academic and the practical.

His approach to an enquiry or committee was, not surprisingly, a consensual one. He would first try and get hold of a good secretary, or possibly two, get papers written and gather up a large quantity of information. When it came to hearing evidence, the Committee would agree the questions in advance and then share them between the members. He found that committee members invariably had a great deal to offer and that a didactic chairman would not get the best out of them. He was not 'a great dictator', and always tried to elicit the initial views of colleagues at the outset of a mission (Interview, 11 June 1993).

He was more inclined to be radical in suggesting new techniques than in suggesting major institutional changes. In a Lords debate on the Annan Report on broadcasting he said 'Of the four committees of enquiry that I have chaired, at the beginning of every one, I can truthfully say that I said 'We are not going to make recommendations for changes just for things that are desirable, but only for things that are really necessary' (Hansard, Lords, 1976-7, Vol. 383, Vol. 980, 19 May 1977). He did, however, propose the establishment of the Civil Service Department to take over the staffing and personnel functions of the Treasury and also suggested to Edward Heath, shortly before he became Prime Minister in 1970, the idea of setting up the Central Policy Review Staff (CPRS), to be attached to 10 Downing Street but to offer broad strategic advice to the Cabinet collectively. This proposal stemmed from his experience with the Central Economic Planning Staff which gave him an appreciation of the value of teamwork, of a group of people with expertise but no line responsibilities or departmental loyalties, in improving decision-making. In being one of the main pioneers of the Whitehall managerial revolution he not only invented new techniques but also contributed to the recognition of the significance of medium-term planning and forecasting.

A unique feature of Edwin Plowden's career as a fixer is that it was reflected in much of the public service undertaken by his wife. She was not a self-starter and her public service involvement, initially at least, owed much to her husband's position and contacts. But she quickly established her own separate identity and reputation, becoming a Dame of the British Empire and of all the reports that bear the name Plowden it is hers on primary education that most readily springs to mind and which has the highest public profile. *Children and their Primary Schools* appeared in 1967 and sold some 146,000 copies over the next five years, adding 'her name to the vocabulary of education' as *The Times* put it (7 August 1967).

It was not until her family of two sons and two daughters was grown up that Lady Plowden became deeply involved in non-domestic activities, though she had been on a couple of charitable committees for many years, and had been involved with the Girl Guide movement and some amateur social work. When she first moved out of the domestic circle, it was to that familiar starting point for middle-class women, the juvenile bench; and then - rather less run of the mill - to a directorship of Trust House Hotels 'rather like housekeeping' she said (Interview, 3 March 1993).

Both she and her husband were very modest and extremely averse to publicity but were possessed of strong social consciences and a well-developed sense of public service. The spotlight of publicity first shone on her when she was appointed chairman of the Central Advisory Council on Education's enquiry into primary schools.

This was not an enquiry set up to deal with an emergency, problem, or dilemma facing the government of the day, nor in response to public or political pressure. The Central Advisory Councils - there was one for

Wales too - were continuing bodies with a changing membership. The enquiry was announced in June 1963 by Sir Edward Boyle probably only because secondary education had been thoroughly studied in previous reports (first by Crowther, then by Newsom): it was now the turn of the primary sector. These reports had never been radical documents. They did not lead but gave official approval to current thinking about what changes should be made. Before she was offered this opportunity, she had chaired nothing more important than her local WI, but it was a 'dream come true' (Interview). She had no influence over the membership, apart from insisting that someone from an independent school should be included.

The committee was a very large one with a membership ranging from A.J. Ayer to Timothy Raison and Michael Young. There was also a large full-time secretariat; a major research programme was undertaken and research findings played an important part in its writing. Not all the members knew anything about the subject of their deliberations, but a strong group feeling developed which was largely attributed to Lady Plowden's drive, energy and chairmanship skills. Most of the drafting was done by the secretariat, though the chairman herself made the main decisions about the shape of the report and how it should be written. One hundred and ninety-seven recommendations were contained in the report, many of them relating to quite minor matters and costing little or nothing. The one which had most impact was that which called for the establishment of Educational Priority Areas (EPAs) - in effect a demand for positive discrimination in favour of deprived areas. This, though distinctive and radical, had an appeal both for those on the Council who favoured selection at eleven plus and for those who opposed it. The report also wanted, while stressing the role of parents in schooling, an expansion in nursery education, which would be facilitated by the introduction of 'teachers' aides' and would partly be paid for by a flexible approach to the age of entry to primary school and of transfer from primary to middle school. The report also recommended the banning of corporal punishment in schools.

In the short run these proposals had little effect. Anthony Crosland, the Education Secretary, was pre-occupied with extending the introduction of comprehensive schools throughout the secondary sector of education, but £16m was allocated for the EPAs which Michael Young strongly supported. The report was generally well received by the press, with the exception of the *Daily Telegraph*. *The Times* called it 'a social document of the first importance' (10 January 1967), while *The Economist* described it as 'showing such clearminded progressiveness that there seems to be no room left for the professional grumbler' (14 January 1967). It was received with something like rapture by the teaching profession, not only at home but also abroad, especially in the USA, reinforcing as it did contemporary progressive ideas on primary education and 'turning radical sociology into conventional wisdom' (Kogan, 1973, p.102). In the longer run its progressiveness was to be severely criticised by later educationists who favour a return to a core curriculum and a more formal pedagogy, although widespread nursery school provision remains an acceptable goal and the educational needs of deprived urban areas a continuing cause for concern.

Lady Plowden was co-opted onto the ILEA where she remained for six years, and was immediately at the top of the list of guest speakers at educational conferences. She defended the recommendation of the committee on corporal punishment at a National Association of Head Teachers' conference. She also confronted the prep school heads (*The Times*, 9 September 1967), telling them to update their curriculum, get better training and warned them not to allow their children to become a 'race apart'. What was more, unlike most other committee chairmen, she held a review meeting on the first anniversary of the report's publication, and called for a more positive response by the Department of Education and Science to the EPA recommendation. Nor did she shrink from pressing other educational matters - e.g. the training of teachers and half-day schooling for new schoolchildren among them, but always and especially the role of the parents in the education of the young child. She later changed her mind on the question of nursery schooling, preferring the pre-school playgroups association of which she became chairman in 1972 and feeling that the paramount importance lay in parental involvement. In spite of this change of heart she remained a staunch defender of child-centred learning.

A measure of the impact on the profession of the report and Lady Plowden's associated activities was that 'Plowden conferences' were held every year from 1969. Organised initially by Michael Young and later by Goldsmiths' College, these small and informal gatherings continued for fifteen years. If the impact on policy was limited, it was due to lack of interest at ministerial level.

She was later, in keeping with the time-honoured system of the great and the good, a member of the 1974 Houghton Committee on Teachers'

Pay along with Robin Leigh-Pemberton, future governor of the Bank of England, and Maurice Kogan who had been the secretary to her own enquiry.

In 1970 she was appointed vice-chairman of the BBC governors in succession to Lord Fulton. She seems to have aroused a good deal of resentment in her five years there. Her natural bossiness did not go down well, especially in current affairs departments where she was seen as an Establishment figure. Educational television was something she favoured and promoted so she was popular in those parts of the Corporation. She had shown herself to be someone who appreciated the problems of broadcasting.

These, almost inevitably, are rarely far from the contemporary political agenda given the power of the mass media, the questions of ownership and monopoly, the speed of technological change and - not least - the always uneasy relationships between broadcasters and politicians. This was as true of the 1970s as at any other time but the particular issues of the decade focused on the renewal of the legislation governing commercial television and the BBC's Charter, and the questions surrounding the creation of a fourth television channel. All of these were politically highly-charged matters.

She had established her reputation as a very skilful and strong chairman and consequently in 1975 she was appointed to succeed Lord Aylestone as chairman of the Independent Broadcasting Authority. It was an especially demanding role calling for fixer-like qualities, requiring as it did the reconciliation of a wide range of interests, involving businessmen and politicians, programme makers and the viewing public. The Annan Committee was in session deliberating on the future of broadcasting and after it reported in 1977 plans for Channel 4 could be laid. Lady Plowden presided over this and her term of office was extended for a year to enable her to guide the allocation of the new franchises in commercial television which, compared with later exercises of the same sort, went very smoothly. She also supervised the plans for the introduction of breakfast television and the larger extension of commercial radio. On her departure from the IBA she said she had learnt a lot and commented 'one is always grateful for having been involved' (*The Times*, 29 December 1980). She would go on, she said, 'with the gypsies, the preschool playgroups, and go back to my old ladies'. She was an old lady herself by this time, and the gypsies by some accounts did not especially appreciate her attempts to improve their education (Wilby, 1979).

However, she went on to join the board of the National Theatre and succeeded Lord Denning as president of Relate, the marriage guidance organisation.

Her own marriage was remarkable not only for the extensive public services rendered by the couple themselves but also because of the genetic inheritance they were to pass on to their offspring. Their eldest son William has followed a twin-track career as civil servant and academic being variously a principal in the Board of Trade, a lecturer at LSE, a founder member of the CPRS (which his father had suggested to Edward Heath) headed by Lord Rothschild, and Director General of the Royal Institute of Public Administration. His younger brother Francis, a director of Coopers and Lybrand Deloitte, was seconded to work in the Financial Management Unit set up in Whitehall as part of Lord Rayner's endeavours to improve civil service efficiency. (One of their sisters, Anna, is an accomplished art restorer and is in her own way therefore something of a fixer!). Edwin Plowden was one of the pioneers of the post-war school of public management who provided not just ideas and techniques but also two sons equipped to carry on with the mission.

4 Arnold Goodman: A Quick Fixer

Arnold Goodman might have stepped straight out of the writings of C.P. Snow. Born a Jew and a lawyer by training, he occupied his middle and later years in the Oxbridge groves of academe and in the rooms off the corridors of power - they being so much more important than the corridors themselves. From modest origins he reached his eightieth year as Baron Goodman, CH, QC, confidant and professional adviser to members of the Royal Family, a clutch of leaders from all three main political parties, industrial magnates, newspaper and television tycoons, theatrical impresarios and numerous other personages. In addition to these discreet ministrations, over a period of two decades he undertook a variety of official roles that embraced the worlds of the arts and the mass media, charity law reform and housing, as well as being entrusted with a number of more covert missions on behalf of governments of both parties. His position during that epoch has been succinctly summarised, with only a touch of hyperbole, by Francis Wheen when reviewing Lord Goodman's memoirs:

> When not firing off writs, he more or less ran the country. He advised the leaders of all the main parties (Harold Wilson, Edward Heath, Jeremy Thorpe) and acted as a Lord High Everything Else in the Britain of the 1960s and 1970s. No quango was complete without Lord Goodman on its board, preferably in the chair: the Arts Council, the Housing Corporation, the Newspaper Publishers' Association, the Industrial Reorganisation Corporation, the National Building Agency, the British Council, the South Bank Theatre Board, the English National Opera and many others ... When a government found itself impaled on some particularly sharp spike - Rhodesia, for instance, or private patients in NHS hospitals - Lord Goodman would be called in to "mediate". (*Literary Review*, September 1993).

Unlike Lords Franks, Plowden and Young his span of influence was shorter, more compressed and therefore seemingly more dramatic; this possibly stems from the fact that he was a relatively late starter - not bursting into the public arena until he was over fifty. The reason for this delayed entry was in part due to the war. Although commissioned in the army he was declared unfit for overseas service because of his obesity. Like Franks, Plowden and Young he thus avoided front-line duty, but unlike them, being stationed first on an anti-aircraft battery and later in an ordnance depot, he did not benefit from the launching pads provided for the other three at the Ministries of Supply and Aircraft Production, and PEP which were all at the very centre of events. Arnold Goodman would have to establish his own network of key actors and clients in the more laborious and pedestrian environment of peacetime.

As an undergraduate he attended University College, London where the young Hugh Gaitskell's lectures put him off studying economics, opting instead for the law. Simultaneously, he spent part of the day as a solicitor's articled clerk. After graduation he studied for an LLM, before going up to Cambridge where he acquired two further law degrees, both with first class honours, specialising in the recondite field of Roman Law. While at Cambridge he cultivated what was later to become a major preoccupation for him, the cinema and the theatre. The solicitors firm where he completed his articles was Rubinstein Nash, well known for its extensive literary, musical and artistic clientele. He began his professional career working for Roy Kisch who introduced him to Edward Heath, then a young sixth-former, at his home in Broadstairs. In sowing such early seeds for later networks to flourish, luck can play a vital role: Gaitskell and Heath were already in the bag.

After the army he resumed working with Roy Kisch and later merged the firm with Rubinstein Nash, becoming the third partner in seniority, specialising in litigation; J.B. Priestley, Victor Gollancz, Graham Greene and Evelyn Waugh were among his clients. Four years later, restless to be his own boss, he moved again to form Goodman Derrick and Co., which would become renowned as a formidable practice, specialising in libel cases and exploiting the new business opportunities that sprung from the birth of commercial television which, as the media tycoon Lord (Roy) Thomson admitted, was effectively 'a licence to print money'. Arnold Goodman's career was about to take off.

He was born in 1913 in north-east London, the younger son of lower middle-class parents, themselves the offspring of east European Jewish immigrants. His father carried on a business as a shipper, arranging for British textiles and garments to be bought on behalf of South African wholesalers and retailers and thereafter taking responsibility for the onward transportation of the purchased goods; he was a 'middle man' working on a commission basis. According to Lord Goodman, it was a very bookish home - not uncommon in the Anglo-Jewry of the time. His elder brother forsook formal academic qualifications, but was self-taught in music, opera, literature, the theatre and the arts in general, and he imparted both his knowledge and his enthusiasm to his brother. Their father was self-effacing, seeking compensation for his tedious trade in voracious reading; he kept the high holy days of the Jewish calendar but was otherwise not religiously observant.   Their mother was altogether different, being strongly archetypal. A former schoolteacher, she was a good mother, who kept a reasonably kosher home, and was highly ambitious for her two sons, her only children.   She busied herself extensively with Jewish, Zionist and other more secular causes, serving on a variety of committees and often taking the chair. She was thus to provide a more influential role model for the young Arnold than his father.

For his secondary education he attended the Grocers' School in Clapton, which had a glorious role in advancing the prospects of talented Jewish boys from the east-end, who included leading playwrights, like Harold Pinter, a clutch of successful academics two of whom were destined to become heads of Oxbridge colleges - Barry Supple and Arnold Goodman. While not a star pupil at the school, Goodman clearly shone very brightly at university.

Though Arnold Goodman did not have a 'good war' that could have accelerated his career as a man of affairs, he did, however, have the good fortune to meet Lt. Col. George Wigg who was later to become a Labour MP and play, as Paymaster-General, a shadowy, fixer-type role in Harold Wilson's first government.   He always studiously maintained an independent, non-party stance, both in the House of Lords and in his later public utterances and he also expressed considerable disdain, bordering on contempt, for politics and politicians. Whether he always held such views or merely developed them as a result of his experience, he kept them to himself in the early and middle years of his professional life, for he clearly spent considerable time and energy assiduously cultivating those of significance in politics. He does not seem to have endeavoured to infiltrate the Whitehall mandarinate, for his attention was focused pretty much on elected politicians and, initially at least, those in the Labour party. In this he may have had little choice for, in the late 1950s, Anglo-Jewry had yet to feel comfortable with the Conservative party (Finchley nearly went Liberal in 1959), while for their part the Conservatives were not disposed to welcome Jews warmly until after the demise of its aristocratic leadership and the arrival of its grammar school leaders in the form of Edward Heath and especially Margaret Thatcher, whose cabinet was at one point to record an historically high proportion of Jewish ministers numbering five in all (cf. Alderman, 1983 passim). Prior to the 1970s political activism and partisanship on the part of the Jewish community had been very largely confined to the Labour party, with some lesser involvement with both the Communists and the Liberals.

In 1957 the *Spectator* weekly magazine ran a story that at the annual conference of the Italian Socialist Party held in Venice three prominent Labour personalities, Nye Bevan, Richard Crossman - both front-bench MPs - and Morgan Phillips - the General Secretary - had been intoxicated. Goodman, although wary of libel proceedings, acted for all three; the jury found in their favour and awarded damages of £2,500 each plus costs. But the story did not end there. Much later, in 1981, with the three plaintiffs and leading counsel involved all dead, Crossman's posthumously published diaries revealed that he and his colleagues had been drunk in Venice, and it also emerged that he had previously admitted as much at a *Private Eye* lunch. The allegation was made that perjury had been committed and Bernard Levin held that it was one of the greatest legal scandals of the century commenting: 'I know that justice is supposed to be blind, but on this occasion she seems to have been blind drunk.' (*The Times*, 10 March 1981). In his autobiography, Goodman in defending the integrity of his clients, and particularly his favourite Bevan, was somewhat sniffy about Crossman's characteristic indiscretion but expressed the view that resurrecting the case when the three Labour personalities were all dead was the work of extreme right propagandists.

Goodman was again to represent Labour's interest in 1962 in another controversial case involving an action for breach of copyright against the *Manchester Guardian* which had been regularly publishing leaked papers from the party's National Executive Committee. Hugh Gaitskell pressed Goodman to pursue the action because the compulsory 'discovery' or disclosure of papers would reveal the culprit who was passing on information to the newspaper. Just prior to the process of 'discovery' the case was aborted by Gaitskell's sudden and untimely death when his successor, Harold Wilson, took Goodman's advice not to continue with the proceedings, which would have caused a good deal of consternation within the upper echelons of the party just at the outset of his leadership. Nevertheless, the case rankled among journalists long afterwards because they greatly resented Labour's attempt to use the machinery of copyright law against a newspaper for the sole purpose of tightening up its own internal security.

In the same year Goodman consolidated his position with the Labour hierarchy by advising it on tactics regarding the Radcliffe Tribunal's investigation into the Vassall affair which, in tandem with the Profumo affair, precipitated the downfall of Harold Macmillan as Prime Minister and the subsequent defeat of the Tories under Alec Douglas-Home in the 1964 general election. George Brown, a leading Labour frontbencher, had been thought to be a major source of rumour-mongering about Vassall and Goodman saw to it that Gerald Gardiner QC, later to be Lord Chancellor, would represent Labour before the Tribunal, a device which obviated Brown appearing, potentially embarrassingly, as a witness. George Wigg, his friend from their army days, was a principal actor in the Profumo affair, taking a leading part in the parliamentary and journalistic pursuit of John Profumo. According to Goodman, both Wigg and Harold Wilson sought his advice but largely ignored it.

At this time, ensconced as a trusted legal adviser to the Labour Party, he had his biggest stroke of luck: Labour won the 1964 general election albeit by the narrowest of margins - an overall majority of five, two of whom were the politically unreliable mavericks Woodrow Wyatt (later to become a staunch Thatcherite) and Desmond Donnelly (who was to commit suicide). Nevertheless, after thirteen years, Labour had been returned to power. A pre-war Labour minister, Jimmy Maxton, once observed: 'if you're close to the fountain of power, you're bound to get splashed' - and so it was for Arnold Goodman. At the level of the individual, at any rate, hindsight might suggest he was the main beneficiary of Labour's electoral success; while retaining and even enhancing his reputation as one of the nation's leading lawyers, he was about to extend himself well beyond the boundaries of legal practice by becoming a fully-fledged fixer.

In the immediate aftermath of the election the new prime minister asked him to save the Royal Philharmonic Orchestra from financial ruin and to chair a committee on the financing of the four principal London orchestras. Jennie Lee, Minister for the Arts and Nye Bevan's widow, almost simultaneously invited him to join the Arts Council and then two weeks later asked him to be its chairman, a post he occupied from 1965 to 1972. During his term of office the other members included Henry Moore, Cecil Day-Lewis, John Betjeman, Sir William Coldstream, Sir Anthony Lewis and Lord Snowdon.

Although relatively unknown at the time, he was an appropriate appointment. Schooled in an appreciation of the arts by his brother, he had taken a continuing interest in most artistic media since his Cambridge days. A keen theatre and concert goer, he had acted as solicitor to the National Theatre since 1960, and thus knew both Laurence Olivier and Peter Hall, and had also represented the Royal Opera House and had negotiated with the Musicians' Union. In his seven years as chairman he undoubtedly achieved a great deal and in the first year (1965-66) the Art Council's grant rose from £665,000 to a staggering £3m, a figure that excluded the hefty Covent Garden subsidy. He had endless battles with the civil service but managed to win most of them, with the unfailing ministerial support of Jennie Lee and by exploiting his personal contacts with people such as Roy Jenkins, successively Home Secretary and Chancellor of the Exchequer. The Council's activities expanded, key appointments were made, provision was made for professional training in arts management, new office premises were organised and a potentially difficult examination by the Comptroller and Auditor-General and the Public Accounts Committee was turned to advantage. He initiated preliminary moves in the campaign for a Public Lending Right for authors which eventually ended in success in 1979, and in a similar way by means of initial deployments within the Arts Council he took a significant part in having the Lord Chamberlain's censorship of plays abolished. Not surprisingly, his chairmanship of the Arts Council was to be the appointment that gave him the greatest satisfaction and he was to continue cultivating these interests after leaving it by becoming a director of the Royal Opera House, chairman of the Association for Business Partnership of the Arts, Chairman of English National Opera and assorted other such affiliations.

The skill and energy he so successfully and unstintingly deployed at the Arts Council was all the more remarkable in view of the other public duties, some formal, some informal, some open, others covert, that were pressed on him during the same period.

In 1964 he was largely responsible for bringing to an end a damaging strike between ACTT (the media technicians' union) and the commercial television companies, three of which were his clients. Goodman had previously settled a dispute between the ACTT and the Boulting brothers who produced a series of comedy films for the cinema. George Wigg suggested that the good offices of Arnold Goodman be employed again. The Prime Minister intervened with a plan of his own which, as Goodman predicted, proved unacceptable, whereupon his own formula, negotiated in his flat, provided the basis for a settlement. He shunned publicity for the role he had played but was 'outed' by the *Financial Times* as the mysterious 'Mr X' who had pulled off the deal.

In 1966 he was asked to join the British Council to facilitate better liaison between it and the Arts Council, the relationship between the two having reached an all-time low. From 1976 to 1991 he was its deputy chairman and believed that he served, '... as I have often - a specialised function which is unflattering but useful: that of a troubleshooter.' (Goodman, 1993, p.287). So honest an admission would not have passed the lips of an Oliver Franks who would have recoiled from uttering what he would have regarded as a vulgar self-description. But then Arnold Goodman was quite open about his motives. He had worked hard at positioning himself to expect various public commissions following Labour's electoral success. As he put it himself:

> I was fifty-one at the time of Harold Wilson's election in 1964, and
> I did speculate about whether I might be offered some job to do.
> I had reached a stage in my profession when partial relief from
> legal practice would be welcome ... while I could not contemplate
> retirement from a practice and a clientele to whom I owed heavy
> responsibilities, I was certainly not unwilling to devote a portion of
> my day to some other palatable activity. (op. cit., p.294)

The extensive commercial negotiations on behalf of television moguls, theatrical impresarios and other types of businessmen that were his main preoccupations for most of the 1950s had resulted in a successful fee income and a high reputation within a variety of commercial and legal networks that many would have been happy to settle for. But the satisfactions afforded by these activities were not enough for Arnold Goodman who hankered after deploying on a more public stage the skills and self-confidence he had acquired. This ambition was to be fulfilled over the next decade and a half to a degree he could hardly have anticipated in his wildest dreams, being charged with a wide range of commissions, in both the public and private sectors, that enhanced his reputation as a fixer and which in turn increased the tasks he was asked to undertake, so that the one seemed endlessly to leap-frog the other: this multiplier of reputation and commissions was to establish him as the foremost serial fixer in the history of modern Britain.

In retrospect he was to observe:

> I enjoyed my politico-legal activities and sought to give the best service I could. My activities had no goal and no aspiration, and I had no competitors, which meant that I rapidly acquired the confidence of the leadership of the Labour party. (op. cit., p.211)

By disclaiming both 'goal' and 'aspiration' he meant that he had no specific political agenda of his own that he wished to promote for, like the best of courtiers or fixers, he was primarily on hand to offer advice as to how best the policies of those he served could be executed. His only goal or aspiration was simply to be there at the heart of things. He was also correct to judge that, while there were others in attendance, he had no competitors in the role that fate was in part establishing for him and which in at least equal measure he was so sedulously establishing for himself; and in this he was further helped by being made a life peer in 1965.

Ennoblement, however, was a mere trifle in comparison with his real trump card, his intimate relationship with the new Prime Minister. From 1964 to 1970, at least fortnightly and sometimes more frequently, he would attend at Number Ten to chew over the issues that were currently preoccupying Harold Wilson. His memoirs record these sessions:

> ... I went in at 9 p.m. and often stayed until midnight or past.

> These meetings were largely an opportunity for Harold Wilson to use me as the wall of a fives court against which he banged the ball. I listened patiently. Sitting in the Cabinet Room at Downing Street, with the Prime Minister taking me into his confidence was an exhilarating experience from first to last. I did not regard Harold Wilson as a wit, nor was his conversation particularly spiced with humour, but it was immensely interesting because he would talk to me about his problems and their supposed solutions, and seemingly consult me on the matter - he was a very polite man - although I was conscious that on most political issues my own opinion was pretty well valueless and he recognised that. (op. cit., pp.210-11)

This is a very characteristic and revealing passage about Goodman himself: he admits to the excitement of being privy to affairs of state, offers but faint praise as to the Prime Minister's character, is scornful of his 'supposed' solutions, and seeks self-effacingly to downgrade the worth of his own suggestions by virtue of his disdain for, and total inexperience of, the world of party politics.   The passage says it all about Lord Goodman but still leaves open what was it that he particularly had to offer Harold Wilson and others who sought his advice.

The Labour party, it has to be remembered, had been in the wilderness of opposition for thirteen years so there were few retired elder statesmen left over from the Attlee period to act as guide, philosopher and friend to members of the incoming cabinet. A proxy had therefore to be found for them and was readily available in the shape of Arnold Goodman. By contrast, in 1979 Margaret Thatcher, when she assumed the premiership, had the benefit of the support and advice of two old hands in Peter Thorneycroft, whom she made chairman of the Conservative party and in Willie Whitelaw who served her as a non-competitive, wise and reassuring deputy in the cabinet. The Cabinet over which Harold Wilson presided comprised ministers of high talents, but who also entertained a good deal of animosity towards one another; these tensions only served to nourish Harold Wilson's insecurity and paranoia, while his own 'kitchen cabinet' did not redress the balance since George Wigg, Marcia Williams and Joe Haines were frequently at each others' throats. It is small wonder, then, that Harold Wilson sought a confidant who was above the battle and its machinations and away from the day-to-day hurly-burly of events.

Lord Goodman himself remarked that 'nearly always people need someone' in whom to confide on occasions, and when asked if he thought this was particularly true in the case of politicians replied: 'politicians depend on periodic elections to be returned to office and this induces greater insecurity in them' (Interview, 3 December 1992). He admitted to David Selbourne that he acted as a confessor to both Wilson and Heath (Selbourne, 1993).

Whatever the reasons for the personal chemistry between Wilson and Goodman, it seemed to work remarkably well and by 1968 the Prime Minister sought his advice over Rhodesia, which in 1965 had made a Unilateral Declaration of Independence and seceded from British sovereignty. International economic sanctions had been applied which nevertheless failed to bring down the illegal, all-white regime led by Ian Smith. One evening the Prime Minister mentioned Rhodesia to Arnold

Goodman following the failure of earlier talks between Wilson and Smith aboard *HMS Tiger*. Goodman suggested that Sir Max Aitken, chairman of the *Express* group of newspapers and son of Max Beaverbrook, should be sent on an informal mission to take further soundings in Salisbury because of his close friendship with Smith dating from when both had served in the war in the Royal Rhodesian Air Force. Aitken agreed to go on condition that he was accompanied by Goodman.

Following a round of negotiations in Salisbury, Goodman sat up all night personally drafting a nineteen page document, the contents of which were endorsed by Smith on the following morning. This clandestine mission had been accomplished without publicity. The document formed the basis for further talks between Wilson and Smith on board *HMS Fearless* which, however, again proved abortive, in Goodman's opinion because as he said:

> I am sufficiently egotistical to believe that one of the reasons they failed was that I was not present. Wilson's Cabinet - jealous of a non-political and non-party intruder - had decided not to include me in the team. This was a mistake. (op. cit., p.220)

Edward Heath, as leader of the opposition, must have been impressed by Goodman's role because he asked him if he would return again to Rhodesia if requested. In 1971, with the Conservatives back in office, Goodman duly made four more trips to Salisbury leading a small delegation under conditions of strict secrecy. On the fifth occasion, Sir Alec Douglas-Home, then Foreign Secretary, officially led the British mission but stayed in the background for the most part while negotiations went on which led to the enunciation of the so-called 'five principles' that, it was hoped, would lead to the restoration of constitutional propriety and an internationally recognised independent Rhodesia.

The agreement again failed; both the Labour party and, more importantly, majority African opinion in Rhodesia, found it unacceptable and no solution to the problem was found until the joint efforts of Sir Christopher Soames and Lord Carrington succeeded in 1979, the first year of Mrs Thatcher's administration, with the conclusion of the Lancaster House talks.

Goodman's role in fashioning the five principles was criticised, as he records, on the grounds that in effect he overplayed his hand as a fixer:

> Such was my disposition to conciliation, the argument ran, that the

temptation to reach agreement on any footing was irresistible to me. There is some validity in this ... complaint. I prefer a bad agreement to a prolonged disagreement. This does not mean that I do not believe there are issues where principle is paramount: but there are a great many issues where principle is misguided or even hypocritical, and it is a fair accusation that I tend to suspect this more often than most people. (op. cit., p.226)

Apparently for Michael Foot and other Labour critics, it was acceptable for him to fix things for a Labour government but not for a Conservative one, even when the deal later fell apart; the Conservative Prime Minister, however, acknowledged Goodman's unstinted efforts over Rhodesia by recommending him for the award of Companion of Honour in 1972.

If the Arts Council was his most gratifying post, his Rhodesian excursions must, at times, have been the most exciting, for an acceptable settlement would have been an achievement - in terms of British politics at least - second only to that of bringing peace to Northern Ireland. (In fact his name was suggested as a possible mediator by Terence O'Neill in 1974.) For Goodman himself it also proved he could effectively exercise his negotiating talents in a sphere other than the purely domestic which was otherwise to be his only stamping ground. Although he was careful to place the blame for failure elsewhere, be it his exclusion from the talks on *HMS Fearless*, the professional inadequacy of the Foreign Office over Rhodesia, or the excessive criticism of the five principles by the Labour opposition and liberal opinion in general, he clearly played a major role that, on two occasions, might have succeeded and, as he said, at least paved the way for the 1979 settlement.

Back on the home front his services continued to be in demand. In addition to other calls on his time, in the early years of the first Wilson government, he assisted Richard Crossman, the Housing Minister, to overcome civil service opposition to the introduction of an anti-eviction of tenants bill. Goodman and his old friend Dennis Lloyd drafted a paper in consultation with the civil service which led to the passage of the 1965 Rent Act that sought to outlaw Rachmanite harassment by landlords.

Matters related to housing were to be another strong *leitmotif* in his career, in 1973, with the Conservatives in power, he was invited to become Chairman of the Housing Corporation and stayed in that post for the next four years, coupling it with that of the National Building Agency and waiving the fees payable for both jobs. The aim of the Corporation was to expand the voluntary housing movement and, in a characteristic remark, Goodman told a meeting of the National Federation of Housing Associations that it was his intention 'not to weep for the homeless but to build houses for them' (*The Times*, 24 May 1973). The same year in the televised Dimbleby Lecture he attacked 'the appalling conditions in which too many are forced to live'. 'Courts would have fewer criminals to deal with and more people would get a chance to fulfill their potential if these conditions could be alleviated', thus directly linking crime and social deprivation ('Housing - who is to blame?', *The Listener*, 24 October 1974, pp.520-22).

He was also to continue his interests in the world of the mass media, and in newspapers in particular. Sir Ifor Evans, Provost of University College, London, his first *alma mater*, suggested he join him on the board of *The Observer*, then being edited by David Astor. Almost inevitably, he became chairman a year later, and by 1970 had succeeded Lord Drogheda as chairman of the Newspapers Proprietors' Association (NPA). Lord Robens, a former Attlee minister who later ran the National Coal Board, had been the initial choice but was vetoed by the more extreme right-wing press magnates. Goodman was asked to take over on a *locum* basis for six months, a period that expanded into six years. Unlike Oliver Franks, who turned down a series of more prestigious jobs than any of those ever offered to Arnold Goodman, the latter always found such invitations difficult to refuse.

At *The Observer* he encouraged Astor to drop a story regarding George Brown's - then Foreign Secretary - drunken overtures to the French ambassadress; negotiated, sight unseen, for the serialisation rights of the first set of Svetlana Stalin's memoirs for the then princely sum of £84,000 that embarrassingly turned out to be no more than a eulogy of her father (though a later set denounced him for the butcher he was); and was involved in the sale of the newspaper, first to the oil tycoon Robert Anderson and later to Tiny Rowland of Lonhro, after which he stood down from the board.

At the NPA he was involved in an exhausting series of industrial disputes between the employers and the various Fleet Street unions, whose grip on the industry was so strong that excessive wages and an assortment of archaic working practices led to inflated wage bills and ludicrous over-manning levels. The NPA consisted of a 'most impossible body of men', locked in continuous circulation wars with one another. They included, according to Goodman, Jocelyn Stevens who was unpredictable, Michael

Berry who was stubborn to the point of obstinacy, and Roy Thomson whose sole goal was profit maximisation. They and the other proprietorial representatives apparently could only agree when it came to acquiescing to the latest union demands: '... there was hardly a day of the week when the threat of strike action did not have to be dealt with on a basis of total urgency ...' (Goodman, 1993, p.361). It was doubtless this experience that prompted Goodman to oppose with all his might the Trade Union and Labour Relations (Amendment) Bill that Michael Foot, as Secretary of State for Employment, ventured to introduce in 1974, extending mandatory union membership - the closed shop - to all forms of employment including journalism. Again, he found the newspaper bosses lacking in stamina for the fight. His own opposition, however, delayed the passage of the legislation for eighteen months before it was finally enacted into law, which was later to be reversed by the trade union reforms introduced by the Thatcher government. This battle for the preservation of editorial freedom as he saw it, was one of the rare instances when Arnold Goodman stepped out of the role of fixer, of facilitating other people's policies, to pursue a goal of his own; an example, perhaps, to paraphrase a well-known dictum, that a fixer who hires himself has a fool for a client.

During the 1960s and 1970s there were yet other duties assigned to him, some of which would take him far away from his usual haunts of Whitehall and the West End of London.

In 1966 he was asked by Harold Wilson to help create the Open University. It is interesting to note in his memoirs that he believed Wilson got the idea originally from the US Senator Benton, publisher of the *Encyclopedia Britannica* but, while he emphasised the contribution of both Wilson and Jennie Lee in getting the OU off the ground, appeared pointedly to ignore the early advocacy of Michael Young except obliquely and dismissively saying that the OU was 'for a long time miscalled the University of the Air' - Young's original title. Be that as it may, Goodman despatched himself to New York to meet Benton and to cajole the Ford Foundation into providing funds for an experimental pilot study. The cabinet set up a working party at Wilson's insistence. Goodman was asked to look into the feasibility of the project especially in regard to the costs of the broadcasting of courses on television. He secured the complete co-operation of the BBC from Sir Hugh Carleton Greene and Charles Curran, his successor as Director General. Goodman reported favourably, if hopelessly inaccurately, about the costs of the project, joined its Planning Board and took part in the selection of Walter Perry, the first Vice-Chancellor.

In 1970 he was again involved with the BBC in its altercation with the Musicians' Union over the question of 'needle time', that is the acceptable ratio of recorded to live music. A solution was arrived at and ten years' later he was called in again to mediate between the BBC and the union over the annual Promenade Concerts. The BBC appeared intransigent and the future of the *Proms* was put at risk; in an interim report a parliamentary committee called for a conciliator. Goodman assumed the role and by his deft deployment of unorthodox tactics, which included leaving the respective negotiating teams to unappetising cheese sandwiches supplied by ACAS while he took supper at the House of Lords, success was achieved after days of discussion, with swift and unexpected agreement in the small hours.

Barbara Castle became Secretary of State for Health and Social Security in the second Wilson government and thereupon published a consultative paper entitled *The Separation of Private Practice from NHS Hospitals*. While private pay beds accounted for only one per cent of beds available in the NHS, Mrs Castle felt they were subsidised by the state and enabled those using them to get faster treatment. The proposal provoked the wrath of the medical consultants, as did her related intention of withdrawing outpatient facilities for private use, and they retained Lord Goodman and his partner John Montgomerie to make representations on their behalf. Montgomerie assisted in drafting the consultants' counter arguments to the government's proposals, while Goodman sounded out the possibilities for a compromise. After long and fruitless discussions Goodman withdrew his services from the consultants because they had decided in the meantime to go on strike and he placed on record his own opposition to such tactics in a letter to *The Times* of 22 December 1975. Some weeks later both sides agreed a conciliator should be appointed to deal with the impasse that had arisen, that Goodman was acceptable to both, and a 'phone call from Harold Wilson secured his services in that capacity yet again.

He initially sidelined Mrs Castle by getting the Prime Minister to preside over the first resumed meeting with the consultants. Goodman then came up with a plan for closing 1,000 pay beds in the first instance, with any others to be phased out later on the condition that alternative facilities for private patients were available. Detailed discussions between the two parties followed at a series of meetings that often took place in

Lord Goodman's flat and peace was eventually restored.

Some time later David Ennals succeeded Mrs Castle at the DHSS and he sought Goodman's advice on a scheme to replace the three-wheeled motorised vehicles, then commonly used by the disabled, with a new mobility allowance that would assist them to purchase their own specially adapted cars which offered a better means of transportation. The outcome was provision whereby the disabled paid their allowance into an organisation, Motability, which by borrowing from a consortium of banks, was able to bulk purchase at reduced cost both the vehicles and necessary insurance at rates far lower than the individuals could obtain for themselves; they would, then, in effect lease back the cars via their mobility allowance. In his memoirs, Lord Goodman stated that the scheme was '... the most fortunate thought that ever came into my head' (op. cit., p.243). The scheme ran into financial difficulties in 1995.

Apart from all these major interventions, and there were others of less moment, he continued with his solicitor's practice and in 1975 represented Jonathan Cape, the publishers of the diaries of the late Richard Crossman. The government did not want them published because of the precedent it would cause in terms of breaching the confidentiality of cabinet proceedings and, in particular, circumventing the thirty year rule. After much unproductive haggling no agreement could be reached and in June 1975 the government sought an injunction against the *Sunday Times* to prevent the publication of extracts from the diary. In the subsequent action the Lord Chief Justice found against the government, which settled instead for a committee of Privy Counsellors, under Lord Radcliffe that also included Oliver Franks, to review the procedures for the future publication of ministerial memoirs.

The Crossman case followed closely on the judgement made in favour of Jonathan Aitken, who in 1971 was charged under the Official Secrets Act for disclosing in the *Sunday Telegraph* details of a secret assessment as to the likely course of the Nigerian civil war over Biafra. Goodman strongly supported the Biafran cause and worked closely behind the scenes with Sir Hugh Fraser MP, a fellow supporter who had collaborated with Jonathan Aitken. The outcome of the two cases, in Goodman's view, had the combined effect of severely curtailing future government resort to prosecutions under the Official Secrets Act.

The rapidity of the rise and the extensiveness of the tasks undertaken by Lord Goodman in his career as a fixer can only be described as remarkable but both are reflected in the attributes he brought to the role and the extensive repertoire of skills he displayed.

First, and most obviously, he had the time to spare. He was a bachelor and as is well known, bachelors, like spinsters, have the most amenable and accommodating spouses. There were no home or other domestic ties to compete with his politico-legal activities. Mary Wilson was probably the only woman in his adult life to signal it was past bedtime when he sat discussing with her husband into the small hours at 10 Downing Street. He seems to have been happy, or at least not unwilling, to be telephoned at all hours of the night or day if a problem merited his immediate attention and, even on those occasions when he was unwell, he was prepared to offer his counsel from his sick-bed.

Time could be spared not just because of a lack of domestic constraints but also because he was clearly a workaholic. Before the war, as a young solicitor, together with some professional friends, he spent many an evening in the East End offering free legal aid to those who could not afford the services of lawyers. Every Tuesday, Goodman, Jim Gower and Dennis Lloyd - all three were to have distinguished careers - would be available in the Commercial Road from 6.30 p.m., often till beyond twelve o'clock dispensing advice, a practice that continued for four years. Burning the midnight oil was thus a habit acquired early on in his career and was one which would hold him in good stead at its peak.

It is also true that he had a felicitous knack of combining business with pleasure. His pastimes were music and the arts, one of the main areas in which he was to perform a variety of official duties. Even his lesser hobby, following horseracing, led on the recommendation of the Jockey Club to his appointment to the board of United Racecourses Ltd. to help keep at arm's length or at least minimise any possible depredations his friend Lord Wigg, as chairman of the Horserace Betting Levy Board, might plan to impose on the racing fraternity.

Then, of course, there was the training and experience he brought with him from his profession as a solicitor for which he claimed: 'There is probably no career that gives one a more rounded view of the human race ... in the course of my career, I have encountered such a wide variety of human situations, such a conflict of opinion and decision, that I have had every reason to determine, on a common-denominator basis, the quality of humanity' (op. cit., p.117). He described himself as 'a loner' and behind his cultivated bonhomonious public personality there probably once lurked a shy young man; military service and professional practice brought him into contact with all shapes and manners of humankind, ranging from the humblest at his pre-war free advice surgeries to the tycoons of the commercial and media worlds. While such intercourse would undoubtedly have broadened his horizons and awareness of the foibles and frailties of the human race it would have had less impact but for his innate ability to get behind the outer personality. It is a trait that he himself fully recognised: '... I am rarely, if ever, conscious of people's religions and backgrounds. I *am* (his italics) acutely conscious of their characters, predispositions and interests' (op. cit., p.271). This was reinforced by his fascination with psychiatry.

In the course of his memoirs Lord Goodman did not hesitate to criticise, though always with some individual exceptions, the judiciary, the civil service, diplomats and politicians, but he was less damning of psychiatrists; while he recognised some are charlatans, he took a relatively benign view of their endeavours, while nevertheless praising two in particular. He met Professor Alexander Kennedy and Sir Martin Roth in the course of his professional work, but both were to become his close personal friends. It is very pertinent that the one recognition to come to him from the medical world was that of being elected an Honorary Fellow of the Royal College of Psychiatrists. As he himself once remarked: 'a man who is nothing but a lawyer is not much of a lawyer' (*Sunday Times*, 6 January 1972); it is also true that the best solicitors are equally good psychologists and Arnold Goodman amply corroborates the correlation.

Insight into the personalities of others must be complemented with a non-neurotic capacity for self-awareness and he admitted to 'an invincible optimism and a buoyant confidence in my own notions' (op. cit., p.272). Previously, he had said:

> I don't think I've ever felt under an intolerable pressure from other people's opinions. Perhaps I have an excessive and rather conceited faith in my own opinions, but I was never tortured by doubts. You couldn't achieve anything if you were tortured by doubt. (quoted in Attallah, 1990, p.275)

It was this sense of self-confidence, stemming from a very high intelligence nurtured over the course of a successful professional career that produced the near charismatic presence he exuded in any gathering.

To Anthony Sampson, chronicler of the British elite, '... encountering him is like encountering a physical object, a great rock or tree' (Sampson, 1971, pp.433-4), while Lord Annan, a fellow member of the elite, wrote:

As he enters a party, like a giant tanker edging towards her moorings, bonhomie, goodwill, warmth, friendliness, and even a touch of fantasy, radiate through the room. (Annan, 1991, p.12)

Of all the attributes bestowed on him by nature or nurture there was one outstanding feature of which he himself was acutely aware and that was of being a Jew. He saw it as the defining element in his make-up and the title of David Selbourne's book about him, *Not an Englishman* serves to emphasise the point. Goodman, of course, was not the first prominent member of Anglo-Jewry to have this sense of being semi-detached, of being *in* but not *of* English society. His sense of being marginal might have accounted for his studied disinterestedness - most noticeable in his constant references to disliking party politics, most politicians and the fact that he never joined a political party - and thus fitted him well in his roles as independent arbitrator, trusted confessor, and, though in this he was much less successful, enunciator of edicts. By no means orthodox in his religious observance - he was a member of the Liberal Jewish Synagogue - he was an ardent but not uncritical Zionist, while successive Israeli ambassadors to Britain seem to be almost the only group of diplomats to receive his unstinting approbation. It was Zionist causes and matters Israeli that truly engaged the commitment of both his head and his heart. His multifarious activities in Britain as we have seen, certainly had his concentrated and undivided intellectual attention but despite relishing the wearing of morning dress to receive his CH in a private audience with the Queen, or participating in the rituals of fellowship as Master of an Oxford college, a measure of reserve had been maintained which, he fondly believed immunised him from acquiring the traditional prejudices of the English. But he was acutely aware of these prejudices and of the other characteristics that compose British society as, indeed, are the other fixers described in this book, all of whom in their different ways did not originate from the mainstream elite of that society: marginality, in whatever form it may take, seems to be a *sine qua non* for a fixer.

It is not always easy to distinguish the attributes of a fixer from the techniques he employs in dealing with a specific problem for the one, consciously or not, can be melded with the other. Is, for example, a disdain for party politics, an attribute or a technique? It can, of course, be professed as the one, while actually being deployed as the other as a means of establishing one's objectivity and neutrality. In the case of Arnold Goodman one thing is for sure: whatever the relationship between the two, and however entangled they may have become, he had - to a degree more than other fixers - an abundance of both attributes and techniques. He was a complex character who used to the full all the innate gifts and acquired skills at his disposal.

It was remarked earlier that Arnold Goodman's greatest stroke of luck was the Labour victory of 1964. It is certain that without it he would not have been catapulted quite so dramatically into the cockpit of public life, but there was also an almost equally essential and related, contextual aspect that has to be brought into the reckoning. His career as a fixer coincided with the high tide of corporatism in British politics that from its origins in the war, through the Butskellite fifties, reached its apotheosis during the premierships of Harold Macmillan, Harold Wilson and Edward Heath. Corporatism was meant to usher in concerted agreement on public policy, via tripartite mechanisms such as NEDDY - the National Economic Development Council - between the government, employers' representatives and the trade unions. Corporatism was an attempt to shore up the decaying institutions of the essentially nineteenth century constitution, centred around a parliament based on territorial representation, with a tripartite scaffolding based on functional representation. But if corporatism was intended to formulate agreed policies, it was just as likely, especially in adverse economic circumstances, to lead to deadlock as in the case of the 1974 miners' strike that brought down the Heath government, or the 1978/79 'winter of discontent' that despatched the Callaghan government. More damaging than particular events, however, was the creation of a climate of expectations - of proposals and, often incompatible, counter proposals - not just at the centre of government, with midnight crisis meetings with beer and sandwiches at No. 10 - that permeated other sectors of the economy, of which the newspaper world was perhaps the most notorious. Corporatism, more often than not in Britain at least, gave all parties a veto and no party much real power of initiative, especially government when it came to the crunch. Corporatism meant impasse, and impasse calls for a fixer. For Lord Goodman, then, the 1964 general election may have provided the precipitating factor which launched his career as a fixer, but it was the corporatist *zeitgeist* that enabled it to flourish so profusely.

Like Oliver Franks, Arnold Goodman always, at the outset of a mission, accepted the logic of any situation; he was, after all, nothing if not a supreme pragmatist, who eschewed extremes and took a reasonably liberal stance on the issues of the epoch. He stood for reason and reasonableness and carried little baggage. Unlike Franks, however, he did not enter negotiations with a particular outcome in mind stemming from a prolonged preparatory stint of reading. He took the situation as given, assessed the viewpoints of the conflicting parties, and suggested as a solution not so much a middle way as, in his own words, 'a likely way' (Interview, 3 December 1992). Previously, he had used the term 'midway' in describing the process and how it is arrived at in negotiations:

> I wouldn't say that estimating your opponent is a very profitable activity. What you have to do is to estimate the strength of your case and the strength of a case that comes midway between the two cases, and ultimately it's your job to propound a tolerable solution acceptable to both sides, or all three sides. But you arrive there by instinct. It's not a calculated process. (Attallah, op. cit., p.275)

This description again appears sharply to distinguish his methodology from that of his fellow pragmatist Oliver Franks who would not admit to anything so base as 'instinct'. Franks saw himself as supremely analytical and logical in his approach to problems as befitted his training as a philosopher; Goodman, in contrast, after weighing up the differing standpoints, saw himself in some intuitive or more psychological way splitting the difference, though not always in equal proportions. Thus at the NPA he elicited the upper figure the press barons were prepared to pay out, and sought agreement with the unions at a sum slightly less than that. Such a tactic was in keeping with the times and had been the sort of approach adopted earlier by Sir Walter Monckton, who as a fixer he most closely resembles. Speaking in the Lords, he said, '... on any compromise one must not expect to achieve all that one sets out to do. The effect of a compromise is that part of what you want you do not get' (Lords Debates, 17 December 1970, Vol. 313, Col. 1561). But does the 'one' refer to the conciliator or to the parties at odds with each other? Most likely the latter for, as quoted earlier, he prefers a bad agreement to a prolonged disagreement and that is why he was a quick fixer; a particular resolution might have a short shelf life but after all the parties could always come together again under his aegis.

Although a ruthless exploiter of the contacts he had built up through the construction of his various networks, he was not reliant on teamwork. In this, he was much more like Michael Young in style. Franks and Edwin Plowden, on the other hand, brought up as they were in civil service procedures, tended to establish and work through teams they effectively guided if not totally controlled. Goodman, for the most part, preferred to work alone: 'I have never enlisted a team since I stopped playing cricket' (Interview, 3 December 1992). This meant that like Franks, and to a slightly lesser extent, Young he tended to do his own initial drafting as with Crossman's Rent Act or in working through the night as in Salisbury, Rhodesia.

He, like Henry Kissinger, was adroit at shuttle diplomacy, often conducted in his own flat which offered neutral ground to the warring parties but constituted home ground for himself: he was the impresario orchestrating events.

Unlike almost all of the other fixers he was prepared to threaten resignation or to withdraw his services and await another opportunity. As has been already noted, he threatened to resign from the board of *The Observer* if George Brown's attempt to importune the French ambassadress was not pulled (the reason given being to protect Mrs Brown, a long-suffering good Jewish wife), and withdrew his services from the medical consultants when they took strike action. Both tactics may have been principled, but they also bespeak a predisposition to take a very tough-minded stance when necessary, which would not have come naturally to a more fastidious personality like Franks.

But such tough-mindedness did not extend to financial prudence or cost efficiency. As we have seen he was prepared to settle for inflationary pay awards in the newspaper industry and he believed fervently that the arts should be subsidised at a very high level. He instinctively loathed such bodies as the Comptroller and Auditor-General and Public Accounts Committee and reacted most violently when Paul Channon, then Minister for the Arts, appointed Clive Priestley to investigate the efficiency of the Royal Opera House in Covent Garden. Equally, Lord Rayner's efficiency scrutinies in Whitehall were anathema to him.

Being stoutly politically non-partisan he was somewhat resentful that his career as a fixer ended so abruptly after 1979. After all, *The Times* had earlier endorsed his crossbench status:

> ... while he commends himself to Labour as the Prime Minister's friend and solicitor, few Conservatives are able to remember him

ever speaking or voting for the (Labour) government. (30 December 1968).

This impeccably independent voting record was not sufficiently appreciated by Margaret Thatcher and may be why he was so outspoken about her. He believed she failed to make use of his skills because in her eyes he was 'tarred with a left-wing brush', whereas Barbara Castle clearly saw him as someone who had benefited by being advanced under Labour without paying his full dues by taking the Labour whip in the Lords. However, in the case of Mrs Thatcher, it was probably not so much his crossbench stance or being tainted by an early association with Labour as that he personified 'consensus/corporatist man' and all the things she loathed about her predecessors. What did him most damage in her eyes perhaps, was not his connection with Harold Wilson, but his close relationship with Edward Heath; he was clearly not 'one of us'.

Goodman differed, too, from most other fixers in being happy enough to use the House of Lords as a platform, especially in the case of the one or two issues that constituted his own political agenda. As we have seen, his opposition to extending the principle of the closed shop into newspaper journalism delayed the passage of Michael Foot's bill for eighteen months so that it had to be reintroduced in a second parliamentary session before it became law. Equally vociferous was his advocacy of a single legal profession whereby, as in Canada and elsewhere, the distinction between barristers and solicitors does not exist: as 'a determined fusionist', he enjoyed some success in persuading government that solicitors should have their rights of audience extended to the crown courts and be promoted to the judiciary but he did not live to see his aim of a single profession come about. He would have gained some gratification, however, in being the first solicitor to become an 'artificial silk' on his appointment as a Queen's Counsel.

But he was quite right to have eschewed the formal game of party politics, for his comparative advantage was in working behind the scenes. Although a sparkling debater, he had much less success as a legislator than as a fixer; his considerable self-awareness and self-discipline could not always quite contain his 'buoyant confidence in his own notions' and he could not always resist an audience.

Lord Goodman had a profound and highly developed sense of history in the making, when he was present and even more especially, as on *HMS Fearless* and during the Thatcher era, when he was excluded, but he appeared, in marked contrast to Franks and Young, to have developed little sense of the direction that history is taking or of the historical alternatives that are on offer. Franks felt he saw the need for the advent of a new philosopher-king or management oriented civil servant, while Young had a deep sense that status not social class would become more important and consequently that the individual *qua* consumer would become more important than the individual *qua* worker. For Arnold Goodman, the future would take care of itself; life was for living.

His death in May 1995 brought many and generous tributes, most of which picked out his successes as a fixer and highlighted his contribution to the arts.

Like his fellow fixers, he was in his own way a zealous custodian of his own reputation, possibly because it was his only heir. But, like theirs, it is a reputation that was hard earned and is widely recognised, one of the most generous accolades coming from Harold Wilson (though Arnold Goodman did not reciprocate the sentiment) when he wrote:

> There is a time in the affairs of governments when deadlock becomes total, and ordinary human agencies are impotent to deal with the situation; the superhuman is then invoked and a telephone call is put through to Lord Goodman. (Wilson, 1979, p.191)

5 Michael Young: Lone Ranger as Fixer

Like nature, Michael Young abhors a vacuum so that any gap found in the system has to be plugged. Although he occasionally accepted commissions from government he was, and resolutely remains at eighty, essentially a wide-ranging, self-appointed fixer. He exercises his organisational ingenuity with a very broad brush, that extends across education, community life, consumer affairs, significant phases in the human life cycle, and political realignment. It is perhaps because of the sheer breadth of these activities that his immense contribution to shaping much of what has been good about British life in the second half of the twentieth century has not been more widely recognised. Prophets in their own land are more likely to be acclaimed if they stick to a single task that attracts a particular following; Michael Young could never be accused of that.

Another reason for his relative lack of recognition lies in a certain internal ambivalence in his make-up. Throughout his adult life he seems to have been tugged in two distinct, though not unrelated, directions. Sometimes it is the political activist in him that gains the ascendancy, while at other times and for more prolonged periods it is the social reformer that has the upper hand. In terms of academic disciplines, this duality manifests itself in never quite making up his mind whether he is a political scientist or a sociologist. While it would be mistaken to place too strong an emphasis on such categorisation, these swings from the political to the social and back again are integral to an understanding of his career. In either sphere, however, like the more conventional official fixers, he prefers to work largely behind the scenes, within a custom-built network of contacts and, like them, for the most part he is a reluctant participant in the political mainstream.

This two-faceted quality of his personality unquestionably owes more to early nurture than to any predispositions implanted by nature, for never was a pupil more influenced by his schooling. Michael Young was born in Manchester on 9 August 1915 of an Irish mother, with artistic talents, and an Australian father who was a musician but for the most part unemployed. He spent his first eight years in Australia before returning to England to live in London. His parents separated and in quick succession he attended two state day schools and two private preparatory schools as a boarder, all four being bad experiences. At fourteen he was sent to Dartington Hall School in Totnes, Devon, for which his paternal grandfather had been persuaded to pay the fees only on the condition that he would learn fruit farming in order to return to Tasmania to grow apples.

Dartington had been set up as a progressive school in 1926 by Leonard and Dorothy Elmhirst as part of a wide utopian complex that also included artistic, agricultural and industrial endeavours. She came from distinguished American stock, a millionairess, whose father had been a leading Democrat serving as Secretary of the US Navy. Her husband was born the son of a Yorkshire clergyman, who later became a landowner, and subsequently went to Cambridge and Cornell Universities and was to be greatly influenced by the educational and communal experiments inspired by Rabindranath Tagore with whom he worked for a while in India.

When the fourteen-year-old Young arrived at Dartington there were only twenty-five fellow pupils and in comparison with his previous schools 'it seemed like paradise', for it had 'no punishment, no prefects, no uniform, no OTC, no segregation of sexes, no compulsion to games, religion or anything else including competition'. Bertrand Russell, Aldous Huxley and Sigmund Freud sent their children to Dartington where at various times Bernard Leach taught pottery, Imogen Holst music and Mark Toby painting. It was the first sustained period of happiness in his life. He was to become very closely bonded to the Elmhirsts, their outlook and chosen way of life.

In *The Elmhirsts of Dartington* (Young, 1982) Michael Young has written an eloquent account of his involvement with the place and the people; the book is an act of filial piety. He gives a loving description of the landscape and buildings, but characteristically also supplies plenty of facts and figures about the various Dartington enterprises. He was bound up with the Elmhirsts from the moment of his arrival. 'They are me or a little part of me' he wrote (op. cit., p.6), and admitted that 'detachment is something I have no claim to' (op. cit., p.4).

They were both somewhat odd. Dorothy, though very rich, was also an idealist who had funded a great array of radical causes, including the defence of two Italian anarchists who had been framed on a charge of bombing a Boston store - a *cause célèbre* of its time. A friend and patron of the pioneering anthropologist Margaret Mead, she also had financed the *New Republic* and other publications and become involved with the League of Women Voters, consumer organisations and labour unions in the USA. As a result some of the higher American social circles were no longer open to her. Her husband Leonard was, if anything, even odder and his interests just as wide ranging. He had helped to start the International Conference of Agricultural Economists and was a third world development enthusiast long before the notion had become popular. In Bengal he had helped Tagore start a new university and had also been involved in the setting up of the Cambridgeshire Village Colleges. After their marriage this strange pair transferred their ideas and energies to England.

According to Michael Young, they believed that mankind can be 'liberated through education; a flowering of the arts can transform a society impoverished by industrialisation and secularisation; a society that combines the best of town and country combines the best of both' (op. cit., p.100). These and other principles guided their work but 'they were not so much fountains as channels or conduits through which travelled a constant flow of ideas to find outlets in Dartington, not so much innovators as enablers' (op. cit., p.99). Young internalised their principles and, while he emulated them as enablers, he was also emphatically an innovator.

Although idealistically motivated, the Elmhirsts were neither spartan in their lifestyle nor in any way egalitarian or democratic in their relationships with those who taught at or otherwise worked for them on the Dartington estate. They lived a luxurious life and mixed easily with the wealthy and famous on both sides of the Atlantic. When the young Michael Young - whom they virtually adopted and called 'Youngster' to distinguish him from their own son Michael - proved unsuited to fruit farming, a bursary was found to pay his fees; and when he had nowhere to go in the holidays, they took him in his father's cut-down suit to New York on board *RMS Majestic*. On arrival in New York they were met by a fleet of Cadillacs in which they drove to Dorothy's Park Lane penthouse. The summer house on Long Island had twenty servants and stabling for twenty horses - a stark contrast with life with his father which meant sharing a bed in a one-room flat in Notting Hill. Dorothy Elmhirst had been at school with Eleanor Roosevelt (who, interestingly, had attended Allenswood School - an early English progressive school patronised by the Bloomsbury set) and in 1933 Michael Young himself stayed at the White House and dined with most of the United States cabinet. All this must have made a deep impression on a seventeen-year-old boy, who was experiencing greater extremes of riches and poverty than most people. Dartington not only gave him a family and a moral framework but eventually, after two terms playing around with motorbikes, an education too. A new headmaster arrived; as Young put it, 'he did not want to make the choice that Rousseau and the Elmhirsts made between making a man and making a citizen. He wanted the citizen as well as the man' (op. cit., p.165).

His introduction to high society and high politics was of a kind that would have been commonplace to a scion of one of the great political families of England, like the Marlboroughs or the Cecils, but it must have been a very heady experience for a teenager from humble origins, and it was one that was not lost on him.

On leaving Dartington, Michael Young spent a year in a solicitor's office before changing to read for the Bar. He attended the London School of Economics at the same time and eventually gained a degree in economics. While at LSE he joined the Communist Party, but was turned down for the International Brigade fighting in Spain. Later, he left the party over the Molotov-Ribbentrop Pact, and joined the Labour Party at the beginning of the war. A lifelong asthma sufferer, he was judged only fit enough for the Pay Corps, decided against this and did a brief spell working in one of Oliver Franks' munitions factories.

He then joined the staff of Political and Economic Planning (PEP), an early forerunner of what are now called 'think tanks'. Michael Young's involvement with PEP had begun when he was a schoolboy. Both Dorothy and Leonard Elmhirst had been involved in the start of the organisation in 1931. PEP's aims were always to promote efficiency in government combined with 'a just and harmonious society'. The polarisation of politics did not obviate the need for 'dispassionate non-partisan ... yet highly relevant work'. (Pinder, 1981, Introduction)

One of the bright young men who founded PEP was Max Nicholson who had written a National Plan in 1931 for the *Weekend Review*. It proposed devolution, and changes in the machinery of government. Most PEP members were non-political or anti-party and the work they did was often remarkably farsighted, for example, looking ahead towards a federal Europe. As at Dartington idealism and reform were the order of the day. While still at LSE, Nicholson invited Young to write a PEP broadsheet. These were anonymous, and a note on the back of each stated: 'PEP asks for the continued support of all who believe in a fact-finding, non-partisan attitude as the most constructive way of dealing with problems of public affairs'.

Young wrote *Broadsheet No. 133: Manpower Planning* in November 1938, and thinks this is the most influential paper he has ever drafted. Based on a book by Humbert Wolfe on labour regulation in the first world war, it stressed the importance of distinguishing between efficiency and regimentation: the chief problem is 'how to overcome the arbitrary and unnecessary identification of freedom with inefficiency and of effective organisation with state compulsion' and to preserve individual initiative and responsibility. The 1914-18 war had taught many painful lessons, including the dangers of indiscriminate volunteering. Drawing on Wolfe's work, the paper set out the essentials of a manpower policy, stressing the need to have the right person in the right job, and sketching a scheme for a national register on punched cards. One of Young's skills, like those of the Elmhirsts, it now appeared, was to take and refashion the ideas of others. In October 1939, just after the outbreak of the war, he produced a second broadsheet *The Home Front*. Now on the staff of PEP, he recognised in the opening sentence the change in the civil service noticed by Franks at the end of the war: 'War has put a new perspective ... on our national life. Perhaps the most significant change has been the switchover from a negative regulatory concept of government, controlling a very limited range of activities, to a positive and constructive type of government taking great responsibilities in every field'.

Though not on active service, life at PEP was far from safe. It is recalled that nothing would disturb Young's 'unshakeable concentration on the details of an editorial session while the bombs fell closer and closer' (Pinder, 1981, p.89). In July 1942 appeared the longest broadsheet of all, *Planning for Social Security*; this was a major influence on the Beveridge Report of 1944. PEP's aim was always to act as a bridge between research and policy making and in the war years there was very close interaction with civil servants. In many ways Young is the personification of such bridge-building and, as earlier remarked, he has moved freely between the two.

There were probably several reasons for his leaving PEP to go to the Labour Party in 1945. One may have been that 'Although sometimes PEP purported to see itself, especially in its early days, as a radical external stimulus to the Establishment, the groups of friends and colleagues who helped formulate and apply that stimulus were as often as not actual or potential Establishment archetypes' (op. cit., p.168).

In any case, reflecting the informal alliance between PEP and the Labour Party in reconstruction planning, Young had since 1943 been writing a series of pamphlets for the Labour party, with such titles as *Will the War make us poorer?*. When he got to Transport House in February 1945 as research secretary and had the main responsibility for the 1945 manifesto he claimed to have 'packed into it as many ideas from PEP as I could decently get past Herbert Morrison' (op. cit., p.96).

Transport House was a lively place in those years. Influential there at this time were, apart from Morrison who was chairman of the policy committee, Patrick Gordon-Walker and Ellen Wilkinson who wrote the first draft of the education section of the manifesto. One colleague, a completely contrasting personality, was Denis Healey, the international secretary destined later to become Defence Secretary and Chancellor of the Exchequer. He remembers Young as 'a sallow intellectual with lank hair and hornrimmed spectacles ... he had an enquiring mind and a roaming imagination' (Healey, 1990, p.72).

In sharp contrast to the Thirties there was a good deal of common ground between the two main parties as the election approached. The Conservatives accepted the need to maintain a high level of employment and make better provision for education (acknowledged in the 1944 Act), to introduce a national insurance system and a national health service, but were committed to removing controls as soon as possible. Labour, stressing they stood for order and for 'positive constructive progress', pointed out the dangers of profiteering and said they would plan 'from the ground up'. At 5000 words, rather shorter than today's manifestos, it was 'written in that vague but uplifting style commonly associated with political publications' (Watkins, 1951, p.12). To the left of the party, it was a 'mild and circumspect document', which contained a less wholehearted commitment to nationalisation than had been demanded by the 1944 Labour conference and the least the leaders could get away with (Miliband, 1964, p.7), but whatever its shortcomings it owed much to Young's drafting abilities and served its purpose. Whenever the manifesto was mentioned in years to come, Young always pointed out that it had been enacted in its entirety.

At this time he came under the influence of Evan Durbin, a member of the Fabian Society Executive from 1945 until his untimely death in 1948. A zoologist turned economist, he lectured at LSE before becoming a personal assistant to Clement Attlee during the war years. He was elected to Parliament in 1945 and became a junior minister. An intimate friend of Hugh Gaitskell, he might well have succeeded Attlee as the Labour leader. Durbin introduced Young to a range of approaches that included industrial psychology and when he left Transport House, after Labour's defeat in 1951, he spent a year at the Tavistock Institute.

While heading the research department at Labour headquarters, the indefatigable Michael Young was simultaneously working for his PhD at LSE under Harold Laski, professor of political science and chairman of the Labour Party during the successful 1945 election campaign. At LSE he met Edward Shils, a young and persuasive American sociologist. In his obituary Young was to write:

> Edward Shils changed my life when he was on the sociology staff of LSE in the 1940s. I was then the research secretary of the Labour Party and still thinking I might try for a parliamentary seat, when he invited me to join his post-graduate seminar over which he presided with irrepressible intellectual brio. By some magic and to my surprise he made me feel I was already more of a sociologist than a politician and should make his strange trade mine. (*Guardian*, 8 February 1995)

Thus Shils temporarily resolved the tug Young felt between the political and the social and Young swopped Laski for Richard Titmuss, one of the founding fathers of social administration as a university discipline. If the Elmhirsts had been surrogate parents, both Shils and Titmuss were to stand proxy as elder brothers and both were to assist him in establishing the Institute of Community Studies (ICS) in 1954 at Bethnal Green. Their intellectual influence reinforced that of the Tavistock Institute so that his focus shifted away from politics towards thinking about non-state action, that is to say, away from government and concentrating rather more on an understanding of society and especially local communities. Born a generation earlier, Young might well have been attracted to the syndicalism of G.D.H. Cole and his fellow Guild Socialists with their emphasis on bottom-up rather than top-down policy initiatives.

By the mid to late 1960s the ICS was perhaps more widely known than any other social research organisation in the country. Started in one room by Michael Young with Peter Townsend and Peter Willmott, a former Bevin boy who had worked with Young at Transport House, within a few months they had moved into the shabby but elegant Queen Anne house in Victoria Park Square where Young still works and which became the first home of so many of the organisations and institutions which he was to bring into being over the next forty years, 'a tree with many nests' as he describes it.

They chose Bethnal Green because, having lived for a time at Toynbee Hall, Young was familiar with the East End. It was also a relatively compact district with a working class population. Young had done some research on the effects of re-housing on family and community life and the topic had been a preoccupation of his since Transport House days. From the outset the ICS was modelled on PEP (Young and Willmott, 1961). Its purpose was to conduct research that would influence policy, but the research would be done by means of field studies, not groups of experts: their purpose would be to explore and pass on their findings about the 'lives, needs and aspirations of working class people' (Willmott chapter in Bulmer, 1985, p.138).   Their motivation was a reaction to their experience at Transport House: policy makers, they thought, needed to be better informed about the needs of their constituents.

The resulting study, dedicated to Dorothy and Leonard Elmhirst, and with a foreword by Titmuss, *Family and Kinship in East London* (1957), was therefore very much Young's book. In many ways the approach was closer to anthropology than to sociology, attempting simultaneously to paint a portrait of the social background of the people of Bethnal Green, to analyse their system of family relationships and to show how the present is shaped by the past. Impressionistic and readable, it displayed what was to be the hallmark of the rest of the Institute's work, the concern with relating social knowledge to social policy. The book was received with acclaim and eventually sold more than a million copies.

The second book, *Family and Class in a London Suburb* appeared in 1960. It also broke new ground. No sociological study had been done in a British suburb before, except on a municipal housing estate. It found that the wider family did not flourish in the suburb as well as in the East End. This was largely due to class influences which detracted from the friendliness, bonhomie and self confidence of Bethnal Green. Published not long after Labour's third successive election defeat, it chimed with the revisionist movement prompted by the Gaitskellite wing of the party, exemplified in the writings of Anthony Crosland, Mark Abrams and others. The findings of the Woodford study supported the so-called 'embourgeoisement' thesis. With an expanding economy and rising incomes, class divisions were no longer based on the workplace but on consumption: 'All classes in Woodford are striving to earn more and spend it on the same things' (Young and Willmott, 1960, p.132).

The ICS studies did not go unchallenged within the profession. One sociologist in particular, Jennifer Platt, attacked the lack of rigour in the studies and their rose-tinted view of working class life. Their emphasis on policy detracted from the value of the work, she argued, though advocacy is widely seen as one of the uses of sociology. Though they have some validity, these criticisms are true of much sociology in Britain at the time and do not detract from the innovative and inspirational character of the ICS which provided an alternative centre to the LSE for social research. Young, Willmott and their colleagues at ICS were always outside the mainstream of British sociology, in spite of the support from Shils and Titmuss. They were not trained sociologists and they wanted to understand social problems, not educate sociologists (Bulmer, 1985, p.147). As a result they were eclectic and pragmatic in their approach. They were not writing for sociologists, but for 'architects and planners, the social workers and the housing managers, the civil servants and the politicians' (Young and Willmott, 1971).

Despite being regarded as being academically maverick he was recruited as a Fellow of Churchill College in 1960 to help establish sociology as a mainline subject at Cambridge. A year later Edward Shils joined him in the enterprise. Whereas the latter quickly went native, moving from King's to Peterhouse, the bastion of intellectual Toryism, Young's brief sojourn at Cambridge was both academically fretful and offensive to his reforming instincts. It was a condition of his appointment that he did not bring the ICS with him: its approach and house-style were not acceptable. For his part, Young was appalled by the elitism of the university and the wastefulness of it being empty of students for six months of the year; his proposal to transfer the activities of Battersea Polytechnic (later the University of Surrey) during vacation times to Cambridge did not endear him to his colleagues. He resigned his lectureship in 1966.

Shils' commitment to Cambridge was never quite total because he regularly commuted there from Chicago, where he held a chair, but when there made himself at home. Young, by contrast, never really left London during his time at Churchill College for, as usual, he was engaged simultaneously in a host of other activities - political, reforming and research.

After leaving Transport House he was relatively inactive politically for most of the 1950s, reflecting perhaps the 'end of ideology' that characterised the decade, Suez and Hungary apart. Labour's third election defeat stirred the activist in him once more and he was a major influence in the modernising, revisionist movement that engaged a large section of the Labour Party and extended more widely into a national soul searching that manifested itself in a series of *Penguin Specials* such as *The Stagnant Society* by Michael Shanks. As we have noted, the ICS Woodford study appeared to validate the revisionist thesis that consumption not class was becoming the main determinant in voter preferences. To support further this contention Young, together with Rita Hinden, the editor of *Socialist Commentary*, commissioned Mark Abrams to undertake an opinion poll the results of which were published as *Must Labour Lose?*. All of this provided ammunition for Gaitskell's attempt to amend Clause Four of Labour's constitution which committed it to nationalisation policies seen to emphasise the class basis of the party's programme.

Young was clearly identified with revisionism, which provoked a fierce reaction from Labour's left-wing, but he wanted to push the case further than most of its supporters. In developing new ideas to bring Labour back from the political wilderness, he wrote a pamphlet which the Fabian Society refused to publish; the general secretary at that time was Shirley Williams, later a founder member with Young of the short lived SDP, but in 1960 unwilling to make the leap which Young was ready for - a new progressive party. Not that he thought the Labour Party was beyond redemption. In this pamphlet, *The Chipped White Cups of Dover* (October 1960), he argued that if Labour was successfully to fight off the challenges of the Liberals, it must return to being a party of reform and adopt an internationalist approach. It also focused on consumption: 'class based on production is giving way to status based on consumption as the centre for social gravity' (Young, 1960, p.11). A reforming party would attack monopolies and restrictive practices and would immediately apply for entry to the Common Market. Education expenditure would rise substantially, more motorways would be built. Labour, if it was to regain its credibility, would have to dispel the impression that it opposed consumer prosperity. He also saw the trade unions as a great liability to the party, 'with smaller and smaller votes behind them in the country to set against their large blocks of votes at the conference'. Internal union democracy must be introduced and the links between constituencies and local union branches should be improved. If all this was too radical even for his fellow revisionists, it was nevertheless a remarkably farsighted piece of analysis. While *The Chipped White Cups of Dover* articulated the importance of the citizen as consumer to a degree not previously stated so forcefully, as a political manifesto it was all-of-a-piece with his research findings and his work as a social reformer which was beginning to reach its climax. In 1957 he created the Consumers' Association with the launch of the magazine *Which?*.

This was an immediate, overnight success and developed into a publishing empire which included books and magazines ranging from *The Good Food Guide* to *Which Way to Health?* catering for all the middle-class preoccupations in between by means of *Money Which? Motoring Which? Gardening Which?* and *Holiday Which?* among others and by 1990 the Consumers' Association had a turnover of £38m.

The inspiration, once again, lay at Dartington, with Dorothy Elmhirst. She had supported the Consumers' Union and Consumer Research in America, providing not only moral support but financial backing. No doubt as a direct result, given the Elmhirsts' close involvement, PEP had earlier done some work on consumer unions between 1934 and 1936, reporting on how the two American organisations operated. It was concluded however (Pinder, 1981, p.68-9), after taking legal advice that the UK libel laws made many consumer issues 'too hot to handle'.

All the same it was an area which had captured Young's imagination and the 1950 Labour manifesto, rather short of new ideas had nevertheless contained a proposal for a consumer advisory service. This, said Young, was the most popular idea in the document and Gallup poll evidence supported him. Harold Wilson, Young said, tried promoting the idea when he arrived at the Board of Trade after the election, but without success. The more immediate inspiration for the foundation of *Which?* was another Dorothy, another American. Dorothy Goodman had married an Englishman, Ray Goodman (Director of PEP 1946-53), and wanting to install heating in her house in the mid-50s was dismayed to find no consumer reports to help her. She accordingly collected a group of people which included a barrister, a solicitor, an engineer and Michael Young to set about starting a consumer magazine, but handed the idea over to Michael Young when she had to return to the US. Eventually a first edition was published. Its editor was Eirlys Roberts, who had been involved in consumer affairs for some time and had written a series of consumer articles for *The Observer*. The first issue of *Which?* was a very amateur affair, which got no press coverage in spite of the fact that they held a press conference. Then the women's correspondent of *The Times* was persuaded to insert three lines about it in an article on something else: there were 10,000 subscribers within a fortnight and work at Victoria Park Square stopped while all available ICS staff were pressed into dealing with the bags of mail.

The consumer movement, especially *Which?* has been criticised as being a very middle class affair. Young himself described the CA as a 'somewhat farouche national institution'. Farouche or not it has had a major impact on producers and purchasers alike, and he saw it as a non-party pressure group dedicated to reform (Young, 1983, p.254). The fact that Young's commitment to the movement was based on something both moral and political was demonstrated in a speech in Oslo in 1964. He argued that the consumer movement should appeal to the privileged to help those less fortunate, especially in the third world. The movement should also stress the need to spend on the environment and bring home to people that they are not just customers, but also consumers of public services. Thirdly, the quality of life should be given as much importance as the standard of living: 'Are we in the consumers' organisation no more than the servants of the washing machine? Is there not a larger aim, the advancement of freedom?'.

As the progenitor of the consumer movement in Britain, he had started something which was to gather considerable momentum, leading successively to the National Consumer Council created by the Wilson government, of which he was the first Chairman, to a Minister for Consumer Affairs appointed under the Thatcher administration and ultimately to the plethora of Citizen's Charters during John Major's premiership.

If consumer affairs were part of the Elmhirsts' legacy he was equally faithful to their principle that highlighted the crucial importance of education. In 1958 he published *The Rise of the Meritocracy* which, like *The Chipped White Cups*, was turned down by the Fabian Society and several commercial publishers. It eventually sold half a million copies in twelve languages, and added a new word to the vocabulary of politics. Though the word is often used, how many remember that the book was a biting satire on selection in education? It describes a future in which selection by merit - i.e. equality of opportunity - is taken to such extremes that the inferior revolt. 'Every selection of one is a rejection of many' in Young's chilling Orwellian phrase. It is a witty and readable book and contains, as so much of Young's work does, very perceptive glimpses of the future. These include the rise of the women's movement, a decline in the relative position of Britain in science and the establishment of a Social Science Research Council (when it was set up nearly ten years later Young was the first chairman). There are compelling turns of phrase: 'the world beholds ... a brilliant class, the five per cent of the nation who know what five per cent means' (Young, 1958, p.103).

Bernard Crick has suggested that the starting point for Young's satire is to be found in Anthony Crosland's *The Future of Socialism*, published two years earlier and widely praised (Crick, 1960, p.368). Crosland was passionately committed to equality of opportunity and educational reform, and acknowledged his debt to Young, with whom he had often discussed the subject (Crosland, 1956, p.235n). 'If the selection is obviously by merit', he wrote, 'this source of comfort disappears (that the system was unfair) and failure induces a total sense of inferiority', or as Young put it 'Educational injustice enabled people to preserve their illusions, inequality of opportunity fostered the myth of human equality' (Young, 1958, p.106). So the nightmare vision conjured up in *The Rise of the Meritocracy*, where every appointment is made according to intelligence, is only the logical extension of Young's own egalitarian views on education and an expression of the dilemma faced by those who like him wish to offer education to everyone equally.

At the time of the book's publication he set up the Advisory Centre for Education (ACE), along the Consumers' Association model, with its own magazine *Where?*, which would act as an educational consumers' adviser and champion. The Director and Editor was Brian Jackson, a colleague from ICS who was also in Cambridge. It was in the pages of the magazine that the idea for the Open University (OU) had its first airing. Michael Young is not the only person who claims paternity of the OU but his claims are better than most. One day the two met on the steps of the University Library, and Jackson said 'You oughtn't to be part of all this. Why don't you start your own university?' 'Ridiculous, of course,' wrote Young, 'but sitting on the steps in the sun we went quite a long way towards imagining what became later and miraculously, the Open

University' (*The Times*, 13 July 1983). It should be remembered at this point that Leonard Elmhirst also played a part in the founding of a new university in Bengal. Young himself was almost obsessed with education, 'that most precious good of all', he called it (*Where?*, Autumn, 1964), and with the need to supply it more abundantly to people of all kinds throughout the world, especially 'those whose needs were not being met by ordinary educational institutions' (*Where?*, Winter 1964, p.17). He proposed a double shift in existing universities. This never caught on except in a small way though a clutch of universities, notably Ulster, Lancaster and de Montfort, are pioneering schemes for year-round working. Secondly, new universities could be established at sites of technical expertise. This did not take off either. The third idea was the 'university without walls'. This was an interesting example of the Young technique of scattering the seeds of many different ideas and then waiting to see which had fallen on fertile ground. Drawing on Soviet experience, where half those in higher education were in correspondence courses but also had access to library and laboratory facilities in local higher education institutes and annual summer schools, and on American practice, where good use was made of TV, he proposed a National Extension College (NEC) which would make use of foreign experience and also improve correspondence courses. (*Where?*, No. 10, Autumn, 1962).

The idea brought a response from Harold Wilson, the newly elected Labour leader in a speech in Glasgow on 8 September 1963, who was later, along with several others, to claim credit for the OU. More importantly, it had also received a positive response from staff in other universities and sponsorship from electronics companies. It would offer a few courses ranging from university level to O-level maths to French and Spanish courses. The response was huge.

The broadcasting aspect also started well with a 7.15 a.m. lecture by Professor Fred Hoyle in October 1963 - 200,000 homes tuned in. In the OU report a year later, Young would stress the importance of 'eavesdroppers', but he also pointed out that the 'university of the air' label was inappropriate: face to face teaching and correspondence were also essential, also very important was the idea of continuous assessment. This report, only about 7000 words long, and written by Young after a Ditchley conference which attracted many from the TV world and from correspondence colleges, represents a quite well worked out plan which compares favourably in its straightforwardness and clarity with many government reports.

The OU and the NEC demonstrated Young's ability to pick up an idea and develop it and find the people to supply the expertise and information needed. He is extremely good at getting people - often quite eminent people - to do things for him, often for very little reward. The OU opened properly in 1972 and led to other ventures in distance learning in the third world. This has been developed a great deal in the ensuing twenty years - for example the Mauritius College of the Air, distance learning in Botswana and Lesotho and in some of the homelands within South Africa - all started off by Michael Young.

At the same time Young was also involved with Lady Plowden's committee on children and their primary schools. Appointed in 1963 by a Conservative education minister, this did not report until 1967, when Anthony Crosland was Minister of Education. At this time a number of academic social scientists were quite influential, in particular Professor Richard Titmuss of the LSE and his proteges; these academics combined the study of social problems and policies with following the egalitarian example set by Tawney and the Fabians (Banting, 1979, p.7). Young was also writing about primary education: *Innovation and Research in Education* (1965) foresaw the impact of modern technology not only on teaching but on the content of education. *Learning Begins at Home* (1968) demonstrated understanding of what makes working class families less likely to take advantage of education, and the difficulties of overcoming these obstacles which could result in a drop in standards and the genuine dilemma over streaming and whether to offer a general education or more vocational courses.

On the Plowden Committee were both Young and a fellow academic, David Donnison of LSE. Together they became the kernel of Working Party No. 2 which looked at social influences on educational achievement. Clearly there was some official sympathy with new educational thinking. The other two members of the working party were Tim Raison and Maurice Kogan. It was from this group and especially from Michael Young that the idea of the Educational Priority Area (EPA) sprang. Though ultimately not a practical success, and not especially appealing to the teaching profession, the EPA idea had more impact than any other aspect of the report. The inspiration came from similar projects in the United States - where in turn the Plowden Report was enthusiastically received.

After the report had been published Lady Plowden continued campaigning. Young and Donnison and a few others, including A.H. Halsey, also pushed the idea in private, including an evening seminar at Crosland's London home. In a sense, all this pressure was successful. £16m was allocated to put the EPA idea into practice. But because of budgetary horsetrading between the Treasury and the DES, almost all of it was allocated to buildings and it was in vain that Young tried to impress upon Crosland - who was pre-occupied with other priorities - that other things were often more important and that allocation of most of the sum to buildings meant sacrificing other more vital aspects of the idea. Another project which took place as part of the Plowden field work was written up in *Learning Begins at Home*. This attempted to link parents more closely with schools, and to make extra efforts to improve education in deprived areas. Though carried out in the familiar area of Bethnal Green it was more interventionist than the traditional ICS field work. For example the Institute paid for a new notice to replace the old one which said 'Trespassers will be prosecuted'. It read 'No Admittance to un-authorised persons. Parents are welcome to see the Head Teacher at any time. Appointments may be made if necessary' (Young, 1968, p.48). Open meetings, private talks with teachers, and home visits, some attended by the researchers, did not result in a meeting of minds. Parents focused confidently only on non-academic matters, but the head dismissed out of hand their request for a Parent Teacher Association. Thus ideals did not match up with reality.

Although most of Young's efforts have been concentrated within Britain, he has always possessed a strong internationalist, and particularly third world, streak in his make-up that harks back to his boyhood support for the League of Nations Union and also to the example of Leonard Elmhirst and indirectly the influence of Tagore.

In 1971 the International Extension College replicated in Southern Africa what the OU and the NEC were doing in Britain. The first centre opened up in Mauritius where he spent a year as its first director pioneering distance learning for adults. He chose Mauritius because it was a relatively easy and peaceful location to start and Harold Wilson provided the letter of introduction to the government there. The initiative was extended to Botswana and Lesotho and later to South Africa, with backing from the African National Council, which led to the formation of the Foundation for Basic Education at Fort Hare University. Currently, Young is endeavouring to establish another distance learning facility - the

University for Democratic Leadership, which he would like to see operating out of the prison buildings on Robben Island that had accommodated Nelson Mandela for twenty-five years.

In 1980 impatient with the evident loss of productive time involved in long-distance commuting by rail, he organised the formation of a series of commuter study clubs which were financed by British Rail. The scheme became known as the 'Brain Train', and provision for teaching modern languages was particularly popular. Two years later, in collaboration with Peter Laslett and others, Young played a major part in establishing the University of the Third Age (U3A) that quickly comprised a network of over 100 programmes designed to cater specifically for older people.

Both of these reflected the high priority he placed on education and his hostility to slack resources and idleness. In the 1980s one of his main research pursuits was to examine the use of time in people's lives and in addition to lecturing on the subject inevitably set up an organisation called the Association for the Social Study of Time in 1983.

The Open College of the Arts was founded in 1987 as the first distance learning institution in the world for teaching the practical skills associated with a wide range of the plastic arts. Neither the OU nor the NEC would undertake such an innovation because both thought the imparting of such skills required face to face contact; Young was determined to prove them wrong. Over 5000 students have enrolled and more than 120 tutorial centres have been formed to back up the distance learning courses.

Then came the Centre for Educational Choice with the aim of studying and promoting small, non-fee-paying schools started by parents' groups, presumably along lines similar to the integrated schools movement in Northern Ireland. His passion for education was combined with a belief in the virtues of small-scale organisations and voluntary initiatives. He consistently defended small rural schools threatened by closure, for he saw the school as the heart of the local community. In 1989 he came up with the idea of the Open School, which would adapt OU methods for school use especially in those areas such as science, mathematics and craft design and technology where there was a national shortage of specialist teachers. Later, with Education Extra, he was also to advocate keeping schools open after regular hours to extend learning opportunities to pupils and to provide them with a protective and supportive environment for creative activity particularly in deprived urban areas. The old solidarities of the working class culture were being undermined by the breakdown of the traditional family, the extensive use of illegal drugs, and the emergence of anti-social teenage behaviour. Young felt impelled to address this evidence of widespread systemic failure with a broad spectrum of remedies, which however well adapted to meet contemporary conditions, derived from Dartingtonian impulses and imagination.

Closely linked both intellectually and operationally to his educational initiatives were those he promoted in the field of community development. In 1971 he helped form the Association of Neighbourhood Councils that aspired to introduce into urban areas the concept of the parish council. Megalopolis, argued Young, needed to be broken down into smaller, more manageable units. Two informal experiments were undertaken: one in Kensington and another one in Birmingham. They were not immediately successful, largely, in Young's view, because the local government boundary commissioners fought shy of such radical reforms. Nevertheless, while Liberal Democrats controlled the London Borough of Tower Hamlets in the early '90s, a highly disaggregated system of Neighbourhoods was constructed which, despite a somewhat chequered existence, remains one of the few bold experiments in decentralised politics. This practical manifestation of an earlier experiment occurred on Young's own doorstep in Bethnal Green.

The Mutual Aid Centre (MAC) was formed in 1978 to facilitate self-help especially in social organisations. It spawned in turn a number of off-shoots including the brain trains, a series of neighbourhood schemes and a chain of workshops using recycled materials for unemployed young people. One of its more successful schemes was the Milton Keynes OK Service Station Ltd. founded in 1978 by Marianne Rigge (a founder of MAC), a community garage that provided hands-on training in local schools. The aims and aspirations of MAC were set out in *Mutual Aid in A Selfish Society* (1979) which stated that it 'was set up to try and apply the principles of Robert Owen and Prince Kropotkin in a series of demonstration projects'. Co-operation it declared is a very general idea, as much ethical as economic.

In futurologist mode Michael Young launched the Argo venture that originated in a lecture to the British Aerospace and Aeronautics Society in 1984 at the height of the controversy over President Reagan's 'Star Wars' programme. If vast amounts of money could be spent on the military uses of space, he asked, why not on peaceful ones? He was hoping to join up with the British Interplanetary Society, he said, to put 10,000 people in space stations. As a start, there would be an attempt to create an artificial environment on earth. This idea was as much an expression of his continuing interest in experimental sociology as of his idealism and interest in the future. The experiment never came to fruition and the idea underwent a metamorphosis, re-emerging as a plan for a space museum in Docklands.

In 1988 Link Age was inaugurated to bring together people of grandparent age without children and children who had no grandparents. It is a kind of adoption agency that skips a generation, and has operated mainly in Tower Hamlets, Oxfordshire and Bristol. As with so many of Young's enterprises it attempts to provide a community solution to family needs.

Language Line was founded in 1990. It provided an interpreting service for Bengalis, Somalis, Vietnamese and Chinese in Tower Hamlets, with the support of various bodies, and became a self-supporting service supplying interpreting facilities 24 hours a day in 140 languages to a range of hospitals, clinics, surgeries and voluntary organisations, mostly in London. The difference this makes to patient satisfaction and medical effectiveness is incalculable: 'Small but effective', says Young with satisfaction.

In 1972 Young worked with Charles Medawar to found Social Audit, a pressure group that sought to persuade industry and commerce to produce social accounts of its activities as regularly as it produced annual financial reports. It was a logical corollary to the Consumers Association, and sought to encourage firms to make automatic assessments of their operations and published them. Social Audit's aims also included developing and applying mechanisms for ensuring the disclosure of information and social accountability in major centres of power including the public sector.

In 1968 Young had also given birth to the National Suggestions Centre, later known as the National Innovations Centre. The idea was to reach out on a national scale to all citizens to encourage them to send in their bright ideas. He felt that the ordinary individual had as much innovative capacity as those more elevated. The problem with British democracy was that it was too 'top-down' and not sufficiently 'bottom-up' as later management gurus were to express it; it was an attempt by Young, to persist with the later idiom, to 'empower' the masses. He had previously suggested that British cabinets should adopt the practice of leaving an empty chair to symbolise the 'Unknown Citizen'. In the event the National Innovations Centre failed to attract a popular response and its proposed magazine *What?* failed to get off the ground. Nevertheless, among its successes was a pilot project in Hull in 1972, providing telephonic assistance to those with difficulties, which afforded a prototype for Language Line eighteen years later.

Another by-product of the MAC was the College of Health which he established in 1983 as a consumers' equivalent to the prestigious Royal Colleges founded by the medical professions; again an example of Young's lateral thinking and one that anticipated the growing awareness of the need to manage one's own health regime. The College has managed to establish itself as a viable management consultancy to units within the National Health Service, but that was not the original purpose.

Over the past thirty years, in addition to belonging to the Plowden Committee, Young has held two official government posts on a part-time basis. From 1965 to 1968 he served as the first chairman of the Social Science Research Council (SSRC), one of the more enduring monuments to Harold Wilson's 'technological revolution'. Although he had long advocated the creation of such a body, the post was essentially a consolation prize for not getting his first preference - the chairmanship of the Public Schools Commission which went to Sir John Newsom, a mildly progressive Establishment educationist. He applied himself to the task of building up the SSRC with considerable assiduity: 'I was paid half-time but worked full-time' he claims. The minister, his friend Anthony Crosland, gave him a free hand in choosing the members of the council. He conducted a poll of thirty to forty people he thought were well qualified - 'Who did they think should be on the new body? The civil servants were dazzled by this piece of practical social science!' Apart from a selection of academics, including W.J.M. Mackenzie, he chose Len Murray and Campbell Adamson.

A decade later he was asked to be chairman of the newly formed National Consumer Council set up by Shirley Williams when Minister for Consumer Affairs. Charged with representing the interests of the poor and disadvantaged, it is non-partisan, but nonetheless lobbies whenever it can within its limited resources. He had just returned from a period in Africa and was not fully attuned to the role of the new agency, allowing the civil service to recommend its members. But he did strive to guide it to look at the provision of goods and services from the perspective of the poorer sections of the community who did not read *Which?*

Michael Young's official forays into government were clearly not among his happiest experiences. He is by nature neither a civil servant nor a politician. He is too much of a gadfly to settle down for the routine hard slog which in their different ways both roles require for successful fulfilment, preferring to expend his considerable energies over a wide range of activities, though this did not prevent him from attempting both from time to time.

After leaving Transport House at the beginning of the 1950s he devoted himself to academic writing and pamphleteering, and did not become involved in politics till the end of the decade, as an ultra-revisionist. Apart from this, his only other intervention was to return temporarily to Transport House to provide backroom assistance during the successful 1964 general election campaign. Thereafter followed a long period of political non-involvement. He accepted a life peerage in 1978 becoming Lord Young of Dartington and taking the Labour whip. Given his track record in the later 1950s it was inevitable he would break away from the Labour Party in 1981 and join with the Gang of Four to found the Social Democratic Party (SDP); he had, after all, sketched out its prototype in *The Chipped White Cups of Dover*. His main contribution was to form the think tank of the new SDP: the Tawney Society was Young's idea. The name was chosen, so it is said, to irritate Labour party friends. But Young has a lot in common with Tawney: opposition to privileged institutions, a commitment to equality and enthusiasm for education Tawney had been a strong supporter of the Workers' Educational Association and an early advocate of comprehensive education.

During the 1980s he responded and contributed to the highly volatile electoral mood of the nation. His over-riding concern for the values of community life were at variance with the prevailing Thatcherite emphasis on the individual and its corollary that 'there was no such thing as society'. His reaction was to participate in attempts to maximise the anti-Conservative vote by means of tactical voting. Tactical Voting '87 was formed to mobilise Lib-Lab collaboration, which later successively became Common Voice in 1988, Voting Reform Information Services in 1993. Michael Young was only directly involved in the first of these, though in parallel with the formation of Tactical Voting, he helped launch the magazine *Samizdat*, to provide theoretical discussion and support, which in its first issue proclaimed itself as fostering 'the popular front of the mind'. But the ebbing electoral fortunes of the SDP, the failure of the Alliance in the general election of 1987, followed subsequently by the failure of David Owen's leadership drove Young back into the Labour Party. Perhaps he had never wholeheartedly joined it, nor wholeheartedly left it. Instead, he had exemplified Raymond Aron's remark that the trouble with British sociology was that it was 'an attempt to make intellectual sense of the political problems of the Labour Party' (Halsey, 1985, p.151).

His outbursts of rather frenetic and short-lived political activism - more recently he was involved in a successful tactical voting campaign in 1994 to rid the Millwall ward of Tower Hamlets of its National Front councillor - illustrate that his real centre of gravity is as a social theorist and reformer. He has, as a life peer, the formal status of legislator but it is a role he largely eschews. He attends and/or participates in the work of the House of Lords only when there is a topic on the agenda that is of direct concern to one or other of his interests. Education, consumer affairs, the health service and community care will see him contributing or in attendance. But the House of Lords is too elitist, too centralist, too remote and too irrelevant to engage him. Even if its composition were to be radically altered, it is doubtful if it would appeal much more to him. By temperament, like his fellow official fixers, he is not naturally part of the political infantry: he belongs more to the political equivalent of the Special Air Service.

To continue the military metaphor, he sees success, in the main, as being a matter of intelligence gathering, strategy formulation and critical personnel selection (that is the legacy of PEP), in combination with forming new platoons and special units that, in the experience gained from their scouting and forays, might suggest how new regiments could be formed.

His activities have covered such a broad range that the spectacular successes have inevitably been accompanied by some half-baked schemes and a few failures, one or two of which scarcely got off the drawing board. All however have demonstrated physical energy, intellectual and imaginative curiosity and a remarkable entrepreneurial capacity.

He invented the consumer movement that was eventually to encompass not just the testing of consumer durables but was also to embrace educational and health choice. He was the main inspiration behind the Open University. He was the first to appreciate the need to understand the dynamic forces threatening and shaping contemporary family and community life. Much later, following official neglect of these institutions, realisation dawned in the exhortatory call for 'back to basics' on the part of John Major, which because it lacked any basic policy substance, fell immediately flat, and also in the more thought-out recent communitarian ideas of Amitai Etzioni. But Young was decades ahead in his thinking, in his practical experimentation and in his appreciation of the significance for policy of these forces.

His mission has been to identify the problems that face ordinary people, to scan ahead and see how they can be solved or ameliorated. The coherent linking of theory and practice and of the exemplary effects of small-scale experiments for the wider agenda are among his most consistent preoccupations. Unlike most of his generation he is fully aware of the finite limitations of state action and associated national panaceas, being conscious that these had to be complemented by local, and often voluntary, initiatives. He faithfully followed the Elmhirsts in backing other people's good ideas - of being an enabler or facilitator - but, even when a magpie, he invariably put his own idiosyncratic imprint on any such proposals. But he was also an originator in his own right.

His originality was not just in formulating and developing ideas, but also in devising schemes to put them into practice - a process that included selecting individuals to run them and, if successful, to take them over. As a fixer, he was an innovator, not a routine operator. Often he made mistakes in his selection of people, but overall he built and nurtured an extensive network of like-minded colleagues. As with most utopians, in seeking to advance the lot of humankind in general, he could be somewhat authoritarian, exploitative and manipulative of those with whom he selected to work and not a few relationships ended in personality disputes and tears, a few of which could not be repaired. But the great majority of his acolytes, however exasperated by him at times, retain a very warm feeling and high regard for him and his work.

Oliver Franks saw the need for a new breed of planner-manager to operate the formal institutions to which he was so attached. He anticipated the shape of things to come but he played very little, if any, direct part in forming such a cadre; most noticeably, while widely esteemed by his peers, he did not recruit his own disciples. Michael Young did, in the sense that he created a diaspora of people who had been attracted to, or had been selected by, him and who shared the same values as his for community, voluntarism, education and the empowerment of the ordinary person in the street.

But there also are marked commonalities between Franks and Young. Both, by origin, were outsiders in terms of the Establishment. In different ways, they were intellectually imaginative and powerful. They shared a belief in the good ordering of business. Attention to detail and prior preparation by reading the relevant documents, and bringing people round to agree a particular outcome was the hall-mark of Franks' technique. For Young, it was more free-floating and relaxed but the aim was the same and a premium was placed on the drafting of documents, whether they were the products of research or the framing of policy proposals.

On leaving PEP he advised that it:

> ... must employ on its staff only people who can write with reasonable clarity. It is a delusion to think that bad drafters can be trained ... In choosing new staff it should be realised that the only essential qualifications are (1) drafting ability, (2) intelligence. (Pinder, 1981, p.96)

Both were rather austere, retiring and even shy personalities who nevertheless could overcome any innate reticence to exude a persuasive and irresistible charm that would secure support for a steely single-minded purpose. Franks thrived in the habitat of officialdom and formal ceremony; Young rejected most of that but sought to create a new, freer-ranging but ultimately equally sign-posted and articulated environment; Goodman couldn't care less, in the confidence that he could operate whatever the ground rules and whatever the context.

6 A Tale of Two Retailers: I
Derek Rayner

In this chapter and the next we analyse the role and methods of two retailers, whose contributions mark a very distinctive mutation in the development of fixers and fixing. Together they stand mid-way between the traditional fixers such as Franks, Plowden and Goodman and the new breed of corporate fixers in the form of management consultants. In some respects they resemble the traditional fixers but also have much in common with the new style of men and women. Like the former they were seen as individual personalities, while their *modus operandi* were much closer to those of the management consultants.

Rayner and Griffiths brought the market disciplines, cost consciousness and most important, management techniques of the private sector to government and to the NHS. Like the management consultants who followed them, they were 'agents of change'. The management models they promoted were committed to permanent revolution, while the old control models still holding sway in government defended the *status quo* and viewed change as a special event. The inflation of the 1970s had exacerbated the twin problems which beset modern governments throughout the world - overload and the control of public expenditure. Following the oil price shocks of 1974 and Britain's recourse to the IMF in 1976, a new sense of reality swiftly dawned that provoked a new approach to the business of government. Though now strongly identified with Thatcherism, it was seen as far away as the antipodes and arguably made its first appearance before the 1979 election in the UK. The reforms introduced in the 1980s were made up of three elements: the drive for less waste and greater efficiency, the wish to cut public expenditure and the aim to reduce the size of the public sector.

This school of thought - sometimes known as the New Public Management - favoured privatisation but also showed a strong drive towards introducing private sector methods and models into the residual public sector. Economic pressures were one reason for the new approach, but another contributing factor was that the civil servants who had lived through the Fulton era, almost a decade earlier, had now reached the top of the Whitehall tree. The approach was also reinforced by ideas that had been incubating in various right-wing think tanks during Mrs Thatcher's time as Leader of the Opposition.

What was required was a catalyst that would graft private sector methods onto the procedures of Whitehall. One person who had both a knowledge of the civil service and a record of success in a well-known and profitable private sector company was Derek Rayner, said by some to be the most influential outsider in Whitehall since World War II (*The Times*, 15 December 1982). Uniquely, Rayner is the only fixer to have had an -ism added to his name.

An only child born in 1926, Rayner was schooled in Norwich, before national service in the RAF Regiment 1946-8, becoming an adjutant in the Middle East command unit. He had been destined for the Church and went up to read theology at Selwyn College, Cambridge, an established conduit for ordination in the Church of England. In his final year a crisis of conscience occurred, a loss of vocation, and receiving little support or compassion from his tutors, he left university without taking a degree. But the training left its mark, if only in the number of biblical references he made use of; for example he was only 'the sower of the seed' he said of the FMI, in a valedictory lecture in 1984; his *Note of Guidance* for his teams of Whitehall scrutineers was popularly known as the 'Gideon's Bible'. He joined Marks & Spencer as a management trainee and was soon spotted by Marcus Sieff who short-circuited the firm's training practices and had him transferred to its head office in Baker Street to work as his personal assistant. M & S used such appointments, as indeed does the civil service, as a means of bringing on the future top managers. On this fast track he ultimately became a board director specialising in food products. His success in rising to the top is striking and at the time unprecedented since he is neither Jewish nor a blood relative of any of the ruling families of the M & S empire.

Years before the term 'Raynerism' was coined its eponymous originator had a spell of working in Whitehall. In 1969 and early 1970, as part of his preparation for office, Edward Heath, then Leader of the Opposition, received advice from a Businessmen's Team which included management consultants and top people from companies such as Shell, Unilever, and RTZ. He approached these companies, including Marks & Spencer, for people who could be seconded to government. Without consulting his colleagues, Marcus Sieff decided to 'make a sacrifice' and send a really good man - Rayner. He attended seminars and meetings and undertook a detailed study of procurement before the election. Though his contact was at this time mostly with Lord Carrington and Sir Keith Joseph, he also had direct access to Heath as he later would to Margaret Thatcher.

Once the Conservatives had taken office, he was asked to write a report on defence procurement: this appeared in April 1971 *Government organisation for defence procurement and civil aerospace* (Cmnd 4641). It recommended the establishment of a procurement executive, which was set up with Rayner in charge, with the status of a permanent secretary. The Marks & Spencer director was a success as a top civil servant, though he chose to stay for only a short time. Lord Carrington found Rayner an exception to his general view that Heath's cross-fertilisation ideas had not worked at all well in practice, partly because businesses would not agree to part with their best brains for any length of time, but also because the businessmen found a far higher calibre of civil servant than they had expected (Carrington, 1988, p.234). The procurement executive dealt with buying £1000m of equipment annually; an operation in which value for money was clearly a top priority. Rayner was astonished by the lack of financial management in an enormous undertaking of this kind and the experience was to colour his views when he was called upon by Mrs Thatcher in 1979.

No high politics attached to his role at this time as there were later, and he had no responsibility for strategy as such. He was struck by the many similarities between Marks & Spencer and the civil service: no-one ever 'made a quick buck', staff well-being was a high priority and careful planning always preceded innovation. As a result of his M & S experience, he said, 'public service came quite naturally'. Nevertheless the structure and activities of M & S could not have been more different from those of Whitehall. It was a relatively simple organisation, with a single head office and no separate divisions, concerned with only two main areas - textiles and food. It employed less than 50,000 people in 1980 compared with more than twice that for one large government department. There was an emphasis on quick and decisive action, with little need for consensus building or elaborate justification of policies (Howells, 1981, p.344).

In 1972 Rayner returned to M & S but stayed in touch with Whitehall by means of membership of one or two departmental committees in the

DHSS and MoD. He was also a member of the Security Commission and deputy chairman of the civil service pay unit. The suspicion that if someone were really top class his company would not let him go was proved triumphantly mistaken in his case. He became joint managing director of Marks & Spencer the following year, the first not to be a member of the Sieff family.

Looking back on his experience, in a talk to the Civil Service College, he stressed the importance of leadership, training and career development. Excessive monitoring should be avoided and there should be freedom to choose suppliers. He would apply these principles both to public and private organisations, but he commented rather bitterly that for government, only failure is news. He also felt strongly that civil servants, often of high ability, were impeded by the structures within which they worked. (Rayner, 1973, p.75).

So, when asked within days of Mrs Thatcher's election victory in May 1979 to advise the new Prime Minister on improving efficiency and the elimination of waste, he was not only no stranger to Whitehall, but had firm views on how government organisation could be improved. The lack of proper accounting systems was something he had noted. The new Prime Minister thoroughly approved of Marks & Spencer and indeed was an enthusiastic customer.

The new government was committed to cutting civil service numbers and costs. The Prime Minister's attitude to civil servants was one of thinly veiled contempt. She was determined to remove their privileges and introduce changes. Rayner and his new boss had both been impressed by a book published the previous year by Leslie Chapman entitled *Your Disobedient Servant*, which gave a detailed catalogue of waste and extravagance in various government departments and agencies - and also of attempts to keep these things secret.

Rayner was to find that the cost of running government was literally an unknown quantity. He made a presentation to the cabinet, which approved his appointment. He now had the money, the political backing and all he had to do was to win round the civil service (Rayner interview, 25 November 1992). Rayner moved into 70 Whitehall on 8 May 1979, less than a week after the general election, committed as he said later to getting good management accepted as 'a higher policy in its own right' (Rayner, 1984, p.1). His familiarity with Whitehall methods meant that he could immediately get on with the task in hand. He knew the ways of the mandarin and indeed was widely trusted. He was therefore employed

- though unpaid and ostensibly part time and initially only for six months - to do an inside job. He knew that reform could not be 'applied externally like an ointment' (op. cit., p.5). He had no general advisory role; his remit was efficiency alone. In view of this his influence was even more remarkable. The Rayner Unit had a tiny staff - he was said to see himself as a David combatting the Goliath of Whitehall, with only two senior civil servants and two or three secretaries; with so little by way of substance a heavy stress on symbolism was likely to be an important aspect of his strategy. What was crucial, and this was recognised by all concerned at the time, was the continuing active support of the Prime Minister. She made it clear that his status was equal to that of Armstrong and Wass, Secretary to the Cabinet and Permanent Secretary to the Treasury respectively; and in the House of Commons in March 1980 she called him a 'remarkable and wonderful person'. He called her 'Madam', in the characteristic manner of the avuncular retailer.

Rayner's first (secret) report to the Prime Minister was made in the autumn of 1979. She circulated it to the whole cabinet and he was summoned to meet them. He brought along two of his scrutineers, Norman Warner and Clive Ponting. She accepted his main proposals which were: first, that ministers should actively manage their departments; secondly, that the cabinet should annually review the whole administrative cost of central government; and thirdly, that each department should scrutinise a section of its work. He also argued that the conventions of government should be reviewed - including minister/civil servant relations and those between the Treasury and other departments. This meant a question mark over the status and position of the Civil Service Department (CSD), which had been set up immediately after the Fulton Report in 1968.

The CSD affair demonstrated his considerable influence, despite the fact he did not immediately get his own way. Though she herself had doubts about the CSD, Mrs Thatcher was known not to favour tinkering with the machinery of government, but the Rayner exercises were effectively by-passing and therefore side-lining it. Rayner favoured abolition because he thought it was lacking in management expertise, and he wanted to bring the control of manpower back into the Treasury - a view that would have been endorsed by Sir Edward Bridges, a former head of the civil service famous for his staunch defence of its traditions. But Sir Ian Bancroft, the permanent secretary, due to retire shortly, strongly opposed abolition and he was supported by some former senior civil servants such as William

Armstrong, Lord Croham and Sir Anthony Part, and others such as William Plowden of the RIPA, who argued that the Treasury, having fewer management functions than any other government department apart from the Cabinet office, was not the appropriate one to introduce management reforms.

The Commons' Treasury and Civil Service Select Committee also decided to interest itself in the matter and took evidence from Armstrong, Allen, and Crowther-Hunt - a leading member of the Fulton Committee. The debate was quite heated and occasionally spilled over into the correspondence columns of *The Times* (e.g. Armstrong letter, 8 July 1980). Rayner was also summoned and, though he admitted that management had improved since he was last in Whitehall, told the committee that the centre could not be 'a robust instrument of management' without unification of the two departments; the management of manpower and of money should be under one minister. The problem of overburdening the Chancellor was not a serious one in his view. He argued that a single central department was necessary to keep the other departments in line. A separate personnel department 'blunted the strength of central management and impeded original thinking' (*The Times*, 30 October 1980). When questioned by the Committee, he said 'I've never known a business organisation with two headquarters at opposite ends of the street. It's crazy'. (Fry, 1985, p.91). Bancroft fought hard to save his department, which was reprieved for a while. But eventually in November 1981 after a civil service strike which lasted for months, the Prime Minister followed Rayner's advice to close down the CSD. It was still a compromise, however, for though the old department's manpower and pay functions went to the Treasury, efficiency and personnel went to the Management and Personnel Office (MPO) in the Cabinet Office till 1987 when they were re-absorbed into the Treasury. The MPO made the running on civil service reform, sponsoring the FMI and the Next Steps.

Rayner's main line of attack, however, was in the 'efficiency scrutinies', as Mrs Thatcher called them, or 'Rayner projects' as they came to be known. The first scrutineers were handed a copy of *Your Disobedient Servant*, even though Rayner had failed to persuade the author to take part in the first briefing session.

The small size of the unit was not a handicap, for his method was to use civil servants from inside the departments concerned. He chose the brightest he could, not discriminating by age or seniority. From personal experience he knew of the strength of the forces of inertia within departments so that reform had to come from inside: 'Unless the spark is from within you will not get change' (Treasury and Civil Service Committee, 1979-80, p.74). Since it was impossible to look at everything, he chose a 'bore hole' or sampling technique - a sharply focused, cost-conscious look at a specific area of activity. Speed was of the essence: he was determined that his scrutineers should work quickly, ask radical questions and complete their work in sixty days, though this was later extended to ninety. 'The purpose of scrutinies is action not study'. The methods of working were in no sense inquisitorial. On the contrary, they were designed to elicit co-operation. 'Going with the grain' was the phrase they used and the subjects for scrutiny were chosen by the departments themselves; in this way departments were more likely to 'own' the recommendations.

Critics said the topics chosen would be those which would cause the least possible disturbance, but this was not generally true. They did though select areas where there was an *obvious* need for change: where administrative structures had fossilised. Thus the scrutineers' recom-mendations would often be giving force to an idea which had been around for some time rather than coming up with a completely novel one. In this sense he/she was a catalyst, not a critical outsider but someone who spoke the same language. And because the investigators were insiders, they would have to live with the consequences. Ministers would supervise, decide on recommendations and ensure implementation. There was therefore an emphasis on self-examination, a suggestion perhaps that confession is good for the soul. To build up team spirit, which Rayner always stressed, he circulated the names and telephone numbers of scrutineers to each other. For although they acquired a certain status and Rayner protected them, they also felt isolated, and sometimes paid a price for their ambiguous position, lying somewhere between that of a poacher and a gamekeeper.

What each scrutiny aimed for was value for money, fewer queues, less paperwork and greater individual accountability. There would be, it was hoped, a demonstration effect, a sort of teaching by example; some individual scrutinies made headlines, for example the famous government laboratory-bred rat which was shown to cost £30 when private enterprise could produce one for £2. The terms of reference were usually quite widely drawn so as not to restrict the investigation. But it was tightly controlled from the top: the whole programme had to be approved by the Prime Minister and the stages of an enquiry were laid down by the Rayner

Unit. Though Rayner was involved at every stage, especially the implementation stage, he was not committed to winning every battle, and so when recommendations were rejected, which happened now and then, that was often the end of the matter.

The approach adopted in general was a problem-solving one. Though focusing on management problems, implementation of the reforms was likely to come up against political barriers, and up to half of the hoped-for savings were lost at this stage. A prime example of this was one of the early scrutinies conducted in the DHSS on the method of payment of social security benefits. The social security arrangements they found, were outdated and direct payment into a bank or building society could save money and offer greater choice to the public. Savings could also be made if payments were made fortnightly or even monthly instead of weekly. One difficulty raised by these proposals was the loss of income to sub-post offices and the team suggested changes to offset these losses. A presentation to the cabinet took place, the plan had the support of the Prime Minister, but there was a leak (Warner, 1984, p.13).

A furore ensued with a press campaign, a television programme, questions in the House and similar tactics being employed. These concentrated as much on hardship to pensioners and poorer mothers as on the threat to rural sub-post offices. The consequent modification of the proposals cut the savings by more than half. What might have seemed on a superficial level to be a simple management issue became a highly charged political one. This was not necessarily due to a lack of sensitivity on the part of the civil servants, but rather to the symbolic and political strength of the sub-post offices. Indeed, Warner argues that the effect of using administrators for scrutinies and Rayner's insistence that scrutineers should also implement made for 'a more holistic and politically aware approach'. One view from a senior civil servant was that the shock treatment of the Rayner scrutinies 'made more immediate and useful impact on efficiency in Whitehall than all the techniques purveyed in the 1960s ...' (Delafons, 1982, p.269). But the loss of momentum for political reasons was quite common, and the savings over several years were still minute when set against total government costs.

Though there were warnings that the programme could become little better than a 'staff suggestions scheme' and some predicted that Whitehall would have its usual success in converting 'such irritating grit into an elegant but irrelevant pearl' (*Economist*, 20 October 1979), Rayner's ambitions went further than these individual scrutinies. He wanted to change the 'culture of Whitehall'. There were several large-scale scrutinies which covered a number of departments. One which attracted a good deal of attention was that related to government forms. Rayner saw them as an important communicative link between government and governed. In 1982 the Rayner team collaborated with the Plain English Campaign to scrutinize forms from those departments which communicate most directly with the public: DHSS, Home Office, Inland Revenue, and Environment. This resulted in the White paper *Administrative Forms in Government*, which proposed cutting out unnecessary ones and saving £300,000 immediately. Another money saving idea was to abolish the *Official Paid* stamp after forty-two years (*The Times*, 4 July 1980). These two small examples show one major difference between business and government. This kind of reform - which M & S had carried out - was undoubtedly useful, money-saving and an improvement in efficiency. And in a commercial organisation could make a revolutionary difference -'Retail is detail' - but in a governmental organisation it could only save marginal amounts. Rayner's model was very much a private sector one in spite of his saying, on leaving the civil service to return to Baker Street, HQ of M & S:

> There is no risk whatsoever of my assuming that government is like running Marks and Spencer either in content or execution. Government has to provide services which no sane business would undertake and whether it is more or less of government that the nation needs, a government will have to deal with those issues which private enterprise and voluntary activities cannot handle. (Rayner, 1983, p.3)

He did, however, greatly increase cost consciousness in all government organisations by introducing the idea of charging for services which had previously been provided at no cost to the users: office space, light, heat and stationery for instance. He told the Select Committee: 'I am firmly of the view that the obligation to pay for what is consumed is a pre-requisite to sound management and cost-consciousness ...' (Treasury and Civil Service Committee, 1981-2). So this was not just a cost-cutting exercise but also a step towards those lasting reforms. It did however create an immense amount of paperwork.

Although those who attacked the reforms said that the Rayner view of efficiency was a limited one, paying attention to costs rather than outcomes, there was another novel aspect. His retail background also made him anxious to please the customer: the Administrative Forms scrutiny is a prime example of this, being an attempt to focus on the recipient of government services which pre-dates the Citizen's Charter idea, an early introduction of a greater awareness of the consumer in government practice.   Other multi-departmental reviews included personnel work, running costs and statistical services, which covered twenty-two departments.   So there was in a sense a shift from nuts and bolts to broader issues.   The Next Steps report itself was the result of a scrutiny of scrutinies.

But overall, the culture of Whitehall was less receptive than he had expected, possibly because the idea of a single Whitehall culture is a serious misjudgment: it is as 'federal as a collection of Swiss cantons', (Massey, 1993, p.36).   The senior civil servant was still not as conscious of the need to manage as he should have been.   Nor indeed were ministers, except Michael Heseltine, who at the DoE had been developing his own management information system (MINIS), which had started life as a Rayner exercise.   Heseltine had also been involved with a large department when he was Minister for Aerospace 1970-74, and MINIS was in large part a result of that experience.   It was first set up as one of the early Rayner scrutinies, the intention being to provide systematic information about the department's work, which would help to decide priorities and staffing and to assess effectiveness, thus helping to see where cuts could best be made.   Heseltine insisted it was not just about staff cuts, but 'costs, priorities, and accountability' (Heseltine, 1987, p.25). He did achieve large staff reductions, but the most visible change was that the role of the permanent secretary and other top officials had increased; one critic described MINIS as 'the equivalent of the blunderbuss - unrefined, blanket coverage, unwieldy, unmanoeuvrable' (Metcalfe and Richards, 1990, p.217).

Whatever its shortcomings in other respects, MINIS provided the germ for the Financial Management Initiative (FMI), Rayner's next and last assault on the traditions of Whitehall: it took the scrutiny principle further into the realm of 'lasting reforms' that Rayner so dearly wished to achieve by combining it with the MINIS concept.

The FMI was coolly received by other departments.   The lack of enthusiasm on the part of both ministers and mandarins might have defeated Rayner, even with Prime Ministerial backing, but the idea was given a further boost by the Commons Treasury and Civil Service Committee, which in its April 1982 Report *Efficiency and Effectiveness in the Civil Service*, followed the Rayner line enthusiastically. Tighter management systems were needed and 'ministers should realise that ability to manage their departments is as important to the country as their performance on the floor of either House or in Committee' (*The Times*, 2 April 1982). A MINIS type system should be introduced in all departments, the committee said. Rayner told the committee that it should not be possible for a ministry *not* to have a system. The doomed Sir Ian Bancroft, asked by the committee why this had not already been done, replied '... there are not all that many Mr Heseltines around' (Fry, 1988, p.8). In spite of resistance from Whitehall, the Financial Management Unit was set up in May 1982, bringing in management consultants from well known firms.

The FMI was much broader than previous scrutinies and reviews, much nearer to being a general strategy for reform. Never more than six in number, the Unit included senior civil servants, mostly accountants by training, and management consultants from four well-known firms - Arthur Andersen, Coopers and Lybrand, Peat Marwick and Hay-MSL. Francis Plowden of Cooper's was only following in his father's footsteps as he wrestled with the difficulties of controlling public expenditure. The consultants had mostly had previous experience of working in government departments; they were developing top management systems of the MINIS type, introducing, often experimentally, budgetary control systems and handling the expenditure programmes of quangos. It continued the Rayner *modus operandi* - though an instrument of the MPO and Treasury, it would only work with departments and would not impose itself on them. Its work was intended to be as much as possible focusing on problems and issues common to all departments, to avoid the reinventing of the wheel all over Whitehall (Russell, 1984, p.150). Introduced throughout the whole civil service in 1983, the FMI had three main aspects, all familiar to the private sector: setting of objectives; the collection of information on costs; and the clear spelling out of responsibility. These aspects of budgetary control were relatively unknown in Whitehall, and many new accounting systems were introduced so that, to some the FMI became more an accounting initiative than anything else (Massey, 1993, p.50).

Rayner's idea was to strengthen line management, to push responsibility down to the point where the costs are actually incurred, but at the same time to put greater responsibility on ministers for the overall management of their departments. Simultaneously however he wanted a central agency to be able to insist that departments operate management systems. A resolution of the conflict between financial devolution to the periphery while retaining general control at the centre was never really arrived at. Freedom to manage could not become a reality for managers if the Treasury kept a tight hold on purse strings. In some cases the new initiative resulted in more control not less, becoming 'a club to bash departments with' (op. cit., p.51).

Even though freedom to manage was only permitted within strictly defined limits - 'a little bit of freedom and a lot of grief' said one official (Gray and Jenkins, 1991, p.57) - for some, the changes threatened constitutional proprieties and raised questions about ministerial responsibility. At the same time it could be perceived as the continuation of a familiar theme. Robert Armstrong saw it as 'a crystallisation' of all the changes going back to 1969 and earlier. Embryonically present in the Plowden Report of 1961, the Fulton Report of 1968 and PAR of the 1970s, the FMI was seen as a watershed in British public administration. It was different from those earlier attempts at reform because of its firm political backing but mainly because of the greater commitment to better management emanating from the very top of government. At the same time its limited impact in actually devolving responsibility paved the way for the Next Steps innovation.

One problem with the Rayner approach was its disproportionate concentration on controlling running costs at the expense of thinking about objectives, which had been one of Plowden's concerns, hence the notion of 'forward looks'. This emphasis was deliberate because Rayner realised that PAR had foundered by focusing almost exclusively on policy analysis.   In its attempt to achieve fundamental change throughout Whitehall, FMI tended to be over standardised, in a way more appropriate to a company like M & S, than to the variegated patterns within government. Next Steps was to recognise the essential heterogeneity of the different elements that make up the machinery of the state.

In 1986 a National Audit Office (NAO) study found that progress was being made in developing budgeting systems, but that a 'cultural change' could not be said to have taken place. According to accountants Peat Marwick, there was nothing very new in it; it had not shifted the emphasis to evaluation, as hoped.   But focusing on delegated budgeting and managing programme expenditure (of quangos) *was* a challenge, since so many civil servants lacked the basic skills which they would now have rapidly to acquire.

At the end of 1982 Rayner left to return to the less complex world of M & S. His place was taken by Sir Robin Ibbs, an ICI man, who tried to continue the permanent revolution, the 'sense of urgency' that Rayner had managed to generate, which seemed to be necessary to keep Whitehall interested in management. It was argued by some that as soon as the instigator had gone, the approach which bore his name collapsed. By others, that despite real achievements little responsibility had been handed down, and management had not really caught on in the upper echelons of the civil service (Hennessy, 1990a, pp.620-1).

However limited success had been, Rayner's working methods survived. The Next Steps report (better known as the Ibbs Report) was the result of a scrutiny like many before it. It took ninety days, the scrutineers talked to ministers and officials, reviewed past scrutinies and reports on management in the civil service. The findings were that the civil service was too large to be managed as a single organisation; and that FMI had barely scratched the surface. The prescription was to hive-off governmental services into agencies. But control over manpower and budgets would remain - and so would the constitutional position on ministerial responsibility. The project manager for the Next Steps programme was an accountant, Peter Kemp, who was happy to have pinned on him the label 'civil service SAS'. In practice, the separation of operational and policy matters was more complex than anticipated, and there were problems with accountability, so the question would not go away: How can managerial freedom be reconciled with at least some element of continuing ministerial direction and control, let alone trying to render it compatible with the traditional conventions associated with the doctrine of individual ministerial responsibility? A doctrine dismissed by Rayner as 'an absurd convention'.

Just as Rayner bequeathed a *modus operandi* to his successors, he had also left them his impatience with all such moribund constitutional niceties. The Next Steps team, a small highly skilled group of the sort with which Rayner liked to surround himself, was attempting to 'co-ordinate, stimulate, facilitate, and sometimes push Whitehall departments towards change' (Gray and Jenkins, 1990, p.165), in the same way that the Rayner Unit had done. In urging rapid implementation of their proposals, that required no formal legislative approval, they were indifferent to any of the constitutional implications of their work (Massey, 1993, p.55). Accountability of the Next Steps agencies has raised many doubts.   Parliamentary Questions relating to their activities are now referred to their Chief Executive rather than answered by ministers but, as with the old public corporations that ran the nationalised industries, the agencies can still be subject to ministerial interference and strict Treasury control.

To conclude, Rayner's achievement was to bring management in government - albeit a restricted definition of it - to the top of the priority list and to keep it there. The FMI may not have been as innovative as it was painted but it was widely applied. He made ministers responsible for the efficiency of their departments. 'We are all managers now' wrote Sir Patrick Nairne in 1982, a phrase Rayner was happy to echo - and there was a good deal of truth in it. He may have been pushing at an open door, but he succeeded where others failed because he had the support of a strong Prime Minister, because the ground had been prepared over preceding years and because the time was ripe for it. But his methods of teamwork, openness and persistence all contributed to his success.

The M & S corporate culture is probably as powerful as any other and Rayner became thoroughly imbued with it. Marks and Sieff were both great believers in MBWA, Management by Walking About, and Rayner's 1979 instructions to his 'Raiders', when the scrutiny programme was first set up, reflected this. They were not to stay at their desks but to go and see things being done. Marks and Sieff, and Rayner too, believed strongly in the importance of leadership in creating team spirit, and in delegation, which helps it develop: 'communication must go down as well as up'. The company was committed to paying great attention to detail and to treating its employees well. It also took seriously its commitment to the community: in the arts and health in particular, and Rayner became involved in this. The running of the company had been revolutionised by cutting out most of the paperwork and civil servants went to Baker Street to learn about it at first hand (Sieff, 1990, p.140).

Though he gained a great reputation as a management expert, he had received very little formal training, apart from a few short courses. He was influenced, however, by contemporary management theory and, in particular the writings of Peters and Waterman. He was fond of saying, 'Don't make it perfect, make it Tuesday'. He was a team worker: on the procurement study in 1970 he assembled a small skilled group, a scientist, an admiral, and an administrator (Rayner interview). He liked to use specialists where he could, but initially did not like management consultants except as experts and recognised that inside knowledge is often vital. 'Stick to the knitting' in Peters and Waterman jargon. Team work is fine as long as he is in charge. He looked after his scrutineers, but he supervised them closely, laying down in great detail the working methods and was invariably closely involved in the design, conduct and reporting of a scrutiny. He insisted reports should be short and gave detailed notes on how to compare the savings which resulted from their recommendations, and indeed on how to write the reports. He was aiming at 'read across' - indicating a desire for the standardisation inculcated by Marks & Spencer. His teams saw themselves and were perceived as such by others as an elite with a certain *esprit de corps* - an amalgam of the RAF Regiment and M & S - as was illustrated by their nickname 'Rayner's Raiders'. This kind of personalisation was much more characteristic of the private sector than of the civil service, at least prior to Mrs Thatcher. The teams adopted a problem solving approach which was also a consensual one, 'going with the grain' in order to garner maximum cooperation from all staff in the department concerned and as such very similar to that adopted by management consultants. The individuals appointed to the teams often had a technical background, in economics, statistics or computing in line with Rayner's declared preference for more professionally trained people; later on, greater use was made of specialists and even teams of experts including seconded consultants (Massey, 1993, p.44).

In peacetime most businessmen do not succeed in Whitehall. Rayner was an exception (another is Sir Peter Levene, the efficiency adviser to John Major and previously director of the procurement executive, both jobs held earlier by Rayner), perhaps because there is much of the natural bureaucrat about him. However, the traffic apparently was not all one way: according to one press profile, many detected a 'hardening of bureaucracy' in the corporate style of M & S after he returned to the company (*The Times*, 3 January 1986). His hero was Sir Arthur Salter, an early pre-war technocratic fixer and sometime civil servant, academic, independent MP, and government minister, who exerted great influence as a 'power behind the stage' (Salter, 1967, p.24 and Smith, 1979, pp.32-34).

Like most of the other fixers, he is a non-partisan figure. When asked in 1986 whether he was a political animal, he replied, a touch disingenuously perhaps, 'No, I am a Tory supporter. I believe in the mixed economy'. As Hennessy has commented, he is the only one of Mrs Thatcher's circle who could possibly be imagined advising the PM of a different philosophy (Hennessy, 1990a, p.593). The gospel according to St. Michael - the M & S trade mark - was certainly accepted as being politically neutral; the Labour party made it clear before the 1987 election that they would wish to continue with the civil service reforms that he had helped formulate and implement.

When elevated to the House of Lords in 1983, he felt like a fish out of water in the Chamber, in spite of the attempts of Lady (Janet) Young, a Conservative minister, to involve him in its activities. To him it is a politicians' club. The talk that goes on there is too much like idle chatter and he is too impatient to listen to it. He was, after all, a man with a mission, bent on delivering efficiency and modern management into the business of government. He believed that success required a cause and a crusading spirit, which is not surprising in someone originally destined for holy orders and with a patron saint for a trademark. Like Arnold Goodman he is physically and metaphorically larger than life and less retiring than Oliver Franks or Edwin Plowden, being a skilful manipulator of the mass media and possessing a good turn of phrase.

As a fixer Derek Rayner introduced some of the most radical attempts at reforming the civil service since the proposals contained in the Northcote-Trevelyan Report of 1864. Roy Griffiths was to emulate him, as a cross between the Victorian duo of Edwin Chadwick and Florence Nightingale, in endeavouring to re-shape the National Health Service.

7 A Tale of Two Retailers: II Roy Griffiths

The previous five chapters have reviewed the activities of a set of people who have 'rendered no inconsiderable service to the state'. They brought different attributes to bear on their allotted tasks, some of which were shared with others, while some were more idiosyncratic. In terms of broad categories a distinction has been drawn between official and unofficial fixers and in the next two chapters a further delineation will be made between these individuals and the corporate fixers who as a type are of more recent origin. Among the individuals, however, it is possible, borrowing the typology of André Maurois, to classify them as 'Fattypuffs' or 'Thinifers': accordingly, Lords Goodman and Rayner fall under the former, and Lords Franks and Young, Lady Plowden and Sir Roy Griffiths would join the ranks of the latter, with Lord Plowden somewhere in between. Placing Franks and Griffiths side by side in this manner, not only illustrates a similar lightness of frame but also points up other features they had in common. The most obvious was that they were endowed with formidable, securely confident intellects of a markedly donnish orientation that placed a very high premium on the collecting and sifting of relevant evidence. But many of the qualities and achievements of Roy Griffiths were of a kind to be seen in the work of the other fixers. His reform of the organisation and management structures of the NHS was at least the equal of Franks' overhaul of the system of administrative justice or Plowden's review of public expenditure control. Moreover his ability rapidly and succinctly to draft proposals matched that of Goodman, while his speed of working and paramount concern for effective operational implementation closely paralleled the approach and style of Rayner. Of them all, he was perhaps the most complete fixer and this doubtless stemmed from the fact that by experience and strong theoretical conviction he was the personification of the general manager *par excellence*. He was to draw almost exclusively on this model during his time in Whitehall, where like Rayner but in contrast with the other fixers, he was to be limited to one theatre of operations, that relating to health and health care; he was, however, to do a longer stint than his colleague from M & S.　He died in 1994 still in harness at the Department of Health.

The health service was the largest employer in the whole of Europe.　An immensely complex entity, it was struggling with rising costs and the latest of a wave of successive reorganisations.　A major restructuring had taken place in 1974; the management consultants, McKinsey, invited into the DHSS by Sir Keith Joseph, had introduced a hierarchy with three layers below the level of the department - regional, area and district health authorities and a complex system of planning.　By 1982 the cumbersome nature of this structure had been recognised: there had been 'tears about tiers' as Sir Patrick Nairne put it.　Area Health Authorities were abolished and a unit level inserted below the district.　But doctors retained all their independence and were effectively outside the management system.　Other professional groups, too, effectively managed themselves.　General management functions were carried out through 'consensus management', by a team which included administrator, nurse, treasurer and medical officer. This required many compromises and was, not surprisingly, sometimes rather slow.　Efforts were made to improve efficiency, but the crisis of funding which had really begun in 1976 became almost perpetual.　An array of measures designed to stem rising costs and improve management had been introduced since 1979, including Rayner scrutinies.

The announcement made by Norman Fowler, Secretary of State for Health and Social Security, at the Conservative party conference in October 1982, of an enquiry into the use of manpower in the NHS, was part of the continuing attempt at improvement, as well as a reaction to a barrage of hostile parliamentary questions on NHS staffing.　No details were made public until the following February, when Roy Griffiths's appointment as chairman was announced; four leading businessmen were to conduct an independent management enquiry into the effective use and management of manpower and related resources in the NHS.　They were not to produce a report but go straight for recommendations on management action, which should not require legislation.

Griffiths, who may not have been the first choice for the task, had been approached - like Rayner to all intents and purposes headhunted - by Sir Kenneth Stowe, the permanent secretary at the DHSS, who asked him to head the enquiry.　His appointment was greeted critically by many of the contending interests within the NHS who feared that management reform concealed an agenda for financial cut-backs and staff reductions. He was fully aware of these suspicions because he expressed a number of reservations about the appointment: he was not prepared to be a hatchet man and simply make recommendations about shedding staff. If there was a manpower problem it was a management issue and should be tackled as such; additionally, a general election was only six months away, and he did not want to be 'part of an electoral gimmick'. Having been reassured on all three points, he was told that it would be half a day a fortnight for eight to nine months. Ten years later he still had an office in Richmond House, Whitehall.

He was assisted by three other businessmen from British Telecom, United Biscuits and Television South-West. The group set about reading up what there was on NHS management which was not much and was largely out of date. There were no formal hearings, no evidence was taken; the group undertook field visits to NHS staff of all kinds, and organised informal discussions. There were also many meetings with Norman Fowler and the junior ministers and top civil servants. Griffiths liked the format of a 6.00 p.m. meeting followed by dinner during which the discussion continued. There was nothing random about any of this however; though he liked to organise meetings in an informal way, like Franks, Griffiths knew what he wanted to get out of them. He was impressed by their commitment and he made it clear that he was not considering any structural changes *per se*, but was intent on specifying responsibilities.

Though the original remit was not to write a report, after a few months they were asked to do so by the Prime Minister, partly because of increasing public clamour at the time about the health service. All four were busy in their full-time jobs and had no time to write a fully documented report, so they decided simply to write a letter to the Secretary of State. The twenty-three page document had very little in common with the weighty examples produced by other fixers. As the King's Fund commented, there were almost no facts in the report; nurses and doctors were barely mentioned. The language of the report was simple and direct, even blunt and reads like a management primer, not an encoded missive for mandarin contemplation. The single sentence which has been widely quoted, '... if Florence Nightingale were carrying her lamp through the corridors of the NHS today she would almost certainly be looking for the people in charge' (op. cit., p.12), was picked out because it sums up Griffiths's main criticism of the NHS.   It recommended the imposition of a formal structure of general management at every level in the health service.   In spite of the changes of the previous decade, this was one of the most major shake-ups that had taken place in the forty-year life of the health service.

Action and quickly was the message - the NHS could 'ill afford to indulge in any lengthy self-imposed Hamlet-like soliloquy as a precursor or alternative to the required action' (op. cit., p.24).   'All our recommendations are designed to be implemented without undue delay: none of them calls for legislation nor for additional staff overall; and all of them are completely consistent with current initiatives to improve costs' (op. cit., p.2).   The Commons Select Committee on Social Services later made the wry comment, with considerable justification:

> If the Sainsbury organisation were to receive recommendations for such significant management changes from an external consultant, much more evidence and investigation would be demanded before such recommendations would be acceptable. (First Report, 1983-4, HC 209, p.vii)

In place of a 'morass of unclaimed responsibilities' (*Economist* 24 March 1984), it envisaged an organisation with a small strong centre and clear lines of responsibility.   General managers would manage everyone from top to bottom including the doctors.   Thus although no real structural change in the service nationally was recommended, the most recent one still being in the process of implementation, the proposals cut directly across the tribalism with which the health service was so deeply imbued and challenged the independence of the medical profession as well as removing control of nursing from the nurses.   The report recommended a management board to support the Secretary of State in running the service and appointing general managers for regions, districts and units. This board would consist of members from business, the health service and the civil service and would be chaired by someone who in a rare moment of coyness was described as the Secretary of State's 'right hand man'.   He would be a full-time paid, outsider.   Above this would be another supervisory board, concerned with the 'purpose, objectives and direction' of the health service.   The Secretary of State would be chairman and the board would give overall approval of the budget and strategic decisions.   The other members would include the Health Minister, the Chief Medical Officer and the Permanent Secretary.   The themes which recur throughout the short report all aimed to introduce 'a more thrusting, committed and energetic style of management' (*The Times*, 26 October 1983). These were: to devolve downwards, to pinpoint responsibilities, to develop proper management budgeting in each unit and to involve the doctors in the processes of management. These ideas were neither new nor startling in business terms and apart from the last are familiar enough, being part of the currency of the period in which both Griffiths and Rayner were operating.

Publication of the report was not expected, but it did in fact come out on 25 October 1983, a day when the media were inundated with the news of the American invasion of Grenada. Reaction was extremely mixed and, not surprisingly, not all of the tribes reacted favourably. Many felt that the 1982 restructuring, still continuing in many places, was enough to cope with. The nurses who had struggled for years to acquire full responsibility for their own management, were particularly vehement in their opposition - they said they were in danger of returning to their 'handmaiden' role of twenty years before. The BMA was more welcoming but said it could only oppose the proposal for a nonmedical chief executive. The prophetic comment from NUPE, the main union for the lower paid, was that it would 'mean a health service with more chiefs than Indians' (*The Times*, 26 October 1983).

The general manager idea was at the heart of the report, not only for most commentators, but for Griffiths himself. 'Cost improvement' was to Griffiths central to management, which was doubtless the reason for his being chosen. But this was not enough. In a fashion similar to Franks he wanted dynamic managers, not administrators who merely reacted to events; what he saw in the NHS were administrators who did not question the pattern of service and who did not see the public as customers, indeed who were not oriented to the public at all, but often rather inward looking. But however desirable in principle, the general manager proposal raised two major problems: first, it would sweep away the 'consensus management', criticised as a cartel by Griffiths but widely regarded within the service as a success. It was seen to usher in a more authoritarian style typified by moving 'from the mobilisation of consent to the management of conflict' (Klein, 1989, p.208).

Little indication was given as to how the methods of general management would be reconciled with the professional concerns of nurses and doctors; it was assumed to be axiomatic that general managers would effectively become agents of the government and the 'frontier of control' of decision-making would move away from the professions particularly the doctors. The task of the general manager in obtaining professional cooperation, Griffiths conceded, would be made more difficult if resources were scarce. Griffiths hoped to bring coherence to the NHS, integrating the disparate professions and disciplines; it may have been an impossible task, and his approach was probably too mechanistic.

The proposals for two management boards and a chief executive radically cut across existing organisational structures as they were intended to do. Norman Fowler, who had previously described the Regional Health Authority chairman as 'my health cabinet' denied that the two central boards made the regional system redundant, for the boards would be inside the DHSS and would not therefore constitute a new tier of organisation; the chairman of the management board would be a second permanent secretary within the DHSS. But nevertheless the possibility remained of a counter-productive tension between the centre and the regions.

Then again, if the Secretary of State's authority was to remain intact the board could only be advisory; but Griffiths had said that he should not interfere in operational management matters. Thus the relationship between the Secretary of State and the Chief Executive would be crucial. Implementation of the reforms went badly. Griffiths had made it clear that 'a real demonstration of management will at the centre, will be required if the NHS is to break free from the top-down approach' (Griffiths report, 1983, p.16). Unfortunately it was at the centre that things went most spectacularly wrong. The first chairman of the management board resigned after only eighteen months, complaining of interference by ministers and advisers. 'He felt in an uneasy no-man's land between the department and the service' commented Fowler in his memoirs (Fowler, 1991, p.196) - or perhaps between political and managerial demands. Fowler said the Board could not be free of political control (*The Times*, 3 October 1986).

A new chief executive was appointed, with Griffiths as an unpaid, part-time deputy, but with Tony Newton - the new Health Minister - as chairman of the management board which was the opposite of what Griffiths had recommended. A further problem was that in the rush to implement the new regime across the country district general managers had to be appointed before the top ones were in position.

Contrary to what Griffiths had in mind in seeking to devolve management responsibility to the periphery, continuing financial pressures and intermittent crises were factors that had the effect of reinforcing greater centralisation. Griffiths was adamant that the aim of his report was not to provide a tool with which ministers could cut the NHS, and stressed that funding considerations were not within his remit. But the shortage of funds for the service as a whole and also incidentally the fact that the Griffiths proposals were not cost free and had no funding at district level meant that the implementation of his proposals was seriously compromised by the financial situation. All the district managers could do was to try and keep within their budgets. Notwithstanding the public perception that the NHS was over-staffed with bureaucrats, it was estimated that at this time Sainsbury's management costs were thirteen per cent, a level three times higher than that of the NHS (Strong and Robinson, 1990, p.167).

The introduction of management budgeting went very slowly and was still not widespread in 1992. Griffiths had also underestimated the power of medical consultants whose position seemed little affected; in general, management still stopped at the consulting room door (Pollitt, 1991, p.69) and in some cases divisions between doctors and managers became quite deep. The result was that managers who had responsibility for budgets had no direct control over the medical consultants who were responsible for much of the expenditure and were unwilling to take on managerial posts or become involved in those management budgeting exercises which did not seem useful to them.

The commitment to consumerism - Griffiths wanted management to play an active, not merely a reactive, role in relation to patients and the community - remained marginal (Griffiths Report, 1983, p.22). In view of the constraints under which the service was operating it is not surprising that many staff took a cynical view of what were widely regarded as frills, such as newly painted waiting areas and patient surveys. But it does reflect Griffiths' retail experience and his debt - like Rayner - to Peters and Waterman, whose dictum it was that the successful enterprises are those which get closest to the consumer. The Patient's Charter, introduced during the Major premiership, also recognised this with the concomitant requirement urged on by successive ministers to reduce waiting lists.

In summary, then, the Griffiths report failed to read the NHS system correctly. Although paying lip service to its political sensitivity, (op. cit., p.11) the recommendations never really took proper account of it nor of the difficulty of drawing a line between policy and management issues and devising clear objectives. All the same, the report did have a major impact and as a result of it, managers became much more powerful. The NHS was transformed it was widely admitted, and purposeful and positive management was beginning to be felt (see for example G. Best of the King's Fund in evidence to the Social Services Select Committee, see *The Future of the NHS*, HC 613 of 1987-8), in spite of the lack of agreed aims and objectives and a good deal of confusion about accountability; yet the cultural diversity of the service remained largely untouched.

Overtaken once more by financial pressures and horror stories about the NHS, the Prime Minister, Margaret Thatcher, conducted her own radical review, which culminated in the White Paper *Working for Patients* of January 1989. This, though it had no publicly announced terms of reference, like the two Griffiths enquiries, was produced quite speedily in the course of a year. It was also quite secretively carried out with little consultation. Griffiths was again involved, the only non-ministerial member of the team, alongside Lawson, Major, Moore, and Newton with the Prime Minister in the chair: 'It was an astonishing episode', Griffiths recalled. They began by attempting to arrive at new methods of funding the service, but came to the conclusion that other methods would be worse. Influential in this was the appointment of Kenneth Clarke as Health Minister in July 1988 who joined the group at that time. As a sop to right-wing reformers, the proposal for an internal market emerged, which stressed choice and competition. It was also decided to push forward the 1983 proposals for more devolution, coupled with the resource management initiative. When, after copious leaks, the White Paper appeared in early 1989, it was a glossy but rather slim brochure. The government stuck to its view that the problem was use of resources not levels of funding, and in this Griffiths agreed. If it was an advance for consumerism, it was focusing on choice rather than participation. But in reality, choice is quite limited 'at best exaggerated and at worst purely rhetorical' said one critic (Wistow, 1992, p.69). Management was to be strengthened by putting district general managers on committees appointing consultants and involving them in merit payments, thus reinforcing Griffiths' earlier reforms.

Another aspect of the White Paper related to the management board, arguably the least effective of Griffiths' 1984 reforms. He himself thought that the implementation had been half-hearted (Griffiths, 1991, p.12). It was renamed the management executive and moved to Leeds. The new Chief Executive, Duncan Nichol, had a background in the health service and had joined the Board in 1985. He may have been better prepared than his predecessors from the private sector to cope with the grey area between decisions which are definitely political and those which are definitely managerial. Eric Caines, the new personnel director was also a civil servant. This attempt to 'beef up' (Griffiths' own phrase) the boards was completed in May 1989 when the supervisory board, which had been fading away, was renamed the policy board; three industrialists were appointed to it by Kenneth Clarke who made it clear that the board was not a representative body, which meant that the government's chief Nursing Officer was excluded to the fury of the Royal College of Nursing. This streamlining process was completed in 1993 with the creation of regional 'outposts' of the management executive and the phased abolition of all Regional Health Authorities by 1996.

Simultaneously with his on-going involvement in the management and organisational reforms of the NHS, Griffiths was asked to undertake another commission, to make recommendations for improvements in the delivery of community care to home-bound patients. In the early 1980s economic considerations for once coincided with medical and other professional opinion that it would be better for the long-term sick to be cared for at the primary level - at home or in community provision - rather than in hospitals and other long-stay institutions. Initial steps were taken to move in this direction in 1983 but the results were patchy and had not kept pace with the closures of the large mental hospitals. In 1985 the House of Commons Select Committee on social services had made wide-ranging recommendations for reform, especially relating to provision for the mentally ill and mentally handicapped. Following this up in December 1986 the Audit Commission issued a damning report, *Making a Reality of Community Care*, which found that the £6 billion spent annually on the mentally ill, mentally handicapped and elderly produced very poor value for money, due to deficiencies in planning and fragmentation of responsibility. What was required was a rationalisation of funding, including removal of the 'perverse incentive' towards residential care resulting from the supplementary benefit regulations. The report also recommended co-ordination of social services and community care policies and the establishment of 'a more radical organisational structure'; it added that community care should be encouraged to flourish at a local level and made it clear that things could not remain as they were.

Griffiths followed his customary approach, adopting an informal, businesslike manner, for it was not to be 'a Royal Commission type investigation' (Griffiths report, 1988, p.iii). He conducted the inquiry himself, together with the advice and help of a panel of advisers. The style was relaxed, panel members were listened to and there was no obviously pre-set agenda. The task was 'to review the way in which public funds are used to support community care policy and to advise on the options for action.' (op. cit., p.iii). It would not be a fact-finding enquiry since the facts had been produced by the recent National Audit Office report and the issues for consideration had been clearly identified. He took no formal evidence, but received plenty of unsolicited material. It was not within his remit, Griffiths decided, to suggest policy changes. Similarly with funding - his concern was with the best use of resources, not their level. But many groups involved in community care, said Griffiths, using one of his rare metaphors like an illuminating flare, 'felt that the Israelites faced with the requirement to make bricks without straw had a comparatively routine and possible task' (op. cit., p.iii). And indeed, in the view of one of the advisers, in this enquiry Griffiths faced 'issues even more intractable' than in the previous one (Hulme, 1988, p.65).

He tackled them with determination, pulling no punches. It was an area more than any other, he said, where the gap between rhetoric and reality was enormous. The most important thing was to close that gap so that policy and resources came into some sort of 'reasonable relationship'. Though the problem was more complex, he took a similar line to Griffiths I and once again decided that a major restructuring would be too disruptive. Two main problems presented themselves immediately. One was the rate support grant, which made it very difficult for local authorities to commit definite amounts of money to community care. The second was the system of provision for residential care through supplementary benefit which clashed with the social services method of priorities and budgets, and which, while swallowing vast sums every year, did not take account of individual needs. There was also the question of the closure of the mental hospitals. The main recommendations to cut through these 'road blocks' as he called them, were: first, that a minister should be identified as responsible for community care; and secondly, that funding should be provided by central government to local authorities of say 50 per cent of programme costs; and thirdly, closure of large hospitals should be seen as being of national significance and detailed plans should be made. Apart from this, provision should be done locally and as far as possible individually. The report recognised that any system would have imperfections - there was no neat 'Rubik cube' solution awaiting discovery. The key thing was collaboration and interdependence. Griffiths made it quite clear (for example on p.11 of the Report) that the major responsibility for community care lay with local government for he was keen to encourage local initiative and diversity.

The report was published in March 1988, the day after the budget, when it was expected attention would be on Nigel Lawson's new tax reforms: Griffiths was recovering from an operation. The timing was deliberate for internal Whitehall reaction was cool to his proposal to make local authorities the main agencies for delivering community care because government policy was to reduce the functions of local government. Although no press conference had been called, media attention was plentiful. Apart from going against the grain by enhancing the role of local authorities, the bulk of the recommendations were hardly novel. The fundamental approach was really that of the FMI and Griffiths I: spell out responsibilities, insist on performance and accountability, evaluate and match policy to available resources. What was more, it was realistic in that it recognised that a perfect solution was not available; nor were its ideas startlingly innovative - some local social service departments were already moving in the direction which Griffiths was indicating and in this respect he was going with the grain. Indeed the report gathered around it a remarkable consensus on an intricate social policy issue from professionals and carers alike.

Official reaction to the proposals was a long time in coming. Labour MP and health spokesman Robin Cook gleefully pointed out in the Commons (12 July 1989) that the government had taken longer to respond than Griffiths had to write the report. After extensive argument within the government, the proposal for making local authorities the lead agents was accepted, but the idea of ringfencing the grants for community care was not, except for funds for the mentally ill. (*The Times*, 21 June 1989). Kenneth Clarke said that the proposals were 'eighty per cent Griffiths', testament to his influence on the Prime Minister. But David Blunkett described them as a 'poisoned chalice', predicting accurately that there were problems ahead with the interface between the health and local authorities especially for old people (*Health Service Journal*, 20 July 1989) and an administrative nightmare for residential home proprietors. Sir Roy himself, however, (ibid., 27 July 1989) declared himself 'quite pleased', adding that this White Paper would be less confrontational as there had been ample opportunity for discussion.

The delay between the publication of the report and the government's response, though frustrating, provided time not only for a debate on all the issues raised but also for alliances to be formed and effective lobbying to take place. Griffiths himself participated in a 'road show', addressing professional groups around the country.

The White Paper on Community Care was finally published in November 1989. It allocated planning responsibilities to local authorities, but expected private sector facilities to be used. The funding questions remained unanswered, but there would be no ring fencing of expenditure except for the mentally ill. One commentator said that Sir Roy's 'sensible and humane' proposals could become 'a ministerial shambles'. The man himself commenting to the National Association of Health Authorities' (NAHA) conference said this:

> I had provided a purposeful, effective and economic four-wheel vehicle, but the white paper has redesigned it as a three-wheeler. Leaving out the fourth wheel of ring fenced funding. (*Health Service Journal*, 4 January 1990)

With one wheel off his wagon, the Community care proposals would probably not go rolling along.

There were to be further delays. First, the bill took nearly a year to get parliamentary approval and then the Prime Minister decided to postpone implementation of the community care provisions of the Act until 1993 in order to keep down the level of the highly unpopular poll tax. However, the delays gave an opportunity for further lobbying that succeeded in extracting a government commitment to earmark funds for community care, including some for treating drug and alcohol addicts and £7.5m towards training costs. (*The Times*, 19 July 1990). The fourth wheel had been reattached but the economy continued to be unhelpful so that as the new arrangements went into effect in April 1993, it was not surprising that doubts were expressed about the adequacy of the funding. Nor had all of Griffiths' proposals been carried out. His report had specifically recommended that appointment of a minister responsible for community care: Virginia Bottomley had been the responsible minister when she was Minister of Health, but in 1993 this was shared between herself, promoted to Secretary of State, and *two* other ministers, certainly not what had been intended.

The necessity of deciding on the tasks to be performed and to allocate responsibility is the hallmark of the Griffiths approach; and it clearly comes from his business experience.

Roy Griffiths was unusual for a fixer in coming from a genuinely working class background. The son and grandson of North Staffordshire miners, he went to grammar school and then after a two year spell in the mines himself as a Bevin boy, on to Oxford. He went to Keble College, probably the Oxford equivalent of Selwyn, a Victorian foundation strong on theology. Like Arnold Goodman he took a first in law, then the postgraduate degree of BCL.

Subsequently qualifying as a solicitor, he worked for the West Midlands region of the 'family firm', the National Coal Board. He went on to Monsanto, a large American chemical company as a legal adviser and company secretary. As a company secretary and a solicitor, he was abundantly professionally qualified but in spite of the qualifications he had no interest in being a lawyer; luckily for him US companies at that time regarded lawyers rather as they did MBAs later, as the seed corn of management. So he went into general management, and rose to become Director and Chief Executive of Monsanto Europe. He did a three-month executive development course in 1964-5 at Columbia Business School in New York. Like Franks he turned down the opportunity to pursue a career in America; he did not want to be an American or have his children grow up as Americans. After being headhunted he went instead to Sainsbury's in 1968 and became the first non-family member to join the board.

There he had a great impact; he organised the primitive monthly management accounts, brought in some outsiders and allocated responsibilities. David Sainsbury (now Chairman) went to Columbia on Griffiths' advice; this meant that when he returned they shared a common business school approach. He also achieved an improvement in industrial relations. Good personnel work and tough line management succeeded in reducing delays which, with a high proportion of perishable goods, could be very costly.

He brought both his style and his working methods with him when he left the world of the supermarket to become a fixer. What was required was a management consultant, and less a wise man on the old model. What had been such a success at Sainsbury's was less so in the health service, but his impact certainly proved that it is possible for one man to make a difference. Unlike most of the others he was very far from being a self-publicist, even in a quiet way, though he had an abundance of self-confidence. 'Let's aim for low-key respectability', he said to one of his advisers when the community care proposals were about to be launched.   Informal, modest and quiet, his first report was a plain typescript. The civil servants who helped the enquiry team are listed by name, with no rank or title. The prose was direct and clear - like Rayner he had a weakness for Biblical metaphors. Never a civil servant, he cut through the pomposity of others, and was not above the occasional cutting remark: at a conference he said to the person next to him, 'I hope you have not got any slides. I find people either have slides or ideas, never both'. He was an optimist, but no Candide; he believed not that we live in the best of all possible worlds, but that it is possible to improve our imperfect one.   He refused to be an accessory to any Conservative electoral gimmick and could be irritated by the ways of politicians:

> I do not expect miracles within six days. I can appreciate that the first example of major change was when the Almighty brought order from chaos within that period. He certainly would not have achieved it in even six years, let alone six days, had the House of Commons been sitting at the time contesting every painful inch.
> (Griffiths, 1991, p.24)

He nevertheless retained a faith in the political process in that he realised that patience and a dogged determination would often succeed in gaining political acceptance.

He was the only fixer of his generation not to become a life peer. Perhaps this recognition was denied him because of his preference for local authorities to run community care and certainly his modesty meant he would not press his own case. He had none of the charisma of Derek Rayner and although he gained the affection and respect of those with whom he worked, his colleagues would not have been regarded as 'Griffiths' Gunners' in the manner of 'Rayner's Raiders'.

Throughout the 1980s and on into the present decade, health service provision has been beset with a series of political 'hot potato' crises amounting to an underlying systemic failure. Griffiths was aware of this but he was confident that the proposals he made could do much to remedy these problems. He believed that part of the secret of success lay in the realisation that:

> Good ideas in any organisation are about 25% of the process; the remaining 75% depends on good and effective implementation. (Griffiths, 1989, p.3)

At the same time he displayed a large measure of impatience: 'there is a faint feeling of eternity about the way reports are handled', he remarked to the Commons' select committee and he expressed himself more forcefully when he said:

> I believe that running any organisation is about a careful intellectualism at one extreme - working out what is important and setting precise plans and strategies - and at the other extreme an obsessive urgency of implementation to see that what is planned is actually achieved. (Griffiths, 1987, p.201)

This 'obsessive urgency' may, however, have been counter-productive in respect of 'effective implementation' because changes were too rushed and the goalposts were forever changing.

Both Griffiths and Rayner recognised the considerable differences that exist between government and commerce but both felt strongly that more important was what both sectors had in common. They shared a common management consultancy approach to their tasks but they chose different methods. Griffiths thought that Rayner's detailed inch by inch methods would not be successful. Griffiths was a stickler for detail too, but he took a more overall view. Where Rayner stressed costs, and was often criticised for it, Griffiths, who saw cost improvement as vital, concentrated on outcomes. (Griffiths, 1991, p.19).

In the event Roy Griffiths was over-optimistic but he set in train a series of reforms both in organisation and management in the NHS and in community care that despite many stumbles along the way provided a blueprint, as reasonable as any other that might have been contrived, for the effective delivery of health care. In terms of technological and scientific innovation and the highly political context in which it operates, the NHS exists in a very dynamic milieu. The pressure for results, for example controlling costs and cutting waiting lists, part of his legacy, has created its own problems according to some critics:

> The family business culture prevailing in the NHS is a closed culture, mostly hidden from public view ... the suspicion flourishes that it is a vehicle of political patronage ... This business culture is

profoundly intolerant of criticism ... The accountability of the NHS to its consumers - the patients - has declined ... But the real problem with running the NHS like a grocery is that it does not guarantee excellence in ethics. The new business managers are out to prove their commercial skills. There will be corner-cutting, and there is impatience ... (Kelsey, 1994)

The basic principles of Griffiths' reforms are likely to stand the test of time and he could hardly be blamed if their implementation was too often over-zealous, too politically driven and financially undernourished.

8 Corporate Fixers: I Management Consultants

The rise of the management consultants was one of the distinctive features of the Thatcher years. While the Iron Lady may have succeeded in reducing the power of the trade unions and had sought, less effectively, to clip the wings of the older professions of medicine and the law, her years at No. 10 were halcyon days for the new professionals, the consultants and accountants who were not slow to appreciate and capitalise on the opportunities that beckoned. These corporate fixers were to be among the main beneficiaries of the Thatcher legacy.

Many factors contributed to this new state of affairs. A major cause was political, deriving directly from the revival of ideology which was the hall-mark of Mrs Thatcher's approach to government. Conviction politics presaged extensive radical reform, and significant departures from the former corporatist state and consensus solutions would call for new kinds of institutions, personnel and techniques. As the pace and range of change gathered momentum so an almost Maoist atmosphere was engendered. Public denunciation and denigration of whole groups of people was not uncommon and included most of those in the public sector, and not least the civil service which stood accused of shoring up the old order. Long before, it had been the pre-war Labour Party of Clement Attlee and Harold Laski that had openly voiced its distrust of the civil service, believing it would act as a fifth column undermining the socialist programme of a majority Labour government but, ironically as it happened, it was a Conservative administration of a decidedly right-wing hue that actually internalised and acted upon this somewhat paranoid perspective. In Mrs Thatcher's case, however, it was not so much a matter of political partisanship that worried her but anxiety that bureaucratic inertia would subvert her intentions.

There was some truth in this. The governments of Harold Macmillan, Harold Wilson and Edward Heath had all variously implemented successive reforms which had largely failed, however, in their aims to modernise the British economy and polity alike. Margaret Thatcher did not wish to emulate them. Disbanding as much of the public sector as possible and streamlining what remained was to be an enormous project even over the lifetime of three governments. It required not simply a massive injection of private sector skills but the invention, testing and application of new kinds of expertise. Bureaucratic virtues were not what was required. The hostility to new ideas and methods of doing things which is inherent in bureaucracies meant that outsiders were needed to implement many of the reforms. Ferdinand Mount, formerly an adviser to Mrs Thatcher, gives two examples of civil service incapacity to grasp new methods (Mount, 1983, p.155).

The first was opting out. This concept baffled the DES, they had no 'idea of how to pluralise the system, since all their efforts had been directed towards ... co-ordinating and collectivising it'. The second example was privatisation. A lack of expertise and of self-confidence led to delay and huge expenditure on merchant bank advice. Wholesale privatisation of large-scale nationalised industries had not been tackled before. The same was true when, at a later stage, reforms in other areas were initiated. The split between purchaser and provider authorities in the Health Service and the creation of hospital trusts could be broadly overseen by the Department of Health and the NHS Executive but specialists from outside had to be co-opted to compile and approve the detailed schemes. This was also necessary for the implementation of such programmes as Local Management of Schools which devolved budgetary responsibility away from local government and down to the individual school. None of these changes could have been undertaken solely from within government; outside help was extensively used in both cases. By the same token, the creation of a plethora of Next Steps Agencies, hiving-off many of the executive functions of government away from the day-to-day responsibilities of Whitehall departments and ministers, could not have taken place without the assistance of external management consultants.

Contracting out government work to private sector firms was part and parcel of Thatcherite policies. Indeed the government encouraged the use of consultants not only in its own sphere but also in private industry for which it provided financial incentives. Greater efficiency was a main motive at work. This meant, as often as not, computerisation.

The consultants were also needed to provide a technical expertise which in spite of the managerial efforts of the post-Fulton years was still lacking within the Civil Service itself; this included financial systems, information systems and IT, all of which became very important. In the field of information technology the designing and installation of bespoke computer systems was almost entirely the monopoly of specialist management consultants, of whom Arthur Andersen was among the market leaders. There are often sound reasons to bring in outside skills - reinventing the wheel is an expensive thing to do; and in the latter part of the decade hiring consultants may have been necessary because of the shortage of skilled staff after years of reductions of numbers. This can also make good economic sense; keeping specialist staff is less flexible than bringing outside help for a short period or seconding a few individuals for a longer period.

But in any case the government also wanted specifically to instill 'managerial perspectives and norms' (Henkel, 1991b, p.71). Consultants were operating at the edge, on the boundaries of government, they were independent and could bring ideas and values from the private sector while reducing the size of the government's pay roll.

There were some apparent spectacular successes, notably the Department of Social Security (DSS) project which, in computerisation terms, was the largest non-defence one in the western world. In the words of Eric Caines, 'the DSS project was hugely successful and the systems it introduced are now part of the everyday fabric of the social security operation' (Caines, 1993). Very big sums were involved. In 1988-89, £47m was spent in the Departments of Health and Social Security, of which £42m went on the computerisation of income support and other benefit payments (*The Times*, 22 February 1990). Later, there was a more sober reappraisal of the Social Security project undertaken jointly by the Oxford Institute of Information Management and Imperial College, London. Their study concluded: 'overall, a major risk was that of costs rising out of control. In fact these rose from the original estimate of £700m to over £2.6bn by 1993. It is unlikely that any of the costs savings, estimated in 1989 at £175m, will be achieved.' The Department 'threw money at problems', employing consultants at an annual cost to the taxpayer of up to £22m. (*The Independent*, 9 September 1994).

Prior to 1979, management consultancy had enjoyed a steady but largely unspectacular growth. Both British and American firms were hired in the post-war years for various government projects, including Cooper Brothers (now Coopers and Lybrand Deloitte) and Urwick Orr (later amalgamated with Price Waterhouse). Lyndall Urwick, founder of Urwick Orr, was a pioneer of management consultancy who predicted in 1946 that government would not be able to deal effectively with a changing world 'unless it is prepared to place good management within the machinery of government in the forefront of its agenda' (quoted in his obituary in *Management Today*, February 1984), which echoes Franks' very similar contemporaneous remark. In 1957 McKinsey became the first American agency to set up a London office. Although it sees itself primarily as a private sector operator, and is shy at revealing how much work it does for public bodies, McKinsey's landed some very large government assignments over the years, that included the Post Office in 1966 and reorganisation of the BBC in 1968, and again in 1990 when its Charter was up for renewal.

Throughout the 1980s the public sector yielded a very rich harvest for consultants. The Management Consultancies Association's (MCA) returns reveal that their members' earnings from central government grew from £18m in 1985 to £51m in 1988 - a tripling in four years. These later levelled out somewhat in 1991 when the figure reached £91m, only £1m up on the previous year. It was later reported to the House of Commons Select Committee on Transport that the privatisation of British Rail would cost £1m in management consultants' fees alone in 1992-3, with an estimated rise to £28m by 1996 (*Guardian*, 27 November 1993).

During its relatively brief existence from 1970 to 1981 the Civil Service Department issued annual reports on the number of assignments commissioned by government, though no costings were revealed. The greatest users were the Departments of Health, Environment, Trade and the Ministry of Defence. Overall, the total number of assignments per year varied from a 'high' of 75 in 1969-70 to a 'low' of 28 in 1974-75, with the annual average hovering around 42. Significantly, since 1981 no comparable data has been released but it is nevertheless possible to discern the phenomenal increase in the government demand for consultancy services since then.

Fee income earned by MCA members from central government

1985	1986	1987	1988	1989	1990	1991	1992	1993	1994	YEAR
18	27	34	51	70	90	91	82	93	113	£m

Source MCA Annual Reports

The development, however, was not without one or two downturns as the economic recession of the early 1990s took hold. The MCA (whose membership does not include the whole profession), reported in 1992 the first fall in its members' turnover since the early 1970s with a drop from £843m to £810m; this included a 12 per cent reduction in computer related activity. Fees from the public sector fell by the same margin to £186m, though interestingly there was an increase in the number of public sector assignments undertaken. The Health Service continued to be a lucrative source of income growing by 50 per cent in 1991 and a further 90 per cent the following year. Thus the recession which caused private sector fees to decline was substantially offset by the continuing buoyancy of demand from public sources. In 1994, the central government figure rose by £10m but expenditure by local government increased by more than fifty per cent to £32m.

This is not altogether surprising given that, very early on in Mrs Thatcher's premiership, the MCA specifically and systematically targeted government as a client for its members' services. Ernst and Whinney were awarded a commission in the Cabinet Office. As a result they realised that the future market for management consultants in government was potentially too vast for them to undertake alone. Taking its cue from this revelation the MCA successfully contrived a meeting with the Prime Minister in 1981 and made a presentation about how its members could facilitate the workings of modern government and advance the implementation of formulated policies. (Gray and Jenkins, 1991, pp.41-59). They could offer objectivity and expertise, provide additional staff either during assignments or on secondment (usually to see through the operational implementation of recommended and agreed changes), take on difficult or sensitive issues (such as civil service pay), and develop techniques appropriate to new thrusts in government policy, such as benchmarking.

Following the Downing Street presentation the profession felt greatly encouraged. Coopers and Lybrand, for example, 25 per cent of whose fee income is generated in the public sector, set up its own government division in 1982.

As we saw in Chapter Six, the introduction of the FMI in 1982, following on the value for money approach introduced by the Rayner scrutinies and the introduction of management information systems, was a sea change.   An article in *Management Today* (December 1983) predicted a big expansion in the use of consultants, seeing them as more ubiquitous and powerful today than the engineers seen by Thorsten Veblen as the 'secret unacknowledged rulers of industrial society'.   The government was determined to force through change and change meant business for management consultants.   The disciplines of the FMI and its offspring would not have been possible without IT; these were not very different from those recommended in the 1960s, but by the 1980s they had become technically feasible.

Having received the Prime Minister's endorsement, the MCA moved swiftly to consolidate its position by developing its network of contacts within the civil service.   It could lobby on behalf of its members in ways that individual firms could not; they would be seen by officials as commercial predators whereas the MCA as a trade association was seen to be rather more neutral in its approach.   Government has to avoid becoming too cosy with individual contractors for it cannot be seen to have favourites.   MCA/civil service relations are close and formalised. The MCA's Public Sector Mutual Interest Group, for example, holds four or five meetings a year attended by members and a Permanent Secretary from Whitehall or the chief executive of a government agency together with one or two supporting officials.   The purpose of such meetings is to receive an authoritative update on activities within a particular sector of government.   These briefings are supplemented by a series of small monthly lunches consisting of four or five senior staff from member firms and a very senior civil servant, agency head or politician.   In 1990 MCA guests included Sir Bryan Carsberg from OFTEL, Sir Gordon Borrie from the Office of Fair Trading, Sir Raymond Lygo from British Aerospace and John Redwood, MP from the Department of Trade and Industry (DTI); in 1991 Lord Young, former Secretary of State at the DTI and later Chairman of Cable and Wireless, Sir Terry Burns, Permanent Secretary at HM Treasury and Robert Evans from British Gas were invited; in 1992 Sarah Hogg, then head of the policy unit at No. 10, and Eddie George, then deputy-governor of the Bank of England, were among those who attended these occasions.

Clearly such briefings provide invaluable market research information, but it is by no means all one way. The consultants gain early insight into the ways in which ministerial and official thinking is moving, new problems that are emerging and so on. Ministers and officials for their part glean new perspectives about how recent changes have worked out and they often get a different kind of feedback from management consultants than from staff working in government organisations. There is a two-way, mutually beneficial trade between government and consultants. They are sounding boards for each other and to have such a facility is particularly valuable for ministers and their regular officials at a time when the strains on contemporary government make the role of a minister an increasingly difficult one to discharge.

Management consultancy is conscious of its changed and enhanced status in public affairs. In the early post-war years consultants worked primarily in the private sector, often as firefighters, called in to deal with sudden crises or seemingly intractable problems or problems that for one reason or another could not be effectively handled internally. More recently they have been used more continuously and routinely especially in the public sector. This development is open to different interpretations. For their part the consultants would see this as a perfectly natural sequence of events in moving from 'hired gun' to regular professional. Some sense of this is to be found in the recognised handbook where management consultancy is defined as 'a method for improving management practices ... that ... has been developing into a profession' (Kubr, 1986, p.xii). But without in any way contradicting this observation, it might equally be remarked that perhaps what has happened is that crises have largely ceased to be the discrete, one-off episodes they once were and have instead become an endemic feature of the modern world and to be seen most vividly in its governance. So combustible have things become, in other words, that the firefighters have to be on hand all the time.

The exaltation of management consultancy since 1979 was, as we have said, largely the result of a political revolution, in the form of Thatcherism, coinciding with a technological revolution, in the form of computerisation and especially information technology. If that was all that was involved things would not have turned out the way they did: computer experts would simply have remained computer experts and management consultants would have remained much as they were in the 1950s and '60s advising on pay and rewards, recruitment and selection,

organisational reform, marketing and so on. What the computer revolution did was to place an even greater emphasis on a systems
engineering approach to decision making, necessitated by the imperatives
of the computer itself, but which nevertheless spilt over more generally.
This is to say, the general management consultant, as opposed to the
specialist, became more systems conscious even when dealing with
essentially non-computer relevant issues. This was all of a piece with the
developing technocratic or managerial ethos that manifested itself in
similar developments, such as tighter expenditure control as presaged by
Plowden, the recommendations of the Fulton report and such initiatives
as PAR, MINIS, FMI, etc.

The methodology of management consultancy is said to be based on a
five-phased model consisting of: 'entry, diagnosis, action planning,
implementation, and termination' (Kubr, op. cit., p.13). How far this is
unique, it is hard to say for presumably surgeons, architects and other such 'consulting' professions adopt much the same approach to their
daily work. The bald fact of the matter is that management consultancy
is not and never will be a recognised profession in the sense of dispensing
skills peculiar to itself for it has no core discipline in the way that doctors,
the clergy and lawyers have. It is true that consultancy has forged ever
closer links with accountancy, as accountants have diversified their
activities beyond their traditional auditing and financial advisory roles
illustrated by such mergers as that between Price Waterhouse and Urwick
Orr. But accountancy remains one of many fields of expertise that
management consultants eclectically draw upon in their work. Increasingly, consultancies are following the example of Andersen
Consulting, the world's largest in terms of gross fee income ($6.02bn in
1993), which places a heavy emphasis on training to induct staff into its
own unique house style. Such intensive training, in Andersen's case
amounting to 124 hours per professional or 3.1 million hours in total for
the year 1993, has two primary goals: it makes for greater internal
coherence and corporate unity, while the identifiable house style provides
a useful tool for niche marketing by means of product differentiation that
aims to distinguish the consultancy from its competitors. A desirable
spin-off is that such training provides a surrogate for consultancy's lack
of its own core discipline. An awareness of such lack is implicit in some
of the jargon employed at times to provide an element of mystification,
one of the symbols - but not part of the substance - of professionalisation.
For example, in the standard text it is written:

Intellectually, the consultant needs the ability to make a 'dilemma analysis', because an organisation which uses a consultant is probably faced with a situation that appears insoluble ... In order to make this kind of dilemma analysis, insight or perception and intuition are necessary ... Unless the important factors can be sifted from the mass of detail, and cause separated from symptoms, accurate diagnosis is impossible. (Kubr, op. cit., pp.459-60)

Oliver Franks could not have disagreed with this, though he would have winced at 'dilemma analysis.' Management consultancy has been described as 'packaged commonsense' but banality, by definition, is an expression of obvious truth. The general management consultant is an almost archetypal model of our times. His/her capital, as likely as not, will be based on the foundation of an initial professional training including perhaps the ubiquitous MBA, accumulated experience, and a comparative knowledge of various situations all of which have an increasingly short shelf-life - a condition to which the consultants have contributed and in which they have a very real vested interest - because for them, the more change the merrier. This means, of course, premiums are placed on relative youth - consultants are getting younger than policemen - and on continuous professional training and personal growth so that when confronted with new learning curves the ascent can be rapid and successful. Management consultants, as Peter Hennessy has pointed out, are dedicated followers of fashion, constantly on the lookout for the latest buzzword, or fad, and in his words, 'get through these fashions almost as fast as normal people get through underwear' (*File on Four*, BBC Radio 4, 8 February 1994) There is no doubt that the intellectual excitement, the life style as well as the material and intellectual rewards make consultancy an attractive career for the bright and the ambitious and it is probably recruiting more than its fair share of talent in the western world. There is also the additional *frisson* of being one of 'the powers behind the throne' which was recently articulated in just such terms in a recruitment advertisement (*Independent*, 7 July 1993). This merely corroborates what is felt at large within consultancy:

It would be an exaggeration to say that management consultants influence the course of history. However, they have been the invisible hand behind some extremely important business and government decisions, and their powerful private and public organisations. (Kubr, op. cit., p.11)

The same author later goes on to support the contention made earlier that the public sector is a growing and lucrative market:

> Public sector organisations, enterprises in particular, constitute an important market for management consultants in many countries owing to growing concern about the efficiency of the public sector and the quality of public services. Management consultants tend to be regarded as a useful source of ideas and expertise that could increase efficiency. (Kubr, op. cit., p.307)

These words were written at the height of the consultancy bonanza, but more sober judgements would now prevail following revelations of very costly failures.

In 1989 the National Audit Office criticised Touche Ross - almost half of whose business is done in the public sector - for the work they did over the privatisation sale of water authorities for the Department of the Environment. The worst faults were 'mounting costs, poor communications, delays and the use of junior staff.' The project management system was cumbersome and did not perform as expected. Touche Ross was subsequently forced to deduct £250,000 from the total bill of £1.6m (*Management Consultancy*, March 1992).

Worse was to be revealed about incompetence and skulduggery in two regional health authorities. The House of Commons Public Accounts Committee issued two reports in late 1993 concerning activities in the West Midlands RHA and the Wessex RHA. In the first it found that £10m had been wasted on hiring management consultants who had been appointed without proper procedures being observed. In the second it found that more than £20m had been wasted following the abandonment of the regional information system plan installed by consultants who, again, had not been appointed in accordance with approved regulations and four people were subsequently charged with conspiracy to defraud (*Guardian*, 10 December 1993). In both regions the chairmen and chief executives resigned.

Disturbing though such examples are they are not the main worry about the use made of consultants by government and public agencies and in any case the sums involved are a minute fraction of overall costs. The real issue is guaranteeing that management consultants provide value for money. The First Division Association (FDA) - the top civil servants' trade union - drew attention to this problem in evidence to the House of Commons Treasury and Civil Service Committee in April 1993. Opening with the observation that:

> The proliferation of the use of management consultants throughout the civil service is one of the most remarkable features of the late 1980s and early 1990s. Almost no decision of any importance is now taken without management consultants being used. Indeed, earlier this year, a single management consultancy told the FDA it was being consulted simultaneously by eight different Government departments on performance related pay. The cost implications of this sort of profligacy are self-evident.
>
> Nonetheless, management consultants can provide useful expertise from outside the public sector, provided such expertise is not regarded as infallible. Used sparingly it can be helpful. (T.C.S.C., 1992-3)

The FDA went on to observe that consultants are 'all too often used to "plug gaps" in an entirely unstructured way', are 'too often consulted simultaneously on the same subject by different Government departments, and on a wide variety of subjects by the same Government department.' Furthermore it was likely that '... corporate strategy could soon become the monopolistic concern of one management consultancy ...' in the case of a particular department. The FDA also stated that the perceived expertise of consultants was very often found to be non-existent but their name was used to support ministerial decisions. The expertise and knowledge gained by consultants working in the public sector is not retained within it, while consultants seeking further commissions from a department may be less likely to dissent from perceived ministerial or management views than civil servants would be.

There is a good deal in what the FDA has to say even though, as is only to be expected, there is a measure of 'turf protection' included as the Association seeks to limit any further encroachments by management consultants into its own traditional preserves. There is also some tendentiousness: after all, civil servants, especially those of a reformist, technocratic cast of mind, are as capable of exploiting the interventions of consultants to further their own ends as are ministers and others, while the assertion about effective civil service independence from lines being taken by ministers has not been a notable feature in recent years. Where the FDA was spot on target was in its observation that: 'There is a real problem about the growing lack of accountability of management consultants, and the evidence for this is increasing.'

Eric Caines, a former member of the NHS Executive and civil servant, compared the Wessex RHA fiasco with the success of the Department of Social Security's computerisation of its social benefits system. The former failed through lack of effective project management by public officials, whereas the latter succeeded because the civil servants were put in charge of the project and they 'looked for their management consultants to work as full members of a combined team, not as instructors simply passing on their skills to others ... They treated the consultants and their own staff forthrightly in pursuit of deadlines and the control of expenditure.' (Caines, 1993). Caines believes that unless the public sector trains up to equip itself with the skills necessary to oversee and work alongside management consultants and effectively police contract compliance most of what the public sector does will have to be parcelled out to the private sector to run. Even this apparent success at the DSS, did not last, for as already recounted, a later study reported that costs escalated alarmingly and the Department apparently stopped counting.

In other words, Caines asserts that responsibility lies with the client. Ensuring that goals are achieved and value for money insisted on, as well as good relationships between the outsiders and insiders, are vital prerequisites of success.

These necessary conditions are often not fulfilled, however, as the August 1994 report from the Efficiency Unit under Sir Peter Levene made clear. Hiring decisions were often left to junior officials, who called in consultants in a 'knee jerk' fashion when a pressing problem arose. They did not always put contacts out to tender properly and exhibited little effort to assess value for money. There was also frequent duplication and poor implementation of proposals though the report saw work on privatisation and market testing as successes. Many of these conclusions were not accepted by consultants, though it was widely agreed that better results would be achieved by closer supervision at a higher level. The Report also showed that few savings had been achieved. An expenditure of more than £500m in 1992-93 generated savings of only £10m. Interestingly, only about 20 per cent of this was accounted for by the big firms which make up most of the MCA membership. In-house teams, in contrast, had identified savings of £18m at a cost of £78m. A recent book by Igor Popovich asserts that only about one-third of consultants are worth the large sums they cost, and many are mediocre or even incompetent (Popovich, 1995).

Better project management may satisfy the technocrat, but will it meet constitutional anxieties? More accountants do not necessarily bring more accountability. Doubts about accountability are compounded by those about conflicts of interest. One area where this is most obvious is in the supply of computer equipment. Many large consultancy firms have close links with hardware companies; they may also be advisers to government departments, local government organisations or health authorities and then subsequently get contracts to supply such equipment to them.

Another example of such conflict is that of Coopers and Lybrand Deloitte, where a senior partner was also special adviser to the Minister of Transport who then moved to Railtrack where he is now a director. Not only this, but Coopers have a multi-million pound contract to work out how Railtrack should charge - a mission so difficult to fulfil that it is known as the holy grail. Many believe that there is no rational solution to the problem, since the costs of using the track cannot be traced back to any particular train or passenger. This issue, like many others now entrusted to consultants, is one that appears to be technical but ultimately will be decided on political grounds. The consultants argue that in such cases they merely 'make a contribution' to the decision which will later be taken by the government; but consultancy firms large and small increasingly promote themselves as delivering solutions rather than offering advice. Peter Hennessy sees them as part of the politics of relative economic decline, a new breed of 'soothsayers' following after the economists and accountants of previous decades, which senior officials hope will rescue the nation from its poor performance (*File on Four*, BBC Radio, 8 February 1994). Even after it has become clear that no miracles are on offer, the promise of greater efficiency is still tempting, and as Hennessy added, the political attraction of having advisers on short term fixed contracts and eager to please may be too great for any government to resist.

So, in spite of the questions that were raised following the Efficiency Unit Report, the extensive use of management consultants will remain a significant feature of contemporary government particularly when it has to operate in the context of an outmoded set of constitutional arrangements. Their position is likely to be consolidated rather than undermined. In this historic tension between the pursuit of efficiency and the maintenance of democratic accountability they are an added problem and it is the one problem they should be excluded from solving. It is for politicians and governments to realign the boundaries and procedures of the state.

In the meantime the consultants have been admitted to the Establishment by being accorded the City of London's highest honour in the granting of chartered status to the Guild of Management Consultants formed in 1993, thereby becoming one of the livery companies whose origins date back to medieval times.   (Oliver Franks might not have been surprised and covertly might even have mildly approved.)

More recently, the consultants have received a further accolade with the appointment of Norman Blackwell to succeed Sarah Hogg in 1995 as John Major's policy adviser.   A senior consultant with McKinsey & Co., he previously had a spell in Downing Street as a member of the policy unit from 1986 to 1987.   He also worked for Lord Young of Graffham, the former Secretary of State for Trade and Industry, as had Howell James, director of corporate affairs at the BBC before becoming Mr Major's political secretary.   Thus are the new networks being formed from the interchangeable roles of consultants, *apparatchiks*, think tank staffers, and others from similar walks of life that, as shall be seen in the following chapter, most definitely include the lobbyists.   All of these occupations are coalescing to form the new *nomenklatura*.

9 Corporate Fixers: II Lobbyists

Lobbyists in their present form are even more recent arrivals on the British scene than the management consultants. In so far as their activities are known to the general public, they would be regarded, perhaps, as the murkiest of the denizens of the political deep. Saloon bar opinion might assume they have been lurking in the depths for some considerable time. In one sense this is true enough: lobbying has a long genealogy for it is not too fanciful to suggest that favourites and fools in the courts of ancient and medieval monarchs were early precursors of the modern lobbyist.

Somewhere between the demise of the court favourite and the rise of the professional lobbyist came the development of what S.E. Finer, in his pioneering book *Anonymous Empire* (1958), termed 'the lobby'. This is the world of pressure groups that includes both sectional interest groups, such as trade unions and commercial organisations, and the promotional or cause groups, such as charities and voluntary associations. All, in their different ways, have regularly sought over the years to bend the ears of ministers, civil servants, parliamentarians and even the electorate itself to promote new policies or preserve or amend the *status quo*. The lobby consolidated its position during the course of the Second World War when, in order to mobilise the economy, government employed an extensive variety of corporatist and consultative devices to maximise the war effort. At cabinet level this was reflected in the appointment of Ernest Bevin, General Secretary of the Transport and General Workers Union, as Minister of Labour and National Service, and Sir Fred Woolton, head of Selfridges, as Minister of Food. The large sectional interest groups representing labour and business which dominated the lobby maintained their positions of influence throughout the Butskellite 1950s, and were more formally acknowledged in the tri-partite institutions, such as the National Economic Development Council and similar agencies, that were a marked feature of successive governments of both parties from Harold Macmillan to James Callaghan. Indeed, it was one of the main aims of Mrs Thatcher's time as Prime Minister to dilute the powers and influence of the lobby, especially of the trade unions. While significant parts of the lobby were cut down to size, the activity of lobbying itself continued and indeed expanded during the Thatcher governments which encouraged the establishment of the independent firms of lobbyists. These constitute a significant mutation in the style and character of lobbying. Solemn and binding undertakings of the old-style lobby, agreed over beer and sandwiches at No. 10, may have been excised from the political agenda, but deals - some overt but mostly under the counter - still go on being struck.

In terms of staff numbers, turnover and scope the lobbyists are much smaller than the management consultants but even so their growth has been at least as phenomenal. Lobbyist firms did exist before 1979. One Commander Powell, who described himself as a parliamentary consultant, was a familiar figure on the Westminster scene from the 1950s to the 1970s. Ian Greer, one of the most successful, first set up in business in 1970, but as with the management consultants, it was in the Thatcher years that they really flourished.

Today, total annual fee income is estimated to be £20-25m of which more than £10m is earned by independent lobbyist firms. A dozen or so firms dominate out of perhaps as many as a hundred, but the significant ones number no more than thirty. Some are small, often very small, independent firms, including some of the best known and successful such as Ian Greer Associates and Public Policy Consultants, Westminster Strategy and GJW: others, like Sallingbury Casey, were independent but were bought up by large advertising agencies.

Ian Greer established his new firm in 1980 with a client list which grew from six in 1981 to fifty by 1990, including such well known names as British Airways, Plessey, House of Fraser Holdings, Argyll, Philips and Drew and Johnson Matthey. Staff grew from four to twenty-four and in 1990 fee income had topped £1.8m. GJW and Sallingbury Casey both employ between eighteen and thirty staff and have client lists of about fifty each.

There is considerable volatility in the business with frequent changes of ownership and staff, mergers and breakaways. One clear feature of the scene, however, is the differentiation between those public relations (PR) agencies that have moved in on lobbying, developing their own in-house specialist lobbying function, and the independent lobbyist firms. The former see lobbying as a logical extension of public relations, while the latter see the two functions as being fundamentally different. To the lay observer there may seem little of moment in this distinction but it has generated an almost tribal war between the two. Ken Weetch of the lobbying firm Advocacy Partnership was quoted a few years ago as saying 'As a professional lobbyist I would always separate lobbying from PR as I would separate architecture from mixing concrete' (*PR Week*, 22 August 1991). Lobbyists like Ian Greer and Charles Miller prefer to see themselves acting in the manner of barristers. In *The Right to be Heard* Ian Greer writes:

> A political consultant must be known to and trusted by all political parties and opinion formers. Like a barrister he has to be seen to be completely apolitical and impartial. (Greer, 1985, p.24)

Charles Miller of Public Policy Consultants, in evidence to the Commons Select Committee on Members' Interests in 1988, made a similar comparison. His job, performed in a setting resembling that of a barrister's chambers, involved 'very detailed and high level research, intelligence gathering and advocacy.' Alternatively, Miller and Geraldine I'Anson of Westminster and Whitehall Consultants see lobbyists as management consultants giving political advice. They tend to view the PR lobbyists' techniques with some distaste, accusing them of over-selling themselves in what can be achieved, relying too much on glossy brochures and endless getting-to-know you lunches between clients and MPs or peers which indicates too great a focus on Parliament. The independent lobbyists see themselves concentrating mainly on Whitehall, targeting the relevant civil servants dealing with the particular policy of relevance to their clients' interests.

Both types of lobbyist aim to influence government to promote, amend or stop specific items of legislation. Ian Greer says it is easier to kill a proposal than it is to change or reverse it after it has been enacted; the same is true of cases involving the exercise of ministerial discretion, such as whether or not to refer a merger or takeover bid to the Monopolies and Mergers Commission. At the outset, Des Wilson points out, the decision has to be made whether a campaign should be of a 'public' or 'corridors of power' variety, though the two are not necessarily mutually exclusive (Wilson, 1993, pp.28-29).

In negotiating on behalf of clients, or assisting clients to make their own representations directly, lobbyists are increasingly persuading government - at both ministerial and civil service levels - to adopt a particular line in Brussels with the European Commission and/or in the Council of Ministers; they will also, where appropriate, lobby Members of the European Parliament and liaise with allies in other member states of the European Union and this is an expanding dimension of their work.

Their stock-in-trade consists largely of monitoring trends, anticipating future events and developments and locating key personnel. Painstaking research is their core activity, for as Grant Jordan rightly observes, in making representations to government, 'the construction of a case can be as important as its presentation' (Jordan, 1991, p.57). Whatever the differences of approach and style between the independent lobbyists and their counterparts in PR and advertising agencies, these are likely to lessen as the latter recruit senior personnel such as Tom McNally at Shandwick Public Affairs and Edward Bickham at Hill and Knowlton. It is worth noting too that one of the independents, Westminster Strategy, is owned by the advertising group Lopex and through its affiliation with Grayling is a member of the Public Relations Consultants Association (PRCA). In any case the independents regularly work alongside PR agencies, law firms, accountants, bankers and management consultants. For the moment at any rate, they want to keep a distance, insisting on the distinctive professional stance and skills of the lobbyist.

The old lobby consisting of the large industrial and trade union pressure groups, local authorities and charities, still functions as best it may, but it is noteworthy that many of its constituent elements are increasingly using professional lobbyists to supplement their in-house capacity. A recent example is the case of local authorities who mounted publicity campaigns in an attempt to survive the review of their status and functions being undertaken by the Local Government Commission appointed in 1992. Lobbyists shared this business with the management consultants, and millions of pounds were spent. Quite small towns spent thousands; a group of historic cities which included Oxford, Lincoln and Canterbury retained GJW. Lobbying assignments reached such proportions that the Audit Commission stepped in to warn councils to limit their campaigns. A Commission spokesman said:

> The legal position of councils is extremely grey. The law says that councils can mount campaigns to their electorate if they are

informative, but not persuasive. We are producing new guidelines because of the way councils are spending their money in the course of the local government review. (*The Independent*, 24 August 1993)

In the circumstances it is ironic to note that the Audit Commission's own press office was set up and run for a time by Profile Public Relations and later by Shandwicks (Rush, 1990, p.80). Local authorities are not alone. The TUC, under its new modernising General Secretary John Monks, hired Des Wilson from Burson-Marsteller, for a six month trial period at a cost of £50,000, to advise in a 'behind the scenes role' on campaigning and public relations. Though central government imposed strict limitations on how local government spends its money in campaigning, its own expenditure is subject to no self-denying ordinance. Charles Barker Public Affairs is retained to promote the various Citizen's Charters.

One major battle in which lobby firms were closely involved was that over Sunday trading; the campaign to relax the rules, though backed by the government, took several years to achieve success. In 1986 the government's proposed liberalisation of the trading laws was defeated after a vigorous campaign conducted by an alliance of Keep Sunday Special, a pressure group, and the lobbying firm Extel. In 1993, when the issue came again before the Commons, a free vote was offered to MPs on three options: the tighter regulations favoured by Keep Sunday Special, a limited deregulation of Sunday trading hours desired by shopworkers and chain stores, and total deregulation as favoured by some consumers and consumer groups. In the event, after lively campaigning, the second option won by a narrow margin. In February 1994 an attempt to amend the Bill at Third Reading, so that moderate deregulation would be limited to small shops failed, but only after considerable lobbying of MPs by shopworkers from the large retailers and multiple stores who were fearful for their jobs. Similar pressure was applied by the Shopping Hours Reform Council. Once the law had been changed, chains like the John Lewis Partnership and Marks & Spencer, which had been totally opposed to flouting the law, began to open some of their stores on Sunday so as not to lose market share.

Privatisation and its consequences have provided lucrative work for the lobbyists as well as for the management consultants. Among the early privatisations was the gas industry. A Monopolies and Mergers Commission inquiry was held into whether the industry should be broken up, but after a huge lobbying effort which cost British Gas more than £6m, and involved Ian Greer Associates, Westminster Communications, and Sir Gordon Reece, it was decided instead that competition should be introduced into the domestic market by 1996. Ferocious lobbying ensued both by British Gas and the other companies hoping to enter the market, as well as Age Concern and other groups representing consumer interests (*Guardian*, 17 May 1995).

The Gas Bill was going through its committee stage in the Commons in the first part of 1995, and it was said that almost every member of that committee was being briefed by a lobby firm, and that lobbyists were seen framing amendments in the committee corridor. This was the occasion when Sir Jerry Wiggin MP, being a paid consultant to the owners of caravan parks, tabled questions in the name of Sebastian Coe MP, without his permission, for which subterfuge he was severely censured by Madam Speaker.

Another campaign launched in 1993 had the purpose of making the government stick to its commitment to build an east/west railway link across the capital. The Treasury wanted to postpone the CrossRail project as part of its policy to rein back public expenditure. A variety of interests, including British Rail and London Underground combined to keep the government to its original parliamentary timetable. MPs representing commuter seats were mobilised, the London *Evening Standard* championed the cause, and the Prime Minister was subtly targeted to overrule the Treasury's decision (Wilson, 1994, Ch.7). According to *PR Week* (27 May 1993) getting through the second reading of the CrossRail Bill involved 'virtually every lobbying firm in London'. This success, however, was short-lived because the four MPs who made up the Committee under the old Private Bill procedure threw the Bill out at the committee stage. Both front benches committed themselves to having it re-considered: the lobbying was not easily abandoned, and attempts to revive the project seem likely to succeed.

A reversal of policy was forced on the government again over the Sheehy Report on police pay and organisation in 1993. It contained radical proposals regarding job tenure, more flexible hiring and firing procedures and delayering by abolishing a number of ranks. Sir Patrick Sheehy had been appointed by Kenneth Clarke, when Home Secretary, with a brief to improve the efficiency and productivity of the police in the light of public disquiet regarding continuously mounting crime figures.

The Police Federation (the representative body for officers up to the rank of inspector), having realised the need to improve the public image of the police in order to offset and possibly pre-empt any radical proposals that Sheehy and his colleagues might make, appointed lobbyists Westminster Strategy. Traditionally, the Federation had relied on retaining the services of a single MP to promote its cause in Parliament and with the government of the day. Previous spokesmen included James Callaghan later to become Prime Minister, Sir Eldon Griffiths and most recently Michael Shersby who was previously director of the British Sugar Bureau and hence experienced in PR and lobbying. When the Sheehy proposals were published, an extensive campaign against them at all levels was mounted. The Federation gained the support of the Association of Chief Police Officers and the Metropolitan Police Commissioner. A widespread advertisement campaign was launched, headed by a photograph of Lord Callaghan with an anti-Sheehy text and a plea to 'Ask your MP to oppose Sheehy.' The culmination of the whole effort was a mass rally at Wembley Stadium attended by coachloads of officers from all the UK police forces. Additionally, there was very effectively organised opposition in the House of Lords involving all sides. As a result the hapless Michael Howard, Kenneth Clarke's successor at the Home Office, had to concede defeat and agree not to implement the main recommendations of the Report. The lesson was not lost on the Police Superintendents Association (the representative body of middle management) which appointed Hill and Knowlton as its lobbyist advisers.

A similar success concerned the reprieve of the Royal Marsden Hospital, famous for its cancer therapy, following the recommendation of the Tomlinson Report that it be closed down. Ian Greer Associates organised the opposition to this proposal. They brought in Lady Tryon (a close friend of the Prince of Wales) Marmaduke Hussey (Chairman of the BBC), Lord Stockton (grandson of Harold Macmillan), Fiona Fullerton and Lord Tonypandy (former Speaker) and former health ministers and other MPs. The lobbyists went exhaustively through the lists of ex-patients and wrote to no less than 400 non-London MPs whose constituents had been treated at the Marsden. This was followed by the presentation of a petition of one million signatures and a three day vigil in St. James's Church, Piccadilly. The Department of Health was surprised by the force of the campaign and the government was forced to climb down once again. After Virginia Bottomley announced her decision, a leading campaigner Lady Olga Maitland MP observed that 'it was a triumph of reserved and carefully targeted campaigning by highlighting issues, not exploiting patients, and motivating public opinion' (*The Times*, 11 February 1994). The government's capitulation, however, meant that the reduction in 2,500 beds Tomlinson had deemed necessary for the future overall viability of London's central hospitals would not be achieved. A letter to *The Times* made the point that other hospitals faced with closure might not be able to marshall such famous names and asked whether closure or reprieve would now depend on the skills of public relations firms in influencing government decisions. By the spring of 1995 it seemed possible that the decision would be reversed again.

Another defeat forced on the government was over the privatisation of the Post Office, a centrepiece of the government's legislative programme for the 1994-95 session and a proof of its Thatcherite *bona fides* for many on the right. The Post Office had turned down the services of Sir Tim Bell in 1992; he was taken on instead by the Union of Communication Workers, which had been campaigning against privatisation since then. In classic fashion, Lowe Bell, Sir Tim's newly formed political lobbying company, used both a former adviser to John Wakeham and an ex-Labour researcher to mount the campaign. As in the Royal Marsden case, it was decided to focus on a limited number of MPs - specifically on the fifty most marginal seats. They also concentrated on Northern Ireland which was vulnerable, the campaign suggested, to competition from the Irish Republic. James Molyneaux ultimately made it clear to Major that the people of Northern Ireland were not in favour of privatisation (*Independent on Sunday*, 6 November 1994).

The result of successful lobbying can be fudged government decisions. The Royal Marsden case left the government with a problem of what they saw as an over supply of beds in London. Not dissimilar was the case of Devonport docks, though here both DML and its Rosyth opponent, retained lobby firms. A fierce campaign resulted in victory for Devonport; the political spin-off was highly undesirable for the government, which succeeded in finding some repair work for Rosyth to do, though the starting point had been that only one yard could survive.

One area in which lobbying has been especially intense is that of mergers and acquisitions or competition policy. The main reason for this is that the procedures for monitoring such activity leave so much to the discretion of the President of the Board of Trade. Also, once a bid has been referred to the MMC, it lapses. Both the bidding company and the target company have an interest in preventing or encouraging a reference and will vigorously try to influence all those institutions involved as well as public opinion. The Trade President can choose to accept or reject the advice from the Office of Fair Trading and Parliamentary opinion can be of great importance in this. Again when the proposed merger has been pronounced upon by the MMC, the President has total discretion if the finding is that the merger would not be in the public interest. Other issues can also be aired - such as local unemployment, the suitability of the directors and how the bid has been conducted.

A good recent example of the working of the OFT/MMC/DTI nexus and the many points at which it is vulnerable to the influence of lobbyists is the case of the ship-building firm, VSEL. Both BAe and GEC were bidding for VSEL against a background of shrinking orders and employment anxieties in Barrow and on the Clyde - always a powerful incentive to get MPs moving. In December 1994 both bids were referred to the MMC by the President, Michael Heseltine, though only the GEC one was recommended for referral by the OFT; Cabinet level discussion probably took place. Both companies had board members who had close links with the political parties, Labour as well as Conservative; Lord Hollick and Lord Hesketh were on the BAe board and Lord Prior and Geoffrey Pattie on GEC's. The MoD evidence was expected to be crucial and the Scottish Office and the Department of Trade would also have had a strong interest. BAe and GEC had taken on lobbying firms: Tim Bell was in the GEC corner and Public Policy Unit was working for BAe, and apparently telephoning every MP (*Financial Times*, 5 November 1994). After a wait of several months, the President of the Board of Trade most unusually overruled a majority report from the MMC, which judged that a GEC takeover would not be in the public interest. Instead, favouring rationalisation over competition, he endorsed a minority report which took the opposite view, thus paving the way for a takeover battle and possibly the merger of GEC and BAe. BAe later withdrew from the fray.

Nowadays, as several of these cases bear witness, the Lords are more easily influenced and more influential, so they are increasingly a target. There have recently been allegations by Lord Lester of Herne Hill that questions have been asked in return for cash. One of the Nolan Committee's second round of tasks was expected to be an investigation of a declaration of interests protocol for the Lords.

The resignation in Autumn 1994 of Dame Angela Rumbold - a former minister and deputy chairman of the Conservative Party - from Decision Makers drew attention to another area where lobbying is rife.

Development issues can require much smoothing of paths, but in the Ebbsfleet case, the local authorities in North West Kent took a positive view of the plans to develop what was a scarred area. The matter came to public attention largely because of the disappointed hopes of Newham, which had wanted the international station sited at Stratford, in East London, as the main terminus for the Channel Tunnel.

Lobbyists are a distinct breed of fixer, quite different from the others we have examined for they are unashamedly working at the very heart of the political process. Other fixers, in varying degrees, are disdainful of politicians, legislatures and elections; willingly serving as best they can the government of the day, they tend nevertheless to have a low opinion of the political class and affect to be somewhat allergic to what they would see as the ever present messiness of political life. The lobbyists stand in complete contrast in terms both of attitude and prior experience: they revel in politics, in the intermediary roles they fulfil in negotiating for their clients, and knowledge of the fact that they are particularly practitioners in *realpolitik*. Almost all of them have become lobbyists from jobs elsewhere in the political system.

Ian Greer, regarded by some as the high priest of the profession, worked at Conservative Central Office before setting up as a lobbyist. He makes no secret of the fact that he maintains close links with high-ranking members of the party. These include John Major, whom he has known for twenty-five years and to whom he loaned his Jaguar car during the 1992 general election; he also sponsored the fringe agenda at the 1993 Tory annual conference. His staff of fifty includes some seven overt Labour supporters and twice that number of Conservatives; the Labour complement would be increased in the event of a Labour government.

Across the range of lobbyists, former *apparatchiks* in one form or another are a pronounced feature. The original founders of GJW, Andrew Gifford, Jenny Jeger and Wilf Weeks had previously served respectively in the private offices of David Steel, James Callaghan and Edward Heath - a remarkable example of multi-partisanship and high level experience. A more recent recruit, Nigel Clarke, had worked as an assistant to Tom King MP and then in the Conservative Research Department until 1985 when he joined GJW. Two former Treasury ministers, who lost their seats in the 1992 general election have recently become chairmen of lobbying firms: Francis Maude has joined the Public Policy Unit, while John Maples heads Rowland Sallingbury Casey, a subsidiary of Saatchi and Saatchi, Worldwide Government Communications. He was for a time simultaneously a deputy chairman of the Conservative Party. Sir Marcus Fox MP, Chairman of the backbench Conservative 1922 Committee and Keith Speed, another ex-Tory MP, founded Westminster Communications and were later joined by Lord Carter, a Labour life peer and William Camp who had previously advised Harold Wilson. Edward Bickham was a former adviser to more than one Cabinet Minister and Tom McNally used to be a Labour and then an SDP MP. Charles Clarke, who ran Neil Kinnock's office when he was Leader of the Opposition, has established his own alternative lobbying consultancy, Quality Public Affairs. Its aim is to teach local authorities and other public and voluntary bodies how to conduct their own lobbying, thus avoiding the high fees charged by conventional lobbyists.

Former civil servants are also to be spotted among the ranks of lobbyists. Sir Brooks Richards from the Foreign and Commonwealth Office is Chairman of CSM, while Michael Casey, who had been an under-secretary at the DTI with responsibility for competition policy, was chairman of Sallingbury Casey. Other sources of recruitment have been from broadcasting and journalism and charities. Those with charity experience include Ian Greer, who worked for three years for the Mental Health Trust; Leighton Andrews worked for Age Concern and the International Year of the Homeless before becoming managing director of Sallingsbury Casey and is now Director of Public Affairs at the BBC; and Des Wilson. Indeed, it is the view of Leighton Andrews that many of the skills used by lobbyists originated with the charities who were among the first to feel the need for effective lobbying. This is an interesting contrast: management consultants have brought private sector techniques into government, while experience from the voluntary sector has been imported into political lobbying. By way of recompense, perhaps, many lobbyists offer their skills to selected voluntary bodies to assist in their campaigning *pro bono publico* on a no fee or reduced fee basis: these have included issues such as the plight of Vietnamese boat people in Hong Kong; haemophiliacs and their carers; and lowering the homosexual age of consent.

There was also the long campaign by the Friends of John McCarthy to free him from captivity. It had been going on for more than three years with the support of a handful of MPs but without noticeable progress, and gained a new impetus when Leighton Andrews offered his professional help. Over the next year or so, he had not only helped to gather more than 150 signatures for an Early Day Motion but had also persuaded MPs to ask twenty-nine Parliamentary Questions on the hostage issue. By April 1991 McCarthy was a household name and the Body Shop was giving away yellow ribbons. This, like the other *pro bono publico* campaigns, sought to use public opinion to increase pressure on government.

The new style lobbyists are the latest newcomers to the small world that comprises central British politics, where close proximity means that the lobbying and the lobbied are known to each other. The painstaking and detailed research of the lobbyists' stock-in-trade is carried out in the context of a labyrinth of networks that requires constant maintenance and refurbishment because of the relatively high velocity of circulation amongst the personnel involved. In Charles Miller's view the break up of the old Establishment around 1970 ensured that decisions were no longer made by a close-knit circle. The decomposition of the old order, which had provided Oliver Franks and Edwin Plowden with their networks, put a higher premium on 'know how' and 'know who' so that 'those who can forge links between government and organisations are increasingly indispensable'. (Jordan, 1991, p.52) This is the sociological cause for the emergence of the new style lobbyist.   When the old boy network flourished it was enough to rely on acquaintances in clubland or if necessary to co-opt a peer or former minister to the company board. While such contacts are still used today these are no longer sufficient. A second cause was the technological revolution with its consequent explosion in electronically transmitted information. The monitoring, decoding and assessment of information sources opened up a market which the lobbyists quickly entered. It is true that such activity can be and is undertaken by commercial organisations, voluntary bodies, local authorities and government itself but there is clearly a widely perceived need for additional external assistance of the kind which lobbyists provide. Like the management consultants they can bring a fresh eye to things, unencumbered by office politics or traditional attitudes, a comparative perspective of competitors' or government reactions, and a feel for trends, opportunities, and potential threats. Most major enterprises have created their own departments of public affairs in recent years - there were none fifteen years ago - and it has been estimated that up to forty per cent of chief executives' time is now spent on public affairs. These developments have been prompted by the sort of regulations emanating from Whitehall and Westminster, tightening up codes of practice and issuing guidelines to be followed, as well as by the flow of edicts coming out from the

European Commission. Brussels has added a further dimension to the work of lobbyists and the leading companies now have their own offices or associated companies in there. The nature and complexity of European Union policy-making will offer increasing scope for lobbyists.

The combination of sociological, technological and European factors will ensure a continuing demand for their services. But the question remains why they seem to have been so easily accommodated by officials and politicians alike.

Officials need information to form policy and administer it well; to respond to parliamentary questions (which may of course have been prompted by a lobbyist). Equally, civil servants want to be able to brief ministers in their dealings with both the standing (legislative) and select (investigative) Committees of the House of Commons; the latter were expanded in numbers and scope after 1979. Feedback is an essential component of government by consent in today's complex world. Ministers and departments want to be associated with success, to be seen to have taken all views into account, and to have consulted widely. Many lobbyists and many MPs see it as an essential part of the democratic process - 'The right of the electorate to lobby the elected is fundamental to democracy', said the Select Committee (HC 586 of 1990-91) - though perhaps many would feel that Austin Mitchell MP was going too far when he described it as the only open part of government, 'the place where the arguments are put and tested' (Jordan, 1991, p.9).

It should not be forgotten however that politicians need lobbyists because MPs are under-resourced, certainly by comparison with the USA. A former chairman of the 1922 Committee expressed this clearly when giving evidence to the Select Committee on Members' Interests in 1988: he was very grateful to the aviation lobby, he said, most of whom had been well know to him for 25 years, for their assistance 'in enabling us to have an informed basis upon which to criticise the administration of the day' (HC 518 of 1987-8, p.1).

There are many reasons for government in its various manifestations to welcome contact if not pressure (Charles Miller prefers the word 'inform' to the word 'pressure'). As Jordan points out, 'the professional lobbyists are performing a useful service for the departments in disciplining the representations from the outside in a way that makes them most useful for Whitehall' (Jordan, op. cit., p.30). On this view, the lobbyist is not 'some kind of intruder into the private deliberations of the department: he is just another voice in the constant dialogue between the department, trade association, companies, consumer groups, etc.' (op. cit., p.31). In the course of this dialogue, civil servants hope to gain information which may improve policy and also make it more acceptable. Advice from outside can also sometimes, and this is a reminder of management consultants, bolster a department or person against opponents within the civil service, but lobbyists must maintain contact with them, Miller says. This use of consultants and other lobbyists to channel and control information is a symptom of overload. Information from lobbyists' clients can help departments to design sensible policies and consequently elicit consent to those policies when they are framed and subsequently cooperate with their implementation.

But information of a considered and well prepared kind is also useful to Whitehall because of the increasing fragmentation and complexity of public affairs and because of the diminished state of its own capacity. Its research and intelligence gathering abilities are not what they were due to cuts in staff levels, early retirements and a growing exodus of senior and experienced staff into the private sector. The DTI was an example cited to us (A. Gifford interview, 8 March 1994).

There are those, however, who take a different view about the benign effects of reciprocity and interchange that has been built up between lobbyists and government. Two quite separate questions are raised: one concerned with the cost effectiveness of lobbyists, and the other with whether or not their activities suborn rather than facilitate the democratic process.

Charles Clarke, Neil Kinnock's former aide, sees lobbying as a proper part of the democratic process and indeed has set up his own consultancy to teach public and voluntary bodies how to lobby more effectively on their own account rather than hiring lobbyists who, he judges, are either buying influence and thus are corrupting influences or they are not in which case they are commercially fraudulent. He believes the defence industry and particularly the overseas sales of armaments are areas for concern. Against this some Conservative backbenchers, such as Teresa Gorman, think that most of the money spent on lobbying is wasted; no substantive item of business had been blocked or seriously accelerated by 'the lobbying classes' in her opinion (*PR Week*, 28 October 1993). For each of these views, as we have seen in the case of Austin Mitchell the Labour MP, and Lady Olga Maitland the Conservative MP, there is one who thinks lobbying is effective and necessary. In many types of business such as advertising and even the law it is not easy to measure accurately specific contributions to what are regarded by clients as successful outcomes.

The select committee on Members' Interests, set up in 1969, has regularly reviewed the role played by lobbyists. When the register of interests was established in 1974-5, the primary motive was to 'reassure the public in the aftermath of the Poulson affair, that the House of Commons was not corrupt'. This a quotation from a letter written by Sir Geoffrey Johnson-Smith to Mr Neil Hamilton when *The Guardian* first revealed the visit of the latter to the Paris Ritz (*The Times*, 22 October 1994).

In 1983, three further registers were drawn up, listing lobby journalists, research assistants and all party groups, but these were not open for the public to see and the committee did not at that time consider the position of MPs, of whom there appeared to be a growing number, who were consultants to lobbying firms. The register of members interests did not require MPs to reveal how much they were paid for such work or to list the clients of the firms with which they were connected.

Over the next decade as lobbying activities increased enormously, there was growing doubt concerning these relationships. The Select Committee intermittently investigated the activities of lobbyists and considered whether they should be curbed. What it signally failed to do as the activities of the professional persuaders became more evident was to look to the conduct of members themselves. 'Westminster's lackadaisical attitude looks less like a naïve anachronism than self-serving neglect' commented the *Economist* (24 September 1994). The lobbying firms generally took the line that if a register was required it should be compiled and administered by the Commons, while the PR firms were more prepared to become involved in voluntary arrangements organised by the PRCA. In 1991 the Select Committee decided that a register should be set up but did nothing. After two years delay, on 28 June 1993, the Commons decided to draw up a new register of Members Interests and to oblige lobbyists to register themselves.

As a result of this unusually decisive move, during 1994 several positive moves came from the two lobby groups. The PRCA launched a Code and Register for professional parliamentary advisers, which required lobbyists to identify themselves and their clients as well as any MP who received any payments or benefits from them. It would not however give details of what MPs were paid nor what they were paid for. The inadequacy of this approach was highlighted by the *Sunday Times* 'sting' of two

Conservative MPs apparently prepared to table parliamentary questions for a £1,000 fee. Eventually the Privileges Committee suspended the two MPs for ten and twenty days, but laid some blame at the door of the *Sunday Times.*

Simultaneously the five most prominent lobby firms led by Charles Miller, who had let it be known that they would prefer to be regulated by Parliament, formed the Association of Professional Political Consultants and established their own code. Pouring scorn on the public relations group register as a 'cricketers' golfing society', they decided that payments to MPs must now be beyond the pale. A number of MPs, including Sir Marcus Fox and Menzies Campbell, resigned from Westminster Communications so that their firm could join the group. Others too joined the APPC, but before the Privileges Committee could investigate the matter, the whole issue of the activities of lobbyists and MPs accepting payments exploded unto the front pages, with revelations concerning Mohammed Fayed, the owner of Harrods and two junior ministers Tim Smith and Neil Hamilton. Jonathan Aitken, too, was alleged to have stayed at the Paris Ritz, owned by the Fayeds, at someone else's expense. Mr Fayed had had lengthy involvements with the government both over the 1985 Harrods takeover, which had not been referred to the MMC, and his application for British citizenship which was rejected; but he had also apparently made a large donation to Conservative Party funds. An investigation by Sir Robin Butler had uncovered 'no wrongdoing by Ministers'. However Neil Hamilton left office and simultaneously the Prime Minister announced an enquiry under Lord Nolan, to investigate the standards of public life. The terms of reference were very broad: it would cover lobbying activities, the question of former ministers moving into lucrative jobs and appointments to quangoes. It would not investigate individual cases, but rather draw up rules for future behaviour. A description of the enquiry by Matthew Parris in *The Times* (26 October 1994) as the 'quintessential quango', seemed fairly apt. The membership of the Committee certainly ran to traditional form, with representatives from all three parties, a banker, a diplomat and an academic.

Though the action of appointing it was speedy, and the independence of Nolan had been established in 1991 when he found Kenneth Baker in contempt of court over the deportation of an asylum seeker, the enquiry appeared the least possible that the Prime Minister could have provided in a feverish atmosphere of sleaze.

While transparency and integrity are always to be welcomed, it has to be stressed that such irregularities as have been unearthed have all concerned MPs, not lobbyists. It is ironic that while lobbyists contrive mostly successfully to get a good press for their clients, their own general image comes close to the saloon bar caricature. While, doubtless, some sail close to the wind at times, no lobbyists as yet are part of the alumni of Ford Open Prison. Nothing they have done is remotely comparable with the recent run of commercial scams and scandals, such as the Bank of International Credit and Commerce, Barlow Clowes, the Levitt Group or the Robert Maxwell pension fraud. Nor, apparently, have they been implicated in any political cover-ups - for example, they are unlikely to be cited in the Scott Report on the Matrix Churchill affair. Nor have they been sued for professional incompetence as have some accountancy practices, who are now lobbying the government to change the law on liabilities for audits of troubled companies. The 'Big Six' practices hired Ian Greer Associates to assist in amending the 1985 Companies Act (*Sunday Telegraph*, 10 October 1993) but withdrew from the contract during the 'parliamentary questions for cash' uproar that occurred in the autumn of 1994.

Lobbying will continue to grow especially perhaps in the areas of transport, financial services and health care (Nigel Clarke Interview, 8 March 1994). It is possible that in the future charities like Age Concern will make common cause with insurance and pension companies to secure tax and other benefits. Some lobbyists do not foresee any notable US-style developments in the practice of lobbying in this country because it has neither the weak whipping system of the American Congress nor such a frequent pattern of elections, to which could be added the lack of a strict separation of powers and a federal system all of which make government more accessible to lobbyists.

The US constitution, so potentially unworkable and ungovernable, seems to require the services of some 80,000 lobbyists in Washington, DC - ten per cent of the capital's population - to oil the wheels of the machine. A BBC Radio 4 programme (*Analysis*, 9 February 1993) described them as a 'permanent and pervasive force', so pervasive indeed that no less than thirteen out of a total of eighteen members of President Clinton's first cabinet appointees were former lobbyists. Another main reason accounting for the size of the Washington lobby is the high cost of electioneering in America, so that a good deal of the activity is directed towards fundraising. In Britain the cost of election campaigning is much more subject to legal limitations.

Nevertheless, differences between the two countries, whatever the formal structures, are diminishing in certain respects. John Major's government, returned with its small overall majority after 1992, has experienced great difficulty in whipping rebellious factions into line and has had to conclude compromising deals not only with its own recalcitrant backbenchers but also with some of the minority parties including the Ulster Unionists and, earlier on specific issues, with the Liberal Democrats. The House of Lords, despite its in-built Tory majority, has also successfully forced the government to climb down on numerous occasions. Furthermore, when European and local government elections coincide, as in 1994, they are not so different from the elections occurring in the mid-term of a US presidency, for both are seen as referendums on a government's performance. Some lobbyists, such as Leighton Andrews, see a reflection of American practices emerging in Britain, first because Parliament in the post-Thatcher era has become more assertive and fractious and secondly because of the growing influence of the European Union. (Interview, 9 March 1994). Politics in Brussels is much more like that of Washington partly because of the more legalistic basis of its operations. Increasingly, on this view, lawyers are likely to take on many of the functions currently performed by lobbyists. Clifford Chance, one of the largest law firms in London, has recently created its own lobbying unit.

As in the UK, there has been an upsurge in the activity of lobbyists over the last decade or so in and around all the institutions of what is now the European Union. Many if not all of the main British lobby firms have offices or associates in Brussels and concern has been increasingly expressed about the influence lobbyists have on policy formulation as well as on the deliberations of the European Parliament and even the European Court of Justice.

But the Commission has from the start encouraged the formation of interest groups at European level. At least 700 of these exist at present, ranging from the European Federation of Chemical Industries, an association of consumer groups, to a collection of local authorities. And a recent estimate reckoned that there is one pressure group employee for every Commission official (Grant, 1995, p.98).

As in the UK, overload has something to do with this. Those who work in the Brussels bureaucracy, which is surprisingly small, less than the size of the Scottish Office, are often short on technical knowledge, overworked and therefore vulnerable to pressure, so that a lobbyist who knows his facts and can argue his case convincingly may achieve a lot. The Commission has 1,000 advisory committees which offer opportunities for every imaginable special interest to put forward its own point of view. Also, since Maastricht the legal requirements imposed on the Commission formally to consult with the European Parliament and other agencies, as well as with the Council of Ministers, in the formulation of directives offers additional points at which lobbyists can apply influence. Thus, as in the UK there are symbiotic relationships between civil servants and outside interests; Brussels is still an 'adolescent bureaucracy' which needs to obtain detailed information from national groups and experts (Mazey and Richardson, 1993, p.10), and Brussels staffers are usually quite young.

The widening scope of community legislation and strengthened powers of the European parliament have both increased the need for interest groups and others to exert influence there rather than at home. Monitoring events in Brussels is a major task, especially since reconciling the conflicting interests of so many nations and groups entails constant redrafting of proposals and the legislative programme is subject to frequent changes. The DG structure adds extra complexity, and the unpredictability of outcomes means that quick fix 'fire brigade' campaigns are often required (Mazey and Richardson, 1993, p.96).

The style of politics in Brussels is very different from London, much more open than any national bureaucracy, perhaps resembling Washington more than any European capital in its informality, accessibility and fluidity. However, British interest groups characteristically prefer national methods and channels to those in Brussels, feeling more secure amid the familiar policy communities of Whitehall and Westminster. British companies have been slow to adjust to the opportunities and exigencies of policy making in the EU. There is a good deal of sense in taking this line; influencing national officials remains crucial, and they are strong allies in European negotiations, but it is also necessary to target others, particularly the Commission, since trade offs are often made (Mazey and Richardson, 1993).

Like Washington the Brussels scene is one where 'much depends on informal social contacts, in which power is the currency of social exchange' (op. cit., p.34). This is reinforced by the presence of quite a few American law firms and 'Amcham', the American Chamber of Commerce, which represents eighty US organisations and is probably the most effective lobbying organisation in Brussels (op. cit., p.7). All of these circumstances help to explain why professional lobbyists have in recent years vastly increased their numbers in Brussels. Hill and

Knowlton employs more than twenty consultants and estimates of the total number of lobbyists in town ranged from 3000 to 10,000 in 1993-94.

British and American lobbyists far outnumber those from European countries. Lobbying is also done by other professionals, mostly the law firms, by PR firms, by Euro-federations and other industrial groupings. Professional lobbyists, especially if they can demonstrate political awareness and technical expertise, can find plenty of work to do. Another reason for British interests to hire professionals is that FCO and Cabinet Office officials are accessible only to the most senior business people and the best of the lobbying firms. Lead departments and UKREP are easier to reach; and this is a vital route of influence. Such is the pressure exerted by lobbyists on the European Parliament that attempts are being made to impose some kind of control. In September 1994, immediately after the two UK groups were formed, nineteen consultancies in Brussels launched a code of conduct, an initiative supported by the commission. Though less stringent than the code of the British APPC it prohibits financial inducements to EU officials. The European Parliament was putting in hand some public hearings and it was said that permanent passes would only be available to those who would sign a code of conduct.

US lobbying firms are beginning to try and use American methods - relying more on glossy PR and manipulating public opinion, seeing British methods as 'too analytical' (*PR Week*, 18 November 1994). Though British lobbyists are sceptical about how effective this approach is likely to be, with national electorates much less closely linked to MEPs than US voters are to their Washington representatives or British ones to their MPs, it is certainly the case that in a move away from fairly technical issues on which all groups lobbied the Commission, the balance of power in EU institutions is changing and the atmosphere is becoming more overtly political.

The Nolan Committee published its first set of proposals in May 1995. Six of its main recommendations related to lobbying. First, there should be an independent Parliamentary Commission for Standards to investigate complaints against MPs. Secondly, MPs should be banned for working gainfully for lobbyists. Thirdly, MPs should disclose all earnings arising from their parliamentary activities. Fourthly, ex-ministers should have clearance before taking up appointments in private industry within two years of vacating office. Fifthly, greater protection should be afforded to 'whistle-blowers' in the civil service when revealing malpractices. Sixthly, a tighter code should be drawn up governing the behaviour of Ministers in office. In the immediate aftermath of its publication, the report received a warm welcome in the press though a MORI poll conducted for the Joseph Rowntree Reform Trust (JRRT) revealed that the proposals, in the public's view, were not stringent enough and 67 per cent would have preferred the full force of the law to deal with erring MPs (JRRT/MORI, *State of the Nation*, 1995). In the ensuing Commons' debate, however, some Conservative MPs expressed reservations about revealing earnings, on the grounds of an invasion of individual privacy, and about the desirability of an Independent Parliamentary Commissioner because such an innovation would be contrary to the principle of parliamentary sovereignty.

Over the summer recess the Conservative majority on the select committee, to which the Report had been referred, hardened in its opposition to the main recommendation that MPs should be required to disclose all outside earnings derived from their role as MPs. However, on 7 November 1995 in a free vote in the House of Commons enough Conservatives joined the opposition parties to ensure that all of the Nolan proposals, including the complete disclosure of lobby-type earnings, would be adopted by Parliament and fully enforced in the future.

Following Nolan, whatever mutations may occur in the twilight milieu in which lobbyists operate, their role and functions will continue to form an enduring and vital part of both the British and European political scenes. The difficulties of contemporary government and the decline of traditional institutions and conventions mean that lobbyists in one form or another are an essential part of the *nomenklatura* of the post-modern world.

10 Conclusion: Fixers and the Deficient Constitution

The previous chapters have described the circumstances in which governments have resorted to fixers to deal with particular crises. Individual fixers crop up regularly but more recently, as crises have become not only episodic but also endemic in character, so the system is increasingly dependent on the services of the corporate fixers. Their appearance on the political scene indicates the profound changes that are taking place in the conduct of contemporary government while reflecting a deep-seated political malaise and a growing constitutional deficit.

As was remarked at the outset of this book, fixers and fixing are as old as government itself, though the precise character of both the role and the activity will vary according to prevailing circumstances. The perspective afforded by the last half century reveals both continuity and innovation within an increasingly dynamic and permeable milieu. Some of the turbulence has been internally generated, but most of it is the result of external forces that affect the governing of all liberal democracies. The most significant of these world-wide forces is increasing globalisation including the activities of multi-national enterprises, a growing concern for ecological and environmental considerations, and the tropical growth of information and its simultaneous universal dissemination, also to be seen in the international mass media networks that transmit broadcasts, newspapers and journals across all frontiers.

All of these factors, exogenous to the single nation state, have rendered the art of government far more difficult than in previous eras. Governments have reacted to this loss of control in various ways attempting to recover their authority, or at least to minimise the extent of control loss. Among such endeavours has been a greater reliance on inter-governmental collaboration, of which the European Union is the most developed example, but even then such collaboration is too often only reluctantly pursued. Additionally, there are the related problems of consensus-building, which demand compromise and hence the formulation of policies that fall short of being fully robust.

Within their own domestic jurisdictions the recent fashion has been for governments to slim down to their core businesses, by divesting themselves of what are now defined as inappropriate or peripheral activities. Privatisation has proved a popular policy, using such means as the sale of state-owned industries, putting services previously run by the state out to commercial tender, or at least requiring existing services to be market tested against private sector criteria. The retreat from the modes and methods of traditional bureaucracy is also to be seen in the delegation of executive functions from government ministries to hived-off para-state agencies headed, as often as not, by chief executives on fixed-term contracts with bonus payments for meeting pre-determined performance targets. Within the residual civil service, hierarchies have been flattened and job specifications made more task-oriented and hence less formally demarcated, while bonus payments, short-term contracts and the public advertisement of senior posts to attract recruits with outside experience are all increasingly favoured. (Massey, 1995 and Gray & Jenkins, 1995)

Whatever their benefits, and they are still too recent to be fully evaluated, these innovations are not without their drawbacks. The privatised public utilities may well become more efficient by importing techniques from private business, but as natural monopolies for the most part they will always constitute a potential political minefield for government. They are clearly not the equivalent of other private sector enterprises exposed to the competition of the market, which was part of the rationale for their nationalisation in the first place. The precise nature of the problems they now present may be different from those under nationalisation, but they still largely concern accountability about such sensitive issues as senior executives' remuneration, that were raised in 1994-95, or pricing, as in the case of the electricity industry and the interventions by its regulator Professor Stephen Littlechild. The progressive Conservatives of the 1930s, such as Harold Macmillan, Oliver Stanley and Robert Boothby, fully recognised the inherent political difficulties which the control of natural monopolies presented (Smith, 1979, pp.32-39); they have still to be resolved.

A similar problem exists in the case of the hived-off executive agencies, such as those set up under the Next Steps reforms. Like the privatised monopolies they are essentially in limbo as far as adequate public accountability is concerned, occupying, as they do, a constitutional no-man's land. They are no longer subject to proper parliamentary scrutiny and it seems far from certain that satisfactory provision has been made for ministerial direction and appraisal of these agencies. Managerialist drives in the quest for greater efficiency are no substitute for formal constitutional provision to ensure democratic accountability. Moreover, the capacity of ministers themselves has been further undermined by substitution of the conventional bureaucracy by a swashbuckling technocracy. This can be seen in the personnel policies now prevalent in the higher civil service whose research and advisory roles have been seriously eroded as a result.

R.A.W. Rhodes has summarised the dilemmas thrown up by current trends and tendencies:

> To talk of the hollowing out of the state is to signal there are potentially dramatic changes underway in British government. Government is smaller. Both central and local government are losing functions to other agencies and to the EU. Service delivery systems proliferate. The role of officials is increasingly constrained by new management systems and political controls. The obvious outcomes of these changes are fragmentation and diminished accountability. There is also a less visible but more important erosion of central capability. This erosion, coupled with the arrival of the information polity, enlarges the potential for catastrophe. (Rhodes, 1994, p.151)

Thus, the sovereignty of parliament and the self-determination of central government have been very severely curtailed by recent reforms. These reforms consequently exacerbate the very problems they were meant to resolve by increasing the likelihood of specific crises erupting from time to time while providing fertile conditions for debilitating, longer term afflictions to become endemic. In such circumstances, it is safe to predict that fixers and fixing will continue to play an increasingly important part in contemporary government. Not only is there an irony and an inevitability about this, there is also a circularity built into the process; many of the most recent developments derive from the specific recommendations of individual fixers, such as Lord Rayner and Sir Roy Griffiths and the firms of management consultants, and more generally from the managerialist climate of which they are the personification.

Further difficulties for governments and governing arise from the formation of the mass society as a direct result of the development of the mass media. It follows that political elites now stand in too stark a juxtaposition with the electorate for, with the coming of television, there has been a concomitant decline in the vitality of local political parties, local government, the trade unions, chambers of commerce, Rotary Clubs and other such intermediating and civically energising agencies. Paradoxically, as the distance between the governors and the governed has been dramatically foreshortened by means of television, so the degree of political disaffection on the part of the public has widened (Smith, 1994). Electorates now exhibit much greater volatility in their voting behaviour which adds to the turbulence of the political milieu.

Politicians, in Britain as elsewhere, are acutely aware of the problem and have responded in two main ways. First, there has been a return to fundamentals in the form of the conviction politics that was the hall-mark of the Thatcher/Reagan years and which their ideological heirs in the form of the Conservative Eurosceptic faction in Britain and Speaker Newt Gingrich in America seek to sustain. Secondly, as the political class has felt itself becoming increasingly detached from civil society so it has sought to compensate for this by increasing its grip on the institutions of the state. Both responses have led to a growing ideological authoritarianism and greater political corruption. The latter is nowadays described generically as 'sleaze', a term that refers to a variety of transgressions ranging from ministerial cover-ups, nest-feathering, under-the-counter payments to parties and individual legislators, to nepotism and patronage. Sleaze is not confined to Britain and afflicts most liberal democracies (Smith, 1995). The over-identification of party with state, therefore, has generated a number of unintended and unfortunate, if inevitable, consequences that in turn have led to a further reliance on fixers and a discernible mutation in the activity of fixing.

That mutation is to be seen in the growing interchangeability of fixing roles, while the speed of change is accelerating perceptibly. A striking illustration is provided by the career of Dr Norman Blackwell who has alternated between spells working for McKinsey as a senior management consultant with periods in the policy unit at 10 Downing Street, first for Margaret Thatcher and currently as its head, for John Major; still only forty-two when appointed in January 1995, he has many years left to take on any number of fixing roles. Nor is his career in any way unique. A written answer by the Prime Minister about the thirty-six special advisers to ministers revealed that four were officially classified as non-party political experts; the remainder consisted of nine *apparatchiks* from

Conservative Central Office, five from lobbyist or public relations backgrounds, four ex-management consultants, three henchmen who had worked immediately previously as ministerial aides, two former journalists, one from a think tank, one from a leading law firm, and a residual group of seven from various forms of employment (*Hansard*, 1995, Cols. 243-4, 18 May).

Another feature of role interchangeability is the movement of former civil servants into management consultancy which quadrupled in the years from 1989 to 1993. In 1989 of the 622 officials leaving Whitehall 77 (12 per cent) became consultants. By 1993 of the 372 leaving, 191 (51 per cent) opted for consultancy. According to one press report:

> The rise coincides with a huge increase in consultancy work, with some leading firms like Price Waterhouse, Arthur Andersen and Ernst & Young attracting growing numbers of ex-civil servants and business across Whitehall.
>
> Price Waterhouse, for example, is known to hold an annual party to attract civil servants who may want to leave Whitehall. ('More quit Whitehall to be consultants', *Guardian*, 13 January 1995).

Whereas Franks, Edwin Plowden, Goodman and other individual fixers constituted rare elements in the political life of the nation, the penetration of those from corporate fixing backgrounds into government and *vice versa* is now commonplace. They are all part of the scaffolding used to shore up the hollowed-out state, in part by re-treading those who have been hollowed out.

As striking as this development, perhaps, are the changes involving the judiciary. First, there has been a noticeable shift in its collective mind-set over the past decade, whereby judges are becoming less reticent about their role and are becoming much more prepared to be pro-active in striking down actions of the executive branch of government. One of the underlying reasons for this reorientation undoubtedly includes the increasing recourse to the High Court by aggrieved parties for judicial review of decisions taken by ministers and civil servants; applications for judicial review have risen from 200 in 1974 to nearly 3,000 in 1994. There is, then, growing demand for greater judicial intervention in the decisions of government. The judges, moreover, have shown a willingness, when they deem it merited, to censure ministers severely and where practical to overturn their decisions. Secondly, recent appointments have prompted a more reformist mood: Lord Chief Justice Taylor and

Master of the Rolls Sir Thomas Bingham, for example, are modernisers who support, among other measures, the incorporation of the European Convention on Human Rights into British law. Thirdly, the European Union is providing a further stimulus for, as Mr Justice Sedley has observed '... the House of Lords has now recognised that our constitution knows such a thing as fundamental law - the European Communities Act 1972 - capable of over-riding subsequent primary legislation if the courts find the two to be in conflict'. ('A right to law', *Guardian*, 11 May 1995) The judiciary has had to become more interventionist to compensate for the growing deficiency of the constitution.

The three developments alluded to above are influencing the work of judges in their conventional roles as, what we have termed, routine fixers. Very recently, however, they are being used, in the manner of Oliver Franks, as non-routine fixers. This development is to be seen most starkly in the appointment of Lord Justice Scott to inquire into the 'arms to Iraq' Matrix Churchill affair and Lord Justice Nolan to preside over a committee to formulate new codes of practice regarding the conduct of MPs, and especially their employment by lobbyists, public appointments to government agencies, and other such areas that have given rise to public concerns and accusations of sleaze. These commissions as non-routine fixers go with the grain of greater judicial interventionism but are a quite distinct development. Hugo Young has suggested a reason for this:

> ... for an increasing range of purposes a senior judge, whether a Nolan or a Scott, is held to be the sole reliable possessor of the scarcest commodity of our age: political independence. ('Umpires now turning into players', *Guardian*, 9 May 1995)

Sleaze had reached such epidemic proportions, in other words, that the Prime Minister had no option but to select judges of the highest probity to investigate the issues referred to them. They had to be, and be seen to be, beyond reproach so that their conclusions could not be open to whitewash criticisms of the kind levied against the Falklands Enquiry conducted by Lord Franks. This has not stopped rearguard actions by some parliamentarians to dilute some of the Nolan committee's recommendations, nor a pre-emptive attempt in Westminster and Whitehall circles to rubbish Lord Justice Scott's report, prior to publication, as being politically naïve and questioning the procedures adopted by him as being fundamentally flawed (Smith, 1995). Whatever the specific consequences of Scott and Nolan, the use of judges in such non-routine fixing roles is likely to grow, but this practice, too, is not risk-free as Hugo Young has indicated:

> The shift we are watching, constitutional in its depth, is not towards detachment but engagement. The judges are becoming more not less important, in the political as well as the judicial arena, a trend which exposes an interesting question: for how long can peo-le whose influence depends upon their reputation for neutrality survive, undiminished, their evolution into active players in governmental controversy? (op. cit.)

In the USA the Supreme Court is a highly political actor as guardian of the Constitution, but its independence is guaranteed by strict adherence to the doctrine of the separation of powers. Britain, with an unwritten constitution that rests on a fusion of powers between the executive and legislative branches of government, has nevertheless hitherto maintained fairly successfully the convention that the judiciary should be independent of the other two branches but subordinate to them. The point that Hugo Young rightly addresses is whether as senior judges become more involved in the resolution of politically contentious issues, in both their routine and non-routine fixing capacities, the convention will prove strong enough to preserve a truly independent judiciary: the crucial question is how to make use of its much needed skills to assist in the ever more difficult task of government, while sustaining its integrity and neutrality. If the judiciary ever comes to be regarded as merely one of the many sources which feed into one or more of the numerous policy networks that nowadays shape the public agenda, then it will be clear that the rule of law - one of the bastions of democratic constitutionalism - risks being seriously compromised.

As the constitution has unravelled so it has become fashionable to resort to the concept of 'policy networks' as a means of reimposing some analytical order on our understanding of the workings of contemporary government. Some thirty years ago A.H. Birch perceptively realised that the constitutional theories developed in the preceding hundred years could no longer continue to be pressed into service. Accordingly, he in-geniously reworked Walter Bagehot's distinction between the 'dignified' and 'efficient' elements of the British constitution into what he termed the 'Liberal' and 'Whitehall' languages of the constitution to provide a more relevant interpretation of the operations of government (Birch, 1964). The

Liberal language denoted the collection of ideas, derived largely from the nineteenth century which, with their emphasis on parliamentary supremacy, afforded a means by which the constitution was and still is, for that matter, formally defined. The Whitehall language, on the other hand, offered a more realistic description of modern government with its stress on the significance of the Crown, its ministers and civil servants, and their interaction with political parties, pressure groups and the mass media. Birch argued that both languages were needed to understand contemporary government for the one complemented the other. This is now no longer the case. To be sure echoes of the Liberal language resonate in the arguments of those who oppose moves towards greater European integration, Scottish and Welsh devolution, electoral reform, or implementing some of the main recommendations of the Nolan Committee. But the doctrines of parliamentary sovereignty, ministerial and collective Cabinet responsibility and the like survive more in such rhetoric than in practice.

Much more important, however, is the fact that the Whitehall language is now seriously out-dated: the operations of government and the personnel involved in them are now too disaggregated and strung out to be easily encapsulated within the term Whitehall, while still less could they be accommodated within Bagehotian terminology as the 'efficient' element of government. Hence, the reliance on policy networks as a tool for describing the current configuration of decision-making (Dowding, 1995).

The advantage of such a tool is that it takes into account, and indeed underlines, contemporary reality which can no longer be explained in the terms of a relatively parsimonious vocabulary: the simple dualisms of Bagehot and Birch no longer suffice. The disadvantage is that the catch-all term 'networks' is merely descriptive and thus can make no comment of a normative kind. It cannot, that is to say, evaluate how far the so-called networks, that after all imply more holes than twine, however understandable their emergence or expediency, are an acceptable development in terms of constitutional propriety or democratic accountability. The very ephemerality of networks, as they ebb and flow, disperse and re-form both in terms of issues and personnel in response to ever-changing circumstances, raises serious problems for the proper ordering of public affairs. In the absence of any coherent attempts at re-ordering them, the sheer dynamics and volatility of the contemporary political milieu inevitably lead to ever greater reliance being placed on fixing and fixers, both individual and increasingly corporate, as a fall-back, make-do-and-mend, alternative of last resort.

This raises the question to what extent fixers aid and abet good democratic governance or contrariwise are inimical to it. The late Kenneth Tynan was in no doubt about the matter. According to his widow and biographer:

> There was nothing *laissez-faire* about Ken. When the pragmatists attacked him, he would counter that there was nothing so extreme as the 'tyranny of the middle way'. Typical of this tyranny, he argued, was Lord Goodman, the *eminence grise* behind many a reform movement of the period, and a 'fanatical compromiser'. Of this portly do-gooder and fixer, Ken wrote in 1972: 'When it actually seems as if real democracy might be about to exert some genuine influence on the nation's life, the ruling class produces an antibody to counter it. The antibody in our time is Lord Goodman. A man who has never held elective office, he has wielded more power than anyone in the country, except for the Prime Minister, during the last decade'. (Tynan, 1995, p.240)

Tynan worked for the National Theatre with Laurence Olivier and had clashed with Goodman when he was chairman of the Arts Council. Discounting Tynan's hyperbole, the point is nevertheless well made. As a romantic left-leaning radical Tynan was temperamentally as dismissive of consensus as was Margaret Thatcher from her right-wing viewpoint: conviction politics, from whatever source, by definition is impatient of anything that falls short of the full implementation of ideological goals. But when there is a collision between those with strongly held views from different ends of the spectrum or, less loftily, when warring pragmatists adopt intransigent stances, how are matters to be resolved? Simon Jenkins has provided at least a partial answer in his obituary of Arnold Goodman:

> The present denizens of Downing Street believe they can do without Goodmans. Graduates of the Thatcher charm school believe that government by 'one of us' can get by with no such creatures. The result is that when they hit trouble, as all government does, they turn to merchant bankers, cabinet secretaries or judges, whose talents tend to be investigative, judicial and expensive rather than conciliatory.
>
> ... Faced with *Spycatcher*, or Matrix Churchill, with a Ritz hotel bill or nurses on strike, Goodman would have gone off quietly into the

night and not resurfaced until a deal was done. He was no politician, but he offered politics a talent it surely needs. Without a Goodman, a government is one long slither to a fall. (*Spectator*, 20 May 1995)

This is only a partial answer to Tynan in so far as it stoutly defends Goodman's activities in the 1960s and 1970s. Where it errs is in the assertion that the services of a Goodman in the 1990s could be a magic solvent. The situation has now deteriorated to the point beyond the remedial ministrations of a single crisis fixer however dextrous.

Individual fixers like Franks, Goodman or Sir Ron Dearing are a necessary adjunct to government and perform a crucial service in settling crises of an episodic sort. Their work is impaired to the extent that they are perceived, by routine fixers in the form of elected politicians, as being akin to double agents. The fact that fixers are called in at all is itself a standing rebuff to politicians, because it means they have failed to prevent an issue becoming a crisis or else have been incapable of dealing with it once it had erupted. Fixers are only ever grudgingly brought in as a last resort. They know this as well as anyone, and this awareness often constrains their approach: they seek to do deals, to compromise, or temper their proposals, not just because of the nature of the crisis subject matter they deal with, but also and not unnaturally because they want their proposals to succeed and be accepted by those immediately concerned, which is helped by attracting wider support. If politicians are resentful of fixers, because their very existence reflects badly on them, by the same token they are often highly selective in picking and choosing between the recommendations that fixers make; those they dislike they seek to ignore, dilute or rubbish. The recent outbreak of sleaze in public life has necessitated the appointment of senior judges, like Nolan and Scott, because the dimension of the sleaze crises would have been beyond the capacities and skills of a Goodman: indeed, while calling on someone like him might earlier have contained it, such is the extent of the problem and the degree of public concern generated, that his essentially behind-the-scenes approach would have aggravated the situation and aroused even greater scepticism and cynicism. Where a Goodman might have helped was in his psychotherapeutic role, counselling a Prime Minister increasingly beset by the sleazy behaviour of his ministers and backbenchers.

To the question do fixers aid and abet good governance, then, it is reasonable to conclude that individual fixers are both necessary and, in the main, useful accessories for dealing with systemic crises that inevitably blow up from time to time. The recent and very dramatic rise of the corporate fixers, however, is much more problematic.

Although the term 'lobbyists' has a sleazy connotation the evidence does not support this. While there are occasional lapses from best practice, their role is not subversive of democracy. As was pointed out in the last chapter, their sudden rise can be explained in terms of the dynamics of technological change and especially the growth of electronic information systems, demographic changes within the political class, globalisation and the impact of the EU, and the depletions of the capacity of the regular civil service. There is a general acceptance that they provide good sources of information, advise their clients on campaign tactics, effect introductions and maintain contacts, and other such hand-holding services, though there is little firm evidence to prove that they exercise any real influence of an 'insider dealing' kind in shaping public policy, no matter how hard they try to project such an image. The problems arising from their activities relate more to the conduct of parliamentarians and their select committees in not formulating adequate protocols regulating the relations between lobbyists and Westminster. MPs, including ex-Ministers, have moonlighted as directors of or consultants to lobbying firms and this raised serious concerns, though awareness of these, and just prior to the appointment of the Nolan Committee, led many to withdraw from such direct association with lobbying agencies. With regard to Whitehall, and contacts with ministers and civil servants, the problem is that caused by the 'hollowing out of the state'; the decline in the career civil servant and the corresponding erosion of the Northcote-Trevelyan ethos whereby an impartial bureaucracy saw itself, much to the anger of conviction politicians, as the guardian of the long-term public interest, means there is less of a counter-weight to the importunities of professional lobbyists and indeed all kinds of external pressures.

The management consultants pose problems of an altogether different magnitude: they do influence policy, and procurement in particular; very large sums of money are involved both in the fees they charge and the contracts they advise on; and, as was related in Chapter 8, there have been some notable failures, sometimes due to incompetence but other times resulting from fraud. Management consultants also have an influence in that it is from their ranks that a significant number are recruited to serve in important political posts as henchmen or *apparatchiks*, to head up government agencies, and to lead major pressure groups: they constitute a significant cadre in the new *nomenklatura*. Thus, for example, before becoming Deputy Governor of the Bank of England, Howard Davies had been serially employed as a civil servant and diplomat, worked as a management consultant at McKinsey, run the Audit Commission and been Director General of the CBI.   His predecessor at the CBI and the Audit Commission was Sir John Banham, who had previously spent fourteen years with McKinsey, and later conducted the Local Government Commission.   As noted earlier, Dr Norman Blackwell is now ensconced in Downing Street again while Adair Turner is the new CBI Director General, and both came directly from McKinsey.

To cite these careers is not to complain that McKinsey appears to have more than its fair share of its *alumni* in such key posts, nor is it to imply in any way that the occupants are not capable of maintaining strict 'chinese walls' between their current and previous activities, for the problem is not one of individuals or a particular firm - it is one of their collective attitudes and predispositions.   The infiltration of management consultants into government and the close politics of major pressure groups is further corroboration of the continuing managerialist orientation that has been growing apace in government over the past few decades to the point where the old bureaucratic ethos has all but succumbed before the onslaught of a relentless technocratic ethos.   From a constitutional perspective this is a very significant loss because the criteria of accountability become so much weaker.

The rise of the management consultants is thus one more symptom of the deficient constitution; one more problem to be added to the risks relating to the use of judges as non-routine fixers, and the difficulties arising from the constitutional limbo into which the para-state agencies and privatised utility monopolies have been pitched.   The recourse to judges and management consultants as crisis fixers may be justified as necessary against the pressing needs of the moment but they have long-term deleterious side-effects.   Sir Winston Churchill's physician, Lord Moran, prescribed a cocktail of amphetamines to enable him to perform his prime ministerial duties on important occasions in the 1950s: each time an assessment had to be made of the priority of the occasion because, although they relieved the symptoms of dotage for a few hours enabling the patient to function reasonably well, they would leave him in a worse state than before.   The judges and the consultants as crisis fixers are medications of the same sort; they may work in the short-run, but in the long-run they leave the body politic more debilitated than previously.

As noted in the first chapter there is a growing chorus from all shades of political opinion calling for comprehensive constitutional reform. It is long overdue. Supporters of reform view the increasingly ramshackle operations of government from a variety of perspectives including those of the historian, lawyer, journalist, and political scientist. As well as reviewing the system and its shortcomings in the round they often latch on to particular deficiencies, be they in the fairness of the electoral system, the over-centralisation of political power, the weakness of parliamentary scrutiny, the need for a bill of rights or a freedom of information act and so on. In this book we have examined a hitherto largely neglected aspect of British politics - the nature and role of fixers and fixing and how both have developed since 1945. Not only are they intrinsically interesting but they illuminate in a unique way the degree to which our constitutional arrangements have decayed to the point where a purposeful codification is now an urgent priority. From a political economy perspective Will Hutton has recently arrived at much the same judgement but also points to the difficulty in addressing the problem:

> No state in the twentieth century has ever been able to recast its economy, political structures and society to the extent that Britain must do, without suffering defeat in war, economic collapse or revolution. Only traumatic events on that scale delegitimise the existing order to such an extent that a country concedes the case for dramatic change. (Hutton, 1995, p.319)

It may be that Will Hutton is unduly pessimistic; Spain, after all, managed the transition from the Franco regime to liberal democracy very smoothly, while the Scandinavian states and New Zealand seem capable of reviewing and renewing their constitutional arrangements on a regular basis without major disruption. In Britain the problem lies in the *immobilisme* of its parliamentarians, for the country at large has already embraced 'the case for dramatic change'. The first JRRT/MORI *State of the Nation* poll was conducted in 1991 and repeated in 1995. On almost all counts they reveal a continuing trend in favour of constitutional reform. Whereas in 1991 23 per cent felt that a great deal of improvement was needed in the system of government, four years later this had increased to 35 per cent, and correspondingly the proportion saying the system works well had fallen from a third (33 per cent) to a fifth (22 per cent) over the same period; an earlier MORI poll in 1973 found that almost half the electorate (48 per cent) thought the system was working well, so that the satisfaction rating has plummeted over the past twenty-two years. In answer to a new question in 1995 no less that 79 per cent favoured a written constitution, with only 7 per cent recording disagreement. In a breakdown of these figures Anthony Barnett has re-marked:

> Support for a written constitution is not a middle class, metropolitan opinion. It is higher among so called C2s (74 per cent) than ABs (70 per cent) and among those who read popular newspapers (79 per cent) than those who read the quality press (69 per cent). It is higher every where else in Britain (between 69 - 81 per cent) than in the capital (62 per cent). (Barnett, 1995, p.6)

These figures puncture previously held stereotypes that constitutional reform is a preoccupation of the chattering classes of Hampstead: it now has widespread popular support.

Unless the *parliamentary* will can be mobilised for a written constitution, reliance on fixers and fixing will steadily increase and the civic culture will deteriorate still further. In the meantime, perhaps the best tactic would be to propagate more self-appointed, unofficial fixers of the calibre of Michael Young.

Bibliography

Abrams, M. Rose, R. and Hinden, R. (1960), *Must Labour Lose?*, Penguin, Harmondsworth.

Acheson, Dean (1970), *Present at the Creation*, Macmillan, London.

Alderman, G. (1983), *The Jewish Community in British Politics*, Oxford University Press, Oxford.

Annan, Noel (1966), 'The Franks Report: from the nearside', *Universities' Quarterly*, Vol. 20, No. 4, September.

Annan, Noel (1991), *Our Age*, Fontana, London.

Attallah, Naim (1990), *Personally Speaking*, Quartet, London.

Banting, K. (1979), *Poverty Politics and Policy*, Macmillan, London.

Barnett, Anthony (1995), *The Defining Moment*, Charter 88, London.

Berry, Sebastian (1992), 'Lobbyists: techniques of the political Insiders', *Parliamentary Affairs*, Vol. 45, April.

Berry, Sebastian (1993), 'Lobbying: A Need to Regulate?', *Political Review*, February.

Birch, A.H. (1964), *Representative and Responsible Government*, Allen and Unwin, London.

Birkenhead, Lord (1969), *Walter Monckton*, Weidenfeld and Nicolson, London.

Blackstone, Tessa and Plowden, William (1988), *Inside the Think Tank*, Heinemann, London.

Blom-Cooper, Louis (1993), 'Public Enquiries', *Current Legal Problems*, Vol. 46.

Boyle, Peter G. (1990), 'Oliver Franks and the Washington Embassy 1948-52' in J. Zametica (ed.), *British Officials and British Foreign Policy*, Leicester University Press, Leicester.

Brandon, Henry (1988), *Special Relationships*, Macmillan, London.

Bray, A.J.M. (1988), 'The Clandestine Reformer: a study of the Rayner Scrutinies', Strathclyde Papers on Government and Politics, No. 55.

Brittan, S. (1971), *Steering the Economy*, Penguin, Harmondsworth.

Bullock, Alan (1984), *Ernest Bevin*, Heinemann, London.

Bulmer, Martin (1983), 'Increasing the Effectiveness of Royal Commissions: A Comment', *Public Administration*, Winter.

Bulmer, Martin (ed.) (1985), *Essays on the History of British Sociological Research*, CUP, Cambridge.

Bulmer, Martin (ed.) (1986), *Social Science and Social Policy*, Allen and Unwin, London.

Butler, R.A. (1973), *The Art of the Possible*, Penguin, Harmondsworth.

Caines, Eric (1993), 'Paying for the clash of cultures', *The Times*, 28 October.

Calder, Angus (1969), *The People's War*, Jonathan Cape, London.

Carrington, Lord (1988), *Reflect on things Past*, Fontana, London.

Castle, Barbara (1980), *The Castle Diaries 1974-6*, Weidenfeld and Nicolson, London.

Chapman, Leslie (1979), *Your Disobedient Servant*, Penguin, Harmondswoth.

Chester, D.N. (ed.) (1951), *Lessons of the British War Economy*, CUP, Cambridge.

Chester, Linklater and May (1979), *Jeremy Thorpe A Secret Life*, Fontana, London.

Clarke, R.W.B. (1978), *Public Expenditure, Management and Control*, Macmillan, London.

Cooper, Frank (1986), 'Changing the Establishment', *Political Quarterly*, Vol. 57, No. 3.

Crick, Bernard (1960), 'Socialist literature in the 1950s', *Political Quarterly*, Vol. 31, No. 3.

Crosland, Anthony (1956), *The Future of Socialism*, Jonathan Cape, London.

Crossman, Richard (1975-7), *The Diaries of a Cabinet Minister*, Vols. 1-3, edited by Janet Morgan, Hamish Hamilton and Cape, London.

Dalyell, Tam (1989), *Dick Crossman, A Portrait*, Weidenfeld and Nicolson, London.

Danchev, Alex (1992), *The Franks Report*, Pimlico, London.

Danchev, Alex (1993), *Oliver Franks, Founding Father*, Clarendon Press, Oxford.

Delafons, John (1982), 'Working in Whitehall: Changes in Public Administration 1952-82', *Public Administration*, Vol. 60, Autumn.

Donoughue, B. and Jones, G.W. (1973), *Herbert Morrison: Portrait of a Politician*, Weidenfeld and Nicolson, London.

Dowding, Keith (1995), 'Model or Metaphor?   A Critical Review of the Policy Network Approach', *Political Studies*, Vol. 43, No. 1.

Finer, S.E. (1958), *Anonymous Empire*, Pall Mall, London.

Fowler, Norman (1991), *Ministers Decide*, Chapmans, London.

Franks, Oliver (1947a), *Central Planning and Control in War and Peace*, Longman Green, London.

Franks, Oliver (1947b), *The Experience of a University Teacher in the Civil Service*, OUP, London.

Franks, Oliver (1955), *Britain and the Tide of World Affairs*, (Reith Lectures), OUP, London.

Fry, G.K. (1985), *The Changing Civil Service*, Allen and Unwin, London.

Fry, G.K. (1988), 'The Thatcher government, the FMI and the new Civil Service', *Public Administration*, Vol. 66, Spring.

Flynn A., Gray A., and Jenkins W. (1990), 'Taking the Next Steps: the changing management of government', *Parliamentary Affairs*, Vol. 43, No. 3.

Gaitskell, Hugh (1983), *The Diary of Hugh Gaitskell, 1945-56*, edited by P.M. Williams, Jonathan Cape, London.

Gilmour, Ian (1993), *Dancing with Dogma*, Simon and Schuster, London.

Goodman, Arnold (1972a), *Not for the Record*, André Deutsch, London.

Goodman, Arnold (1972b), 'Patronage Without Pain', *Public Administration*, Vol. 50, Autumn.

Goodman, Arnold (1993), *Tell Them I'm on My Way*, André Deutsch, London.

Grant, Wyn (1995), *Pressure Groups, Politics and Democracy in Britain*, Harvester Wheatsheaf, London.

Gray, A. and Jenkins, W. (1991), 'The Management of Change in Whitehall: the experience of the FMI', *Public Administration*, Vol. 69, Spring.

Gray, A. and Jenkins, W. (1995), 'From Public Administration To Public Management: Reassessing A Revolution', *Public Administration*, Vol. 73, Spring.

Greenleaf, W.H. (1987), *The British Political Tradition*, Vol. III, *A Much Governed Nation*, Methuen, London.

Greer, Ian (1985), *The Right to be Heard*, Ian Greer, London.

Griffith, J.A.G. (1958), 'The Franks Report', *Modern Law Review*, Vol. 21.

Griffith, J.A.G. (1959), 'Tribunals and enquiries', *Modern Law Review*, Vol. 22.

Griffiths, Sir Roy (1988), 'Does the Public Serve? The Consumer Dimension', Redcliffe Maud Memorial Lecture 1987, *Public Administration*, Vol. 66, Summer.

Griffiths, Sir Roy (1989), 'Sir Roy Reflects', *NHS Management Bulletin*, April.

Griffiths, Sir Roy (1991), 'Seven Years of Progress: General Management in the NHS', Audit Commission Lecture No. 3.

Hall, Robert (1989 and 1991), *The Robert Hall Diaries* (2 vols.) edited by Alec Cairncross, Unwin Hyman, London.

Halsey, A.H. (1985), 'Provincials and professionals: the British postwar sociologists' in Bulmer, 1985.

Ham, Chris (1985), *Health Policy in Britain*, Macmillan, Basingstoke.

Hancock, W.K. and Gowing, M.M. (1949), *The British War Economy*, HMSO, London.

Harrison, S. (1988), *Managing the NHS*, Chapman and Hall, London.

Harrison S. et al. (1992), *Just Managing: Power and Culture in the NHS*, Macmillan, London.

Healey, Dennis (1990), *The Time of My Life*, Penguin, Harmondsworth.

Heclo, H. and Wildavsky, A. (1981), *The Private Government of Public Money*, 2nd ed, Macmillan, London.

Henderson, Sir Nicholas (1982), *The Birth of Nato*, Weidenfeld and Nicolson, London.

Henkel, Mary (1991a), *Government, Evaluation and Change*, Jessica Kingsley, London.

Henkel, Mary (1991b), 'The New Evaluative State', *Public Administration*, Vol. 69, Spring.

Hennessy, Peter (1990a), *Whitehall*, Fontana, London.

Hennessy, Peter (1990b), 'The Political and Administrative Background', in *Output and Performance Measurement in Government* by Cave, M., Kogan M., and Smith R., Kingsley, London.

Heseltine, Michael (1987), *Where There's A Will*, Hutchinson, London.

Holland, P.F. (1988), *Efficiency and Effectiveness in the Civil Service - the Rayner Scrutinies*, Pavic Publications, Sheffield.

Horne, Alastair (1989), *Macmillan*, Vol. II, Macmillan, London.

Howells, David (1981), 'Marks and Spencer and the Civil Service: a comparison of culture and methods', *Public Administration*, Vol. 59, Autumn.

Hulme, G. (1988), 'Griffiths on Community Care', *Public Money and Management*, Spring/Summer.

Hunter, David (1984), 'Is Griffiths the last quick fix?', *Public Administration*, Vol. 62, Spring.

Hutton, Will (1995), *The State We're In*, Jonathan Cape, London.

Jay, Douglas (1980), *Change and Fortune*, Hutchinson, London.

Jenkins, Simon (1985), 'The Star Chamber, PESC and the Cabinet', *Political Quarterly*, Vol. 56, No. 2.

Jenkins, Roy (1989), Foreword to E. Plowden, *An Industrialist in the Treasury*, André Deutsch, London.

Jordan, Grant (1991), *The Commercial Lobbyists*, Aberdeen University Press, Aberdeen.

Kellner, Peter and Crowther-Hunt, Lord (1980), *The Civil Servants*, Macdonald, London.

Kelsey, Tim (1994), 'Grocers are bad for health', *The Independent*, 8 February.

Klein, Rudolf (1989), *The Politics of the NHS*, Longman, London.

Kogan, Maurice (1973), 'The Plowden Committee on Primary Education', in R. Chapman (ed.), *The Role of Commissions in Policy making*, Allen and Unwin, London.

Kubr, M. (ed.) (1986), *Management Consulting: A guide to the profession*, ILO, Geneva.

Leigh, David (1980), *The Frontiers of Secrecy*, Junction Books, London.

Likierman, Andrew (1982), 'The MINIS System in the DoE', *Public Administration*, 1982, Vol. 60, Summer.

Mackenzie, W.J.M. (1950), 'The Structure of Central Administration' in *British Government since 1918* by Gilbert Campion et al., Allen and Unwin, London.

Mackenzie, W.J.M. (1963), 'The Plowden Report: a translation' in R. Rose (ed.) (1969), *Policy making in Britain*, Macmillan, London.

Marshall, Geoffrey (1957), 'The Franks Report on Administrative Tribunals and Enquiries', *Public Administration*, Vol. 35, Winter.

Massey, A. (1993), *Managing the Public Sector*, Edward Elgar, London.

Massey, A. (1995), 'Civil Service Reform and Accountability', *Public Policy and Administration*, Vol. 10, No. 1.

Mazey, S. and Richardson, J. (1992), 'British Pressure Groups in the European Community: The Challenge of Brussels', *Parliamentary Affairs*, Vol. 45, No. 2.

Mazey, S. and Richardson, J. (eds) (1993), *Lobbying in the European Community*, OUP, Oxford.

Metcalfe, L. and Richards, S. (1983), 'The Impact of the Efficiency Strategy: Political Clout or Cultural Change?', *Public Administration*, Vol. 62, Winter.

Metcalfe, L. and Richards, S. (1990), *Improving Public Management*, 2nd ed., Sage, London.

Miliband, Ralph (1964), *Parliamentary Socialism*, Merlin Press, London.

Miller, Charles (1990), *Lobbying*, Blackwell, Oxford.

Morgan, K.O. (1984), *Labour in Power 1945-51*, OUP, Oxford.

Morgan, K.O. (1987), *Labour People*, OUP, Oxford.

Mount, Ferdinand (1993), *The British Constitution Now*, Mandarin, London.

Nairne, Sir Patrick (1982), 'Some reflections on change', *Management in Government*, No. 2.

Nicholas, H.G. (1970), review of Acheson's, *Present at the Creation*, *International Affairs*, Vol. 46, October.

Norton-Taylor, Richard (1995), *Truth is a Difficult Concept: Inside the Scott Enquiry*, 4th Estate, London.

Part, Anthony (1990), *The Making of a Mandarin*, André Deutsch, London.

Paxman, Jeremy (1991), *Friends in High Places*, Penguin, London.

Pedler, R.H. and van Schendelen, P.C.M. (eds) (1994), *Lobbying in the European Union*, Dartmouth, Aldershot.

Pimlott, Ben (1992), *Harold Wilson*, Harper Collins, London.

Pinder, John (ed.) (1981), *Fifty Years of PEP*, PEP, London.

Platt, Jennifer (1971), *Social Research in Bethnal Green*, Macmillan, London.

Plowden, Lord and Hall, Sir Robert (1968), 'More light on Priorities I: The Supremacy of Politics', *Political Quarterly*, Vol. 39, No. 2.

Plowden, Edwin (1989), *An Industrialist in the Treasury*, André Deutsch, London.

Plowden, William (1971), 'An Anatomy of Commissions', *New Society*, 15 July.

Plowden, William (1981), 'Whate'er is best administered', *New Society*, 9 April.

Plowden, William (1985), 'What Prospects for the Civil Service?', *Public Administration*, Vol. 63, Winter.

Plowden, William (ed.) (1987), *Advising the Rulers*, Blackwell, Oxford.

Pollitt, Christopher (1984), *Manipulating the Machine*, Allen and Unwin, London.

Pollitt, Christopher (1990), *Managerialism and the Public Services*, Blackwell, Oxford.

Pollitt, Christopher et al. (1991), 'General Management in the NHS: the initial impact 1983-8', *Public Administration*, 1991, Vol. 69, Spring.

Popovich, I.S. (1995), *Managing Consultants*, Century, London.

Postan, M.M. (1952), *British War Production*, HMSO, London.

Ranelagh, John (1992), *Thatcher's People*, Fontana, London.

Rayner, Derek (1973), 'Making Room for Managers in Whitehall', *Management Services in Government*, Vol. 28, No. 2.

Rayner, Sir Derek (1983), 'The Business of Government', *The Administrator*, March.

Rayner, Lord (1984), *The Unfinished Agenda*, Stamp Memorial Lecture.

Rhodes, R.A.E. (1994), 'Hollowing out the State', *Political Quarterly*, Vol. 65, No. 2.

Rothschild, Lord and Benson, Lord (1982), 'Royal Commissions: a memorial', *Public Administration*, Vol. 60.

Rowntree Reform Trust, *State of the Nation*, MORI poll, 1995.

Rush, Michael (ed.) (1990), *Parliament and Pressure Politics*, Clarendon Press, Oxford.

Russell, A.W. (1984), 'The Financial Management Unit of the Cabinet Office (MPO) and the Treasury', *Management in Government*, No. 2.

Salter, Sir Arthur (1967), *The Slave of the Lamp*, Weidenfeld and Nicolson, London.

Sampson, Anthony (1967), *Macmillan*, Allen Lane, London.

Sampson, Anthony (1971), *The New Anatomy of Britain*, Hodder and Stoughton, London.

Sampson, Anthony (1992), *The Essential Anatomy of Britain*, Hodder and Stoughton, London.

Selbourne, David (1993), *Not an Englishman*, Sinclair Stevenson, London.

Seldon, Anthony (ed.) (1960), *Not Unanimous*, IEA, London.

Shonfield, Andrew (1969), 'In the course of investigation' in Bulmer, M. (ed.) (1980), *Social Research and Royal Commissions*, Allen and Unwin, London.

Sieff, Marcus (1990), *Management: the Marks and Spencer Way*, Weidenfeld and Nicolson, London.

Skidelsky, Robert (1992), *John Maynard Keynes*, Vol. II, Macmillan, London.

Smith, Trevor (1979), *The Politics of the Corporate Economy*, Martin Robertson, Oxford.

Smith, Trevor (1994), 'Post-modern Politics and the Case for Constitutional Renewal, *Political Quarterly*, Vol. 65, No. 2.

Smith, Trevor (1995), 'Political Sleaze in Britain: Causes, Concerns and Cures', *Parliamentary Affairs*, Vol. 48, No. 4.

Strong, P. and Robinson, J. (1990), *The NHS under New Management*, Open University Press, Milton Keynes.

Taylor, A.J.P. (1972), *Beaverbrook*, Hamish Hamilton, London.

Tivey, L. (1988), *Interpretations of British Politics*, Harvester-Wheatsheaf, London.

Tynan, Kathleen (1995), *The Life of Kenneth Tynan*, Weidenfeld and Nicolson, London.

Tyson, S. (1990), 'Turning Civil Servants into Managers', *Public Money and Management*, Vol. 10, No. 1.

van Schendelen, M. (ed.) (1993), *National Public and Private EC Lobbying*, Dartmouth, Aldershot.

Wallace, William (1985), 'How frank was Franks?', *International Affairs*, Vol. 59, No. 3, Summer.

Warner, Norman (1984), 'Raynerism in Practice: Anatomy of a Rayner scrutiny', *Public Administration*, Vol. 62, Spring.

Watkins, Ernest (1951), *The Cautious Revolution*, Secker and Warburg, London.

Watkins, Alan (1990), *A Slight Case of Libel*, Duckworth, London.

Wigg, George (1972), *George Wigg*, Michael Joseph, London.

Wilby, P. (1979), 'All Power to Lady Plowden', *New Society*, 26 July.

Williams, Marcia (1972), *Inside No. 10*, Weidenfeld and Nicolson, London.

Willmott, Peter and Young, Michael (1971), 'On the Green', *New Society*, 28 October.

Wilson, Des (1993), *Campaigning: The A to Z of Public Advo*

-*cacy*, Hawksmere, London.

Wilson, Harold (1979), *Final Term: The Labour Government 1974-6*, Weidenfeld and Nicolson and Michael Joseph, London.

Wistow, G. (1992), 'The Health Service Policy Community' in *Policy networks in British Government* by Marsh, D. and Rhodes, R. (eds), OUP, Oxford.

Young, Michael (1958), *The Rise of the Meritocracy*, Penguin, London.

Young, Michael and Willmott, Peter (1957), *Family and Kinship in East London*, RKP, London.

Young, Michael and Willmott, Peter (1960), *Family and Class in a London Suburb*, RKP, London.

Young, Michael (1960), *The Chipped White Cups of Dover*, Unit 2, London.

Young, Michael and Willmott, Peter (1961), Research Report No. 3, *Sociological Review*, Vol. 9, No. 2, July.

Young, Michael (1965), *Innovation and Research in Education*, RKP, London.

Young, Michael and McGeevey, Patrick (1968), *Learning Begins at Home*, RKP, London.

Young, Michael and Willmott, Peter (1971), 'On the Green', *New Society*, 28 October.

Young, Michael and Rigge, Marianne (1979), *Mutual Aid in a Selfish Society*.

Young, Michael (1982), *The Elmhirsts of Dartington*, RKP, London.

Young, Michael (1983), *Social Scientist as Innovator*, Abt Books, Cambridge, Mass., USA.

Official Publications

Administrative Tribunals and Enquiries (Franks) (1957) Cmnd 218.

Committee on the working of the monetary system (Radcliffe Report) (1959) Cmnd 827.

Control of Public Expenditure (Plowden Report) (1961) Cmnd 1432.

Representational Services Overseas (Plowden) (1964) Cmnd 2276.

Aircraft Industry (Plowden) (1965) Cmnd 2853.

Fulton Report on the Civil Service (1968) Cmnd 3638.

Report of Committee on Section 2 of the Offical Secrets Act 1911 (Franks) (1971) Cmnd 5104.

Committee on Ministerial Memoirs (Radcliffe) (1976) Cmnd 6386.

Police Pay (Edmund-Davies) (1978) Cmnd 7283.

Police Complaints (Plowden) (1981) Cmnd 8193.

Administrative Forms in Government, Cmnd 8504 of 1981-2.

Falkland Islands Review (Franks Report) (1983) Cmnd 8787.

Griffiths Report 1983 'NHS Management Inquiry'.

NAO 'The Rayner Scrutiny Programmes 1979 to 1983, HC 322, March 1986.

'Developments in the Next Steps Programme' 5th Report July 1989, HC 348.

OPSS, Efficiency Unit (1994) The Government's Use of External Consultants, HMSO.

Social Services Committee (1983-4), Evidence HC 209.

Social Services Committee (1987-8), 5th Report 'The Future of the NHS', HC 613.

Griffiths Report 1988 'Community Care: Agenda for Action'.

Social Services Committee (1989-90), 8th Report 'Community Care: Planning and Co-operation', HC 580-I.

Select Committee on Members Interests (1987-88), 'Parliamentary Lobbying', HC 518.

Select Committee on Members Interests (1988-89), Evidence, HC 283.

Select Committee on Members Interests (1990-91), 3rd Report 'Parliamentary Lobbying', HC 586.

Treasury and Civil Service Committee (1979-80), 'Civil Service Manpower reductions', HC 712.

Treasury and Civil Service Committee (1980-81), 'The Future of the Civil Service department', HC 54.

Treasury and Civil Service Committee (1981-82), 'Efficiency and Effectiveness in the Civil Service', HC 236.

Treasury and Civil Service Committee (1985-86), 'Civil Servants and Ministers: duties and responsibilities', HC 92.

Treasury and Civil Service Committee (1992-93), 'The role of the civil service', HC 309.

Index